Communication Excel

CW00765521

Ralph Tench • Dejan Verčič • Ansgar Zerfass •
Ángeles Moreno • Piet Verhoeven

Communication Excellence

How to Develop, Manage and Lead Exceptional Communications

Ralph Tench
Leeds Beckett University
Leeds, United Kingdom

Ansgar Zerfass
University of Leipzig
Leipzig, Germany

Piet Verhoeven
University of Amsterdam
Amsterdam, The Netherlands

Dejan Verčič
University of Ljubljana
Ljubljana, Slovenia

Ángeles Moreno
Universidad Rey Juan Carlos
Madrid, Spain

ISBN 978-3-319-48859-2   ISBN 978-3-319-48860-8 (eBook)
DOI 10.1007/978-3-319-48860-8

Library of Congress Control Number: 2017932649

© The Editor(s) (if applicable) and The Author(s) 2017
This work is subject to copyright. All rights are solely and exclusively licensed by the Publisher, whether the whole or part of the material is concerned, specifically the rights of translation, reprinting, reuse of illustrations, recitation, broadcasting, reproduction on microfilms or in any other physical way, and transmission or information storage and retrieval, electronic adaptation, computer software, or by similar or dissimilar methodology now known or hereafter developed.
The use of general descriptive names, registered names, trademarks, service marks, etc. in this publication does not imply, even in the absence of a specific statement, that such names are exempt from the relevant protective laws and regulations and therefore free for general use.
The publisher, the authors and the editors are safe to assume that the advice and information in this book are believed to be true and accurate at the date of publication. Neither the publisher nor the authors or the editors give a warranty, express or implied, with respect to the material contained herein or for any errors or omissions that may have been made. The publisher remains neutral with regard to jurisdictional claims in published maps and institutional affiliations.

Cover illustration: Fatima Jamadar

Printed on acid-free paper

This Palgrave Macmillan imprint is published by Springer Nature
The registered company is Springer International Publishing AG
The registered company address is: Gewerbestrasse 11, 6330 Cham, Switzerland

Foreword

The world we live in is complex, unpredictable and forever changing. In the book the authors talk about hypermodernity and its impact on all our lives. For many organisations this fluctuating instability is one of the key challenges and possible threats to their long-term sustainability and security. It is for these reasons that strategic communication has and continues to see its place strengthening in the eyes of CEOs, boards and top management. That is why this book on communication excellence is so valuable: it helps to understand and interpret how communications can help to contribute to organisational success, and how communication departments and professionals can leverage this potential to a full extent.

The insights presented here are based on results from ten years of empirical research by the European Communication Monitor. I have had the privilege of an early sight of each year's findings as the President of the European Association of Communication Directors (EACD). As an association we are representing more than 2,000 communicator leaders across Europe. I am always fascinated by the insights and observations that the annual reports reveal about our sector, and specifically of the experiences of strategic communicators across Europe. We need more solid, evidence-based knowledge in our field and this work provides that foundation and understanding. It will also be an important spur for helping to professionalise and identify the skills and competency gaps so practitioners can build self-awareness and know how to develop themselves in the future.

It's therefore with some anticipation and excitement that I've read how the analysis and integration of so much research in the last ten years has been compiled by the authors to develop this fascinating book on 'Communication Excellence'.

Excellence is a difficult and potentially controversial topic that the team handles with aplomb. What stands out from the discussions is the depth and level of understanding that the book brings to a complex and much-debated area of strategic communication. In other words not just how to do high-level communication, but how to do it in an exemplary way.

The authors have structured their thinking and analysis in a clear and logical fashion, which adds value to those of us who manage and lead in organisations, and want to know how others do what they do so well.

Using a levels approach, broken down from the organisational to the department and then to the individual level makes absolute sense and we can all understand and interpret these insights. These three levels are then discussed in what the research team calls the 'nine commandments' of excellence, which are explained in detail throughout the book.

It is fascinating how the book then explores the key elements at each level with examples from established chief communicators in high-profile brand organisations. But again this a complex and challenging topic, so it is refreshing that at the end of the book the authors reflect on the models and approaches to excellent strategic communication. They summarise the learnings and discuss the paradoxes that each of these 'solutions' present, making this a thoughtful, insightful and valuable book for executives and senior managers in strategic communication.

Only when you measure and have defined criteria in place is it possible for the notion of 'excellence' to emerge. Now with the knowledge presented in this book we can start to compare strategic communication over time, across regions and industries.

With only one out of five communications organisations considered as 'excellent', there is still plenty of room and clearly a need for further improvement. But for such a young and still fast developing profession, excellence always remains a moving and aspirational target. The authors suggest that the better organisations develop towards increased engagement with their environments and stakeholders; that the high-performing communication departments thrive by having more influence in the decision-making within their organisations; and the communication professionals emerge from these environments as being more sagacious, linked, and solid in their knowledge of the business and profession.

Another challenge for reaching excellence is the fact that there is hardly any other professional in an organisation where the leader not only has to be a good professional and manager in his/her discipline, but also a good coach towards the CEO. True excellence requires strength in both areas and true assessment of excellence in the future will necessitate also seeking the view of the CEO and assessing their level(s) of satisfaction.

As an association we at the EACD are proud to have supported this innovative research project and ultimately to see such a significant contribution to the day-to-day practice of top executives and communicators alike. It is refreshing to see empirical work used in such a pragmatic and practical way to help professionalise and improve the future performance of strategic communication and ultimately our organisations.

European Association of Communication   Dr. Herbert Heitmann
Directors (EACD), Brussels   President

Preface

Over the past decade we have had the opportunity and privilege to talk with many communication leaders worldwide about how they develop, manage and lead their departments. We have explored the status quo and trends in strategic communication through the largest annual survey in the field, including responses from more than 21,000 practitioners in Europe. We have initiated similar studies in Asia-Pacific and Latin America, altogether covering more than 80 countries.

These insights have enabled us to paint a picture of what constitutes communication in organisations today, but also what makes for the highest performance. We believe we have identified and can articulate the core components of *communication excellence* in the best organisations, departments and professionals. We have integrated this developing knowledge based on sound empirical research with theoretical insights and our own understanding as former practitioners in the field. The book addresses executives from top management interested in building an outperforming communication function in their organisation, communication practitioners striving for excellence in their job, and those consulting or collaborating with communication experts.

This book presents a new framework to support the future development of communication departments in companies, non-profits and other types of organisations. To add sense and simplicity to what can be complexity in discussing these issues we have outlined our understanding of communication excellence around nine core commandments. They are explained in the introduction and subsequently explored each in a distinct chapter. We have added case studies from leading brands and organisations that bring to life what we have found and integrate our understanding of excellence with the work and experience of chief communication officers and their organisations.

This work has been driven for the past decade by the five of us as a core team of professors representing the leading universities in the field of strategic communication and public relations on the continent. But it could not have been completed without significant support from partners in the professional field, sponsors, colleagues and academic supporters.

We have benefited from consistent and steadfast backing from the European Association of Communication Directors (EACD), the European Public Relations Research and Education Association (EUPRERA), Communication Director magazine, and PRIME Research, as well as all previous sponsors of the study series. Several individuals have been invaluable to the project. This includes Markus Wiesenberg and Ronny Fechner as assistant researchers and all student assistants working in the team of lead researcher Ansgar Zerfass at Leipzig University. We have been supported by Stefanie Schwerdtfeger, Grit Fiedler and Dafydd Phillips and many more colleagues from Quadriga Media. Many thanks to the authors of the case studies in this book. We would also like to acknowledge all colleagues at numerous universities worldwide, who have supported or continue to support the European, Asia-Pacific and Latin American Communication Monitors as member of research teams or national collaborators.

Ralph Tench
Dejan Verčič
Ansgar Zerfass
Ángeles Moreno
Piet Verhoeven

Contents

Epilogue   193

Appendix   205

Index   211

Authors

Prof. Dr. Ralph Tench is full-time Professor of Communication at the Faculty of Business and Law at Leeds Beckett University, United Kingdom. A former journalist and communications consultant, he heads international research projects and teams on corporate communication, governance and responsibility as well as health communication. He is President elect and past Board Director for the European Public Relations Research and Education Association, Brussels.

Prof. Dr. Dejan Verčič is Professor and Head of the Centre for Marketing and Public Relations at the University of Ljubljana, Slovenia. He holds a PhD from the London School of Economics and Political Science and he was a Fulbright scholar at San Diego State University, United States. His research covers international and intercultural communication as well as various aspects of public relations and strategic communication.

Prof. Dr. Ansgar Zerfass is Professor and Chair in Strategic Communication at the University of Leipzig, Germany, and Professor for Communication and Leadership at BI Norwegian Business School in Oslo, Norway. He worked as a communication and management executive for ten years before re-entering academia and has since published 34 books and more than 300 articles, book chapters and study reports about corporate communications.

Prof. Dr. Ángeles Moreno is Titular Professor at the University Rey Juan Carlos, Madrid, Spain, and Board Director for the European Public Relations Research and Education Association, Brussels. Her work achieved awards at major academic conferences in Europe, Latin America and the Unites States. She belongs to the scientific board of international prestigious journals, congresses and national agencies.

Assoc. Prof. Dr. Piet Verhoeven is Associate Professor for Corporate Communication at the Amsterdam School of Communication Research (ASCoR) at the University of Amsterdam, the Netherlands. His research focuses on corporations and the news media and empirical explorations of organisational communication practice. He started working as a scientist in 2002 following a career in public relations practice in renowned companies.

List of Figures

List of Tables

List of Boxes

Introduction

Within the past 100 years, strategic communication has become a core management function in companies, non-profits and other types of organisation. Some call it public relations, some corporate communication, communication management, reputation management, integrated communication or simply communication(s). But all these names cover the same function: organisations purposefully use communication to fulfil their missions.[1]

The authors of this book are members of a research team that since 2007 conducted the largest annual survey in professional communication in the world: the European Communication Monitor (ECM).[2] In the past ten years we interviewed over 21,000 communication practitioners in 43–46 countries in Europe. In 2014 we extended the project to the Americas with the Latin American Communication Monitor and in 2015 into Asia-Pacific. We are developing a truly global comparative research, which covers more than 80 countries worldwide.

Besides conducting surveys, we have interviewed chief communication officers of the largest European multinational companies, organised presentations and workshops, produced reports and articles, and regularly discussed our findings at both academic and professional conferences. But we are not only researchers. We have personal backgrounds as communication executives and consultants – with more than 100 years of experience between us.

---

[1] Hallahan et al. (2007).

[2] See the last chapter of this book for details on the methodology of this research. Full reports for each annual study along with articles, web videos and other content explaining key results are available at www.communicationmonitor.eu.

We are also active members of national and international professional associations.

For the tenth anniversary of our empirical research in professional communication practice in Europe we decided to digest our findings and write a book on *Communication Excellence*. In this volume we build on previous work in general management theory and practice, as well as on more specific investigations into communications and public relations. Our intention is to present a framework to help practitioners develop *excellent communication*.

Communication in Management

Management used to be about command and control, and the role communication played was to transmit information (command) from the top to the bottom, and provide a feedback loop (for control). It may have never been so simple in reality, but textbooks endeavoured to make it appear so. An illusionary simplicity that never existed in any reality.

The world we live in is complex, and humans living in it are – more often than not – confused. Management is a messy business in which organisational leaders are trying to make sense of fuzzy environments in organising processes aimed at sensibly impacting many stakeholders inside and outside organisational borders – if these can be differentiated at all.

In pre-modern times people lived in traditional aggregations where everybody knew everybody else and any other person was immediately stigmatised as a 'stranger'. Time was slow and change was something to avoid. Rulers ruled and the ruled obeyed, or they were punished. The natural order of a primeval community is reflected in the animal kingdom with a known pecking order, and in which members learn their position at birth.

Management is a product of modern times, and modern times value progress. All humans can become better, they are all born equal (free) and they can all aspire to a heavenly nirvana (happiness). This is the essence of the Western conception of democracy (people can equally rule only because they are of equal faculties), but also of its inherent instability and change. At the turn from the nineteenth into twentieth century there was a promise of management as social engineering (science and technology) to bring organisational order out of societal chaos. It comes as no surprise to learn that one of the first books on management, Chester Barnard's *The Functions of the Executive*, originally published in 1938 and still in print today, is about the importance of communication in and for formal organisations and their success (see Box 1).

Box 1 Three constitutive elements of formal organisations[3]
1. Communication
2. Willingness to serve
3. Common purpose

Throughout the twentieth century, management theory was primarily about communication. But the notion of communication in modern management was mainly about control. This is apparent in acronyms used to capture the essence of managerial work: POEM (plan, organise, execute, monitor/measure), POCCC (planning, organising, command, coordination, control) and POSDCORB (planning, organising, staffing, directing, coordinating, reporting, budgeting). Managerial work was adapted to large scale organisations and fitted the production processes they used with a centralised chain of command.[4] Such approaches, which also shaped communication for a long time, were designed to operate machines but, as it turned out, human organisations are live organisms that need care and cultivation.

Under the influence of the information and communication technology (ICT) revolution that started in the 1970s, postmodern culture developed and changed the way organisations had to work. Postmodern organisations needed to be flexible, knowledge was their main source of competitiveness and ICT their most important technology.[5] Also the liberalisation of the economy instigated a new phase of globalisation of production and consumption. Postmodern culture and postmodern organisations relied more heavily on communication than their modern predecessors so communication and letting go of control gained importance in the last decades of the twentieth century.

Today some say we live in hypermodern times, a term introduced by the French fashion sociologist Gilles Lipovetsky.[6] In hypermodern times modern and postmodern organisations still exist and have to adapt to this new phase of cultural development. A hypermodern society is a society in overdrive. It is

---

[3] Barnard (1968/1938).
[4] Roberts and Armitage (2006).
[5] Roberts and Armitage (2006), pp. 559–565.
[6] Lipovetsky (2005).

characterised by hyper consumption, hypermodernity and hyper narcissism. Consumption is central in hypermodernity and so is production. An increasingly large part of life is characterised by consumption. A majority of people consume with great pleasure; they are turbo-consumers.[7] Hypermodernity is also modernity in overdrive; continuous change and flexibility are key to our times. Furthermore the individualisation that started in modern times has shifted to a hyper narcissism. This has raised the expectations society has of individuals. Everybody is expected to get the best out of himself or herself and to behave responsively.[8] Continuous reflection is expected of everyone and every organisation as well. Hypermodern organisations are hyperflexible, meaning that their size can change rapidly depending on the market situations, their key source of competitiveness is acceleration and they rely on the Internet and mobile communications. They are also transient – their existence can be brief depending on their activities and their context.[9] Obviously not every organisation is a hypermodern organisation right now. Modern and postmodern organisations keep on existing in our hypermodern times. Especially when you take a global perspective.

The global society in overdrive is essentially mediatised, meaning it is saturated with media, and permanently reflecting on itself and on everything else. It is also full of paradoxes, another key characteristic of hypermodernity.[10] For example organisations have to be open and flexible and at the same time managing and controlling their internal and external environment in order to reach their goals. They have to be authentic and strategic at the same time. And, simultaneously, be ethical and make as much profit as possible. These paradoxes raise questions about how to run an organisation and how to communicate for it. To deal with the paradoxes of hypermodernity value-driven management, business and organisational ethics, and corporate social responsibility (CSR) came to the forefront of organisational policy.[11] Good ethical business that goes hand in hand with strategic calculation is the overall paradox organisations of all kind have to deal with. This and other paradoxes create a big communication problem: How to communicate about this double siddedness to stakeholders and the global mediatised audience? Organisations and their communication departments need, increasingly, to be excellent in order to do that.

---

[7] Rendtorff (2014), pp. 279–287.

[8] Rendtorff (2014), pp. 279–287.

[9] Roberts and Armitage (2006).

[10] Lipovetsky (2005); Rendtorff (2014), pp. 279–287.

[11] Rendtorff (2014), pp. 279–287.

Communication Excellence

The notion of 'excellence' entered the language of management as a sign of aspiration. When 'scientific management' did not deliver on its promise that it can bring order out of chaos and determine once and for all how to run organisations to their full potential, and some organisations succeeded and others failed, a question was raised: Why is it so, why are some organisations better than others? How can we make our organisation better? A series of books, mainly by researchers and consultants from the United States, explored the issue.[12] Their key insight was that organisations are not just machines. They are composed of people who in interactions form cultures. While hard (machine, structural) parts of organisations are easy to imitate, it is this soft (human, cultural) part that is unique and practically impossible to copy.

Excellence in management today stands for 'an outstanding practice in managing the organisation and achieving results'.[13] Organisations look for characteristics that contribute to higher performance and benchmark against them to see where they are weak and where they are strong with an aspiration to improve. In Europe, many organisations use the Business Excellence Model proposed by the European Foundation for Quality Management (EFQM), while in the United States they prefer the Malcom Baldridge National Quality Award and in Japan the Deming Application Prize.

In the ECM project we developed our own excellence framework for communication practice. We have applied it in our surveys based on self-assessment to identify outstanding communication departments. We have used statistical analysis to differentiate excellent from non-excellent communication departments, and after obtaining the two groups, we looked at characteristics on which they differ.[14] This is in line with excellence approaches from management mentioned

---

[12] Peters and Waterman (1982); Peters and Austin (1985); Collins and Porras (1994); Collins (2001).

[13] Martin-Castilla and Rodriguez-Ruiz (2008), p. 136.

[14] The comparative excellence framework for communication management has been introduced and used by Zerfass et al. (2014), pp. 133–149; Zerfass et al. (2015), pp. 106–125; Zerfass et al. (2016), pp. 108–125. For a more detailed explanation see Verčič and Zerfass 2016. The framework builds on the self-assessment and benchmark logic of organisational excellence approaches and applies it to the field of communication management by using established indicators from public relations research. Communication departments were identified as excellent along four indicators: advisory influence (senior managers take recommendations of the communication department (very) seriously); executive influence (communication will (very) likely be invited to senior-level meetings dealing with organisational strategic planning); success (the communication of the organisation is (very) successful); and competence (the quality and ability of the communication department is (much) better compared to those of competing organisations). Only organisations clearly outperforming in all four dimensions (values 6 or 7 on a 7-point Likert scale) were considered as excellent in the benchmark exercise. Approximately one out of five departments was identified as excellent in various applications of this framework.

Fig. 1 The comparative excellence framework for communication management

above. It differentiates our framework from previous attempts in public relations theory which have been criticised for defining excellence normatively.[15] The comparative excellence framework, which has been successfully used in the European, Asia-Pacific and Latin American Communication Monitor research, is presented in Fig. 1.

The communication function is often explained as a boundary-spanning function, linking the 'inside' with the 'outside' of an organisation. Internal capabilities of communicators are intended to influence organisational decision-making, while external performance through competent practitioners enables success. This is not an objective category, but the extent to which communicators are perceived as useful and contributing to the overall success. Competence, on the other hand, is a combination of knowledge, skills and personal attributes.[16]

Influence of the communication function, however, is an expression of the power communicators have in an organisation. They can be excluded from having any influence on managerial decision-making, they may be asked for opinion and exert advisory influence or they can be included in

---

[15] E.g. the seminal works on Excellence in Public Relations and Communication Management by Grunig (1992); Grunig et al. (2002).

[16] Tench and Moreno (2015).

the decision-making processes and thus exert executive influence. This is often visible in the position of the top communicator and his or her title of, for example, Vice-President for Communication or Senior Vice-President for Communication, but often it is done without any formal positional recognition. What matters is an effect: does communication contribute to organisational decision-making? And, if so, how? And, if not, why not?

Our analysis consistently shows through the years that approximately 20 per cent, or every fifth organisation in our sample, is considered as excellent, while 80 per cent, or four–fifths, are not. We have explained our data and analysis elsewhere.[17] Interestingly a similar ratio of outstanding and normal communication departments has been identified in other regions of the world, where the same method was applied.[18] We take this difference between organisations with excellent communications departments and those with non-excellent communication departments as a starting point for this book. When we divided our sample between excellent and non-excellent, we focused on characteristics that we found as critical. Our framework/model, the ECM Communication Excellence Model, comprises nine characteristics, which we call 'commandments', that every organisation must consider if it is interested in developing and nurturing an excellent communication department.

Levels and Commandments of Communication Excellence

An excellent communication department is dependent on the right communicators working in the right organisations. Our analysis has led us to distinguish between three levels at which communication excellence can be observed: individuals, departments and organisations (see Fig. 2).

On each level, three key characteristics can be identified. When turning those indicators into requirements then nine commandments of excellence emerge. These are presented in Fig. 3. The figure visualises how to understand and manage excellence in strategic communication. Only simultaneous efforts at all three levels can produce optimal results:

- Excellent organisations are connected to their environments and stakeholders, which requires them to be globalised, mediatised and reflective.

---

[17] Verčič and Zerfass (2016).
[18] Moreno et al. (2015); Macnamara et al. (2015).

Fig. 2   Levels of excellent communication

- Excellent communication departments are influential within their organisations. This means they have to be embedded, datafied, and strategised.
- Excellent communication professionals are ambitious; this includes being sagacious, linked and solid.

Excellent Organisations

Organisations that nurture excellent communication departments can be labelled connected organisations, and this connectedness consists of three characteristics: globalisation, mediatisation and reflection.

Globalisation is not an expression of size as digital technology allows even the smallest organisations to operate globally. It should also not be misunderstood as a particular ideology like neo-liberalism, favouring the elimination of all barriers to trade and mobility of capital, goods and services, and people. Globalisation is much more an expression of open-mindedness and humbleness: organisations today, at least potentially, compete with all other organisations wherever they are in the world, so they have to be observant and globally connected to be able to see and understand what goes on.

Mediatised means that organisations understand that the reality they are facing is constructed and influenced by communication. Organisations are

COMMUNICATION EXCELLENCE

Fig. 3 Nine commandments of excellent communication

therefore dependent on communication. They use communication not only to move messages inwards (monitoring) and outwards (messaging), but organisations themselves are communicatively constructed, they exist in communication and this communication materialises in media. Traditional mass media still hold significant power in the world. Collaborating with journalists (so-called earned media) and using advertising (paid media) is a key feature of successful organisations. But social platforms on the Internet (shared media) and corporate magazines or channels (owned media) are gaining in importance, enabling every organisation to become a media producer and distributor.

Reflective organisations are those organisations that understand that they are dependent on many stakeholders for their success or failure and that they have to be able to observe or look back on themselves through their own eyes. They have to observe and listen, be able to visualise the world beyond today and learn from their own and others' mistakes. Reflection and adaptation to ever-changing environments may be the most important characteristics of modernity and communication plays a critical role in the appreciation variability.

Excellent Communication Departments

Communication departments must be influential to matter and have an effect. They can be influential if they are embedded, datafied and strategised.

Embedded communication departments fit in organisations where they can have the highest impact: they are very close to top management, are therefore able to participate and/or affect decision-making, and they are well connected to other functional departments, like controlling, human resources, marketing, operations, sales, etc., to enable synergies and mutual learning. Communication is not something that precedes or succeeds other activities. It must be embedded in every activity an organisation undertakes.

Datafied means that communication departments today are as much about numbers as they are about people. Long gone are the times when 'people who liked people' went into public relations and those that liked numbers went to finance. In our contemporary world, communication practitioners must understand how to collect, analyse and use data, as much as finance people must understand why numbers are collected and how they should use them and with what effect. The Internet has brought innumerable opportunities to collect big and small data and communication is transforming itself from a soft to a hard-wired profession.

Strategised means that communication departments will only have a real impact on organisational life and success when their activities are clearly aligned to overall goals. A decade of empirical research shows that this is still the most important issue communicators face: how to link communication to organisational strategies. Everything communicators do has to be done strategically: listening, planning and messaging,. Communication departments can only make a substantial contribution to organisational success if they are integrated in strategic decision-making, both in the inbound dimension (when influencing management) and in the outbound dimension (when influencing environments and stakeholders).

Excellent Communication Professionals

Everything that is necessary at the organisational and departmental level has to be implemented by *ambitious professionals*, who are sagacious, linked and solid. However impersonal the world in which we live may seem, agents are humans, and individual communicators matter. Professionals who are capable of forming excellent communication departments must strive for excellence: without personal drive and motivation, the search for excellence is void.

Sagacious professionals are knowledgeable, demonstrating reflective wisdom as well as shrewdness and at times applying appropriate mental discernment. High-performing communicators are well educated and experienced, and they possess explicit competencies needed for performance in their jobs. Professional communication is at the intersection of business and social science, and appropriate appreciation of both is becoming a necessary condition for top performing communicators.

Linked professionals are personally and professionally networked individuals who understand the importance of collaboration with colleagues through mentoring and mentorship. Organisations are nothing but sets of relationships between people inside and outside organisations. Communications professionals must develop and nurture interpersonal relationships with their colleagues above, parallel to and below them. A key feature of organisations with excellent communication departments is that they provide a climate fostering mutual collaboration and support.

Solid professionals show a solidity driven by personal, organisational and professional ethics and frameworks. They also explore issues of pluralism and diversity in the workplace to facilitate and deliver satisfaction for themselves and their peers. In a world of declining trust in organisations, it is extremely important to start building respect and reliability of communicators at the interpersonal level. This prepares the ground for excellent communication departments that can help organisations overall to rebuild public confidence and trust without which success is not sustainable.

References

Barnard, C. I. (1968). *The Functions of the Executive*. [first published 1938]. Cambridge, MA: Harvard University Press.

Collins, J. (2001). *Good to Great: Why Some Companies Make the Leap…and Others Don't*. London: Random House.

Collins, J. C., & Porras, J. I. (1994). *Build to Last: Successful Habits of Visionary Companies*. New York, NY: Harper Business.

Grunig, J. E. (Ed.) (1992). *Excellence in Public Relations and Communication Management*. Hillsdale, NJ: Lawrence Erlbaum Associates.

Grunig, L. A., Grunig, J. E., & Dozier, D. M. (2002). *Excellent Public Relations and Effective Organizations: A Study of Communication Management in Three Countries*. Mahwah, NJ: Lawrence Erlbaum Associates.

Hallahan, K., Holtzhausen, D., van Ruler, B., Verčič, D., & Sriramesh, K. (2007).

Defining strategic communication. *International Journal of Strategic Communication, 1*(1), 3–35.

Lipovetsky, G. (2005). Time against time: Or the hypermodern society. In G. Lipovetsky & S. Charles, *Hypermodern Times* (pp. 29–71). Malden, MA: Polity Press.

Macnamara, J., Lwin, M. O., Adi, A., & Zerfass, A. (2015). *Asia-Pacific Communication Monitor 2015/16. The State of Strategic Communication and Public Relations in a Region of Rapid Growth. Survey Results From 23 Countries.* Hong Kong: APACD.

Martín-Castilla, J. I., & Rodríguez-Ruiz, Ó. (2008). EFQM model: knowledge governance and competitive advantage. *Journal of Intellectual Capital, 9*(1), 133–156.

Moreno, A., Molleda, J. C., Athaydes, A., & Suárez, A. M. (2015). *Latin American Communication Monitor 2015. Excelencia en comunicación estratégica, trabajo en la era digital, social media y profesionalización. Resultados de una encuesta en 18 países.* Brussels: EUPRERA.

Peters, T. J., & Austin, N. (1985). *A Passion for Excellence: The Leadership Difference.* New York. NY: Random House.

Peters, T. J., & Waterman, R. H. (1982). *In Search of Excellence: Lessons from America's Best-Run Companies.* New York, NY: Harper & Row.

Rendtorff, J. D. (2014). *French Philosophy and Social Theory. A Perspective for Ethics and Philosophy of Management.* Dordrecht: Springer.

Roberts, J., & Armitage, J. (2006). From organization to hypermodern organization: On the appearance and disappearance of Enron. *Journal of Organizational Change Management, 19*(5), 558–577.

Tench, R., & Moreno, A. (2015). Mapping communication management competencies for European practitioners: ECOPSI an EU study. *Journal of Communication Management, 19*(1), 39–61.

Verčič, D., & Zerfass, A. (2016). A comparative excellence framework for communication management. *Journal of Communication Management, 20*(4), 270–288.

Zerfass, A., Tench, R., Verčič, D., Verhoeven, P., & Moreno, A. (2014). *European Communication Monitor 2014. Excellence in Strategic Communication – Key Issues, Leadership, Gender and Mobile Media. Results of a Survey in 42 Countries.* Brussels: EACD/EUPRERA, Helios Media.

Zerfass, A., Verčič, D., Verhoeven, P., Moreno, A., & Tench, R. (2015). *European Communication Monitor 2015. Creating Communication Value Through Listening, Messaging and Measurement. Results of a Survey in 41 Countries.* Brussels: EACD/EUPRERA, Helios Media.

Zerfass, A., Verhoeven, P., Moreno, A., Tench, R., & Verčič, D. (2016). *European Communication Monitor 2016. Exploring Trends in Big Data, Stakeholder Engagement and Strategic Communication. Results of a Survey in 43 Countries.* Brussels: EACD/EUPRERA, Quadriga Media Berlin.

Part I

Connected Organisations

The first part of the book focuses on the *organisation* and the positioning of communication departments in the wider context of society and revolving around the important theme of being *connected*. Accelerating political, economic, social and, above all, technological changes make our future(s) ever more uncertain and all of us ever more dependent on communication. In the twenty-first century, we have ascended not only from modern to postmodern conditions of life, but even beyond that: we live in a hypermodern world. Today, good organisations not only produce good products or services, they have to behave and communicate in a *good* way too, and the best among them strive for excellence.

In the first of our commandments from the framework we discuss the context and influence on organisations of operating in a *globalised* world. Companies with 'excellent' communication departments live on the global stage: they communicate daily with more countries than their counterpart companies with 'non-excellent' communication departments, indeed 20 per cent of them with 20 or more countries. There is a demand for an intercultural, internationally comfortable, hypermodern communication practitioner who can understand different cultures in addition to political, economic, social and media systems.

When Canadian media scholar Marshall McLuhan described the world as a 'global village' due to media causing its implosion, there was no Internet: and the Internet, we have subsequently learned, has transformed our lives. Companies not only use media to reach stakeholders, they are becoming media producers. Besides advertising, publicity and press relations, new media practices flourish. And the major gatekeepers to media content become the organisation's employees themselves. Our second chapter in this part of the book discusses how organisations respond to this *mediatised* environment when they are in high-performing positions. An in this mediatised global village organisations must establish their own identities, their own selves. This can be done only in communication with others (stakeholders) and it is by looking at oneself through the eyes of the other that one becomes a self-aware subject. As humans, organisations must learn to observe and listen to their environments and understand that it is through their own existence and operation that they co-create the world in which they (and we all) live. We encapsulate this as being *reflective* which we debate in commandment three and which is frequently observed in the high-performing organisations in how they listen and engage with research and information gathering to support organisational strategies and goals.

Commandment 1
Globalised: The World We Live In

We live in a globalised world. Like it or not, we affect people living on the other side of the globe and they affect us. We are interdependent. And public relations is a profession concerned with management of inter-dependencies between organisations and their stakeholders.[1] Political, economic, social and technological changes in the second half of the twentieth century have brought us closer together than ever, and the term evolved to describe this new condition is globalisation. But what does that have to do with excellent communication? Everything. Today, if you want to know how good you are, and furthermore, if you want to become better, you have to compare and learn globally. You don't have to go physically everywhere (although it helps), but you have to be willing to let that 'everywhere' come to you, at least mentally. That said, if you look deeply enough, you will see the whole world coming to us all the time: ideas, food, goods, services, money, plants, animals and people, whatever, sometimes legally and at other times illegally. Globalisation is unequivocally here and winners have embraced it.

Globalisation means different things to different people. Jan Aart Scholte, a professor of global studies in Sweden, identified four redundant concepts of globalisation and proposed the fifth as the transformative one: internationalisation, liberalisation, universalisation, Westernisation and

---

[1] Verčič and Grunig (2000).

© The Author(s) 2017
R. Tench et al., *Communication Excellence*,
DOI 10.1007/978-3-319-48860-8_1

globality (see Box 2).[2] All of them are true and they affect communication. Therefore the first commandment of being excellent is: be globalised. Being globalised in this context means first and foremost that the organisation is connected to its local and global environment through communication. Excellent communication helps the organisation to do that by having an eye for the five aspects of globalisation: internationalisation, liberalisation, universalisation, Westernisation and globality. Excellent professionals are aware of these aspects and how their organisation, small or big, is a part of these developments while at the same time realising the consequences of globalisation for the profession of communication.

Box 2 The G word

Globalisation as

1. **Internationalisation**
   Intensification of cross-border movements of ideas, goods and services, capital and people
2. **Liberalisation**
   Disappearance of restrictions on movements of ideas, goods and services, capital and people
3. **Universalisation**
   Homogenisation of ideas, goods and services, capital and culture(s) everywhere around the globe
4. **Westernisation**
   Worldwide spread of rationalist modernisation from the West (Europe and the United States) to the rest of the world
5. **Globality**
   Transplanetary relations and supraterritoriality: development of transplanetary connections between people developing a social space in its own right that transcends territorial geography.

Internationalisation

There is no doubt that internationalisation is deeply affecting strategic communication practices. In the European Communication Monitor, we found that 8 out of 10 professionals have international communication as a

---

[2] Scholte (2008).

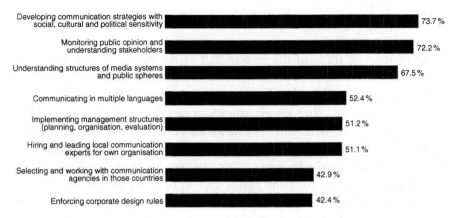

Fig. 4 Major challenges of international communication[3]

part of their daily business, with nearly a quarter of those reaching more than 20 countries in their daily work. If we differentiate between different sectors, more than 90 per cent of corporate Chief Communication Officers operate internationally on a daily basis, while professionals in non-profit and government sectors lag behind.[4]

Communication across countries and cultures is a unique challenge. It is only in the presence of others that we become aware of our identities and limitations. European studies in societal cultures started with explorations of Africa and the Americas. Organisational culture gained in importance with the arrival of Asian products and companies to the United States. International communication poses many challenges. The results of the European Communication Monitor show that communication professionals think that developing communication strategies with social, cultural and political sensitivity, monitoring public opinion and understanding stakeholders and structures of media systems are the most important challenges when dealing with non-European countries (see Fig. 4).

Internationalisation of the communication function follows the implementation of traditional management models for planning, organisation, execution and evaluation, communication in multiple languages, enforcement of corporate values and logos, and the use of agencies in other countries.[5]

---

[3] Zerfass et al. (2013), p. 68. n^{min} = 1,324 communication professionals working in communication departments across Europe who are communicating internationally in their daily job. Q: How challenging are the following aspects when communicating internationally, especially in non-European countries? Scale 1 (not challenging) – 5 (very challenging). Percentages: agreement based on scale points 4–5.

[4] Zerfass et al. (2013), pp. 60–69.

[5] Verčič et al. (2015).

Liberalisation: In the Search of Excellence

Liberalisation of trade in the second half of the twentieth century brought unprecedented wealth to the West, but also unexpected downsides and crises. There was a real shock when between the 1960s and 1980s Japan upgraded its exports from toys through electronics to cars that were cheaper and better than those produced in the United States or Europe. It was this external shock that led many Western management consultants and researchers to study and understand why some companies are better than others. This was the impetus that led to Tom Peters and Robert Waterman publishing *In Search of Excellence: Lessons from America's Best Run Companies*.[6] What they concluded was that organisations are composed of hard (structure and strategy) and soft (systems, shared values, skills, staff and style) elements, and that managers in the West often overlook the soft side, while excellence can be achieved only with the right balance of the two sides. Interestingly, they discovered exactly what they were trying to explain: some companies are better than others because of their culture(s). Japan's success between the 1960s and 1990s was in large part founded in the values and cultures of their key corporations. The most known code of values is the 'Seven Spirits of Matsushita', named after its creator Konosuke Matsushita. They are service to the public, fairness and honesty, teamwork for the common cause, uniting effort for improvement, courtesy and humility, accordance with natural laws, and gratitude for blessing (see Box 3).[7]

Box 3 The seven spirits of Matsushita

Code of values for organisations:

1. Service to the public
2. Fairness and honesty
3. Teamwork for the common cause
4. Uniting effort for improvement
5. Courtesy and humility
6. Accordance with natural laws
7. Gratitude for blessing

---

[6] Peters and Waterman (1982).
[7] Kippenberg (2002).

Strategic communication and public relations can certainly play an important role in developing the soft side of organisations and help to find a balance between the hard and the soft side.

It is a kind of a paradox that Western scholars became interested in business excellence stimulated by the presence of Japanese management practices that were largely developed with the assistance of an American statistician trying to help the Japanese catch-up with the West after the Second World War. His name was William Edwards Deming, and in 1950 he started preaching innovation and quality to leaders of Japanese industry. Today, the Japanese Union of Scientists and Engineers sponsors a global quality award for contributions to total quality management with his name: the Deming Prize.

Excellence models for improvement and self-assessment are one of the consequences of liberalisation and internationalisation: it is only by being in contact with (better) others that we become aware of our limitations and can discover opportunities for growth. As the Japanese industry learned from an American statistician, and American consultants from Japanese businessman, these days Chinese researchers learn from Western scientists: in 2003, the Centre for World-Class Universities, Graduate School of Education of Shanghai Jiao Tong University, China, started studying higher education around the world. They developed six objective indicators to rank world universities and the initial purpose of the exercise was to find the global standing of top Chinese universities.[8] Today, the so-called 'Shanghai list' or 'Shanghai ranking' (officially: the Academic Ranking of World Universities) is the most important and authoritative list of universities in the world. The Chinese developed it to self-assess and improve their universities. Thirteen years later, the fastest supercomputer in the world uses a Chinese-made microprocessor chip: 'Supercomputers are viewed in scientific circles as an indicator of national technology leadership, and they are vital for research in areas ranging from the development of new weapons and medicines, to the design of cars and consumer products'.[9] To know how good you are, you have to go and compare yourself globally.

Universalisation

Between 1992 and 2002, a group of researchers led by James Grunig from the University of Maryland developed and tested a theory to explain how public relations and communication management contribute to

---

[8] ARWU (2016).
[9] Markoff (2016).

organisational effectiveness. They postulated that organisations develop excellence in response to environmental pressures. The theory proposes nine generic principles, or characteristics, that public relations needs to contribute to organisational effectiveness:

1. involvement of public relations in strategic management,
2. empowerment of public relations in the dominant coalition or a direct reporting relationship to senior management,
3. integrated public relations function,
4. public relations as a management function separated from other management functions,
5. a public relations practitioner in a management role,
6. two-way model of organisation-stakeholder relationships,
7. a symmetrical system of internal communication,
8. knowledge potential for managerial role and symmetrical public relations and
9. diversity embodied in all roles.[10]

Based on additional research, Dejan Verčič, James Grunig and Larissa Grunig proposed the nine generic principles as the global, universal principles of public relations valid around the world.[11] They supplemented them with specific (local) applications mediated by five environmental variables: political ideology, economic system (including the level of development of the country's economy), degree of activism (the extent of the pressure that organisations face from activists), culture and media system(s) (the nature of the media environment in a country).[12] This was collapsed from five environmental variables into three factors: a country's infrastructure (composed of political system, economic systems and level of development, legal system and social activism), media environment (with media control, media diffusion and media access) and societal culture.

There are clear tendencies for universalisation of communication functions, as expressed by a Head of Corporate Communication of an Austrian company mentioned in one of our qualitative studies: 'Central structure (with standards and policies) is key! The rest may be democratic, but causes

---

[10] Grunig (1992); Grunig et al. (2002).
[11] Verčič et al. (1996).
[12] Sriramesh and Verčič (2009).

chaos and unwanted "independency" with strange strategies and statements'. But her colleague from Switzerland advocates: 'Aligned decentralisation: meaning headquarters responsible for corporate story (vision, mission, values, global strategy, targets), corporate standards (global messages, policies such as corporate design and key-wording); while regional/national communications units should ensure aligned transformation in regional/national/local statements. However: online communication remains global due to the "flat world" we live in'.[13]

Excellence, as long as it stands for a model enabling self-assessment and comparative improvement, must contain some elements of universalisation, otherwise we can only compare apples to oranges.

Westernisation: Worldwide Modernisation

Westernisation means a particular type of globalisation and universalisation that got its ultimate expression in political scientist Francis Fukuyama's article and book *The End of History*.[14] There can be no doubt that the public relations profession as we know it, originated in Europe and in the United States at the beginning of the twentieth century, and that it has been globalising since.[15] It is easy to underestimate the triumph of Westernisation over the rest of the world: Fukuyama, an American social scientist at the end of 1980s and in early 1990s, when the Soviet Union collapsed and the Berlin Wall fell down, said that Western liberal democracy may present the endpoint of human political evolution and the final form of government.[16] What a difference a decade makes! At the beginning of the twenty-first century, China, Russia or the Middle East, to name just three, present viable alternatives to liberal democracies, and any notion of the end of history is clearly premature, if not completely refuted. The question is whether these presented alternatives are temporary downturns in an ongoing process of 'rising freedom' as the German political scientist Christian Welzel has put forward[17] Based on the World Value Survey, Welzel found evidence for

---

[13] Verčič et al. (2015), p. 790.
[14] Fukuyama (1989, 1992).
[15] Verčič (2013).
[16] Fukuyama (1989, 1992).
[17] Welzel (2013).

multiple trends in the direction of human empowerment and emancipation. These trends are centreing around people gaining more control over their lives in combination with the spread of emancipative values emphasising free choice and equal opportunities. Studying the results of the World Value Survey shows that emancipative values are universal and not just a Western construction. They are driven by so-called action resources (the possibility to act and gain control over your life, especially economically) and by technological developments (e.g. media technology).[18] For communication professionals the question is how to position the profession within these global developments and how to handle these on the level of the individual practitioner, the organisation and the local and global societies.

It is easy to underestimate how Westernised the public relations industry is. While the so-called emergent and developing economies in the second decade of our century overtook the so-called advanced economies in the share of the global Gross Domestic Product (GDP) produced, it is only in 2016 that the first non-Western public relations agency entered the list of top 10 global public relations agencies: Chinese firm BlueFocus ranked 9 in the 2016 Global PR Agency Ranking produced by The Holmes Report.[19] And we are talking about a US$20 billion industry by 2020.

A quick look at the top academic programmes in public relations and communication management at US universities reveals a growing cohort of Asian students and professors, mostly Chinese and Korean. They are also very productive in research, but so far mainly reproducing ideas of their American professors. Their cultural background is still largely absent in their publications, but that is only a matter of time: we can clearly foresee non-Western ideas fertilising public relations and communication management thinking in the very near future.

Anybody who wants to stay at the top of the global communication game has to start paying attention to communication practices beyond the borders of the Western world. Besides that, excellence is also in perseverance and sustainability of one's ambition, consistently communicating the purpose of the organisation and its value to the global society is also part of excellent communication practice.

---

[18] Welzel (2013).
[19] The Holmes Report (2016).

Excellence in Globality

Globality is the term proposed by Jan Aart Scholte to describe the current state of globalisation, characterised by transplanetary relations and supraterritoriality.[20] There can be no doubt that the contemporary global society emerged out of Western modernisation that produced a Westernistic global society[21] with interdependence at its core.[22] Transplanetary relations between people are different from international relations as they are truly transcending borders, while the notion of international relations still carries with it the primacy of countries and relations between them. The British sociologist Anthony Giddens defined globalisation in transplanetary terms a quarter of a century ago: 'Globalization can thus be defined as the intensification of worldwide social relations which link distant localities in such a way that local happenings are shaped by events occurring many miles away and vice versa'.[23] Since then the Internet, social and mobile communications has brought us all even closer and into a network society.[24]

Commandments in Practice: Globalised

Acknowledging and Delivering Globality Through the Communication Strategy

Founded in 1857 as a small, local bank with the aim to foster international trade between the city of Santander in Spain and Latin America, Banco Santander today is one of the most important financial institutions in the world. The leading bank in the eurozone by market capitalisation, it has 3.6 million shareholders and a

---

[20] Scholte (2008).

[21] Debeljak (2012).

[22] Levy (1996).

[23] Giddens (1991), p. 64.

[24] Castells (2010).

retail presence in ten core markets in Europe and the Americas where its 190,000 employees serve more than 120 million clients through a network of 13,000 branches.

Santander believes its business model has been the key to turn itself from a small local bank into a globally renowned financial institution. Many companies in the banking sector have failed over the last few years due to their business models and risk management practices. However, Santander, with a diversified and client-oriented retail banking model, has weathered the difficulties better than others. Its financial strength, risk management culture and profitability have been widely recognised; as well as the bank's retail focus, geographical diversification, subsidiaries model and its brand, which is unified across the markets where the Group is present.

In 2004, after a process of rapid international expansion which began in the mid-1990s, the Group was composed of many local brand names without a common identity. It was missing the chance to make the most out of a strong single brand, which unifies objectives and generates synergies and efficiency. It is also a shield against potential crisis – as was later demonstrated. In April of 2004, the bank's board of directors addressed that need by approving a communication plan to implement common management of its corporate identity in all of its countries, units and divisions with the goal of creating a global brand capable of transmitting the Group's common purpose and values. Aside from setting guidelines to unify the Santander brand throughout its markets, the project put a shared communication policy in place which integrated views from the teams in all its markets.

The plan's main goal was to position the bank internationally to fully exploit the advantages of a global brand. These include a strong corporate culture with goals and values shared by all of the Group's employees; the ability to promote global business and product lines; to increase client loyalty and the value investors place on the brand; to generate synergies and cost efficiencies; to facilitate access to new markets and attract the best talent.

Reflecting internationalisation, in 2007 the bank was moving towards a single brand. In fact, in Spain, Mexico, Brazil and Portugal it was already a reality. Once the Group had created and implemented its single global brand, the next challenge was to place Santander among the most reputed brands in the world. This was the beginning of its 2007–2010 Brand and Identity Plan which was launched with the broad support of the Group's top management. That same year, coinciding with Santander's 150th anniversary, and taking advantage of the synergies generated by a single brand, Santander started the cooperative project 'Santander is you', aimed at communicating to all its employees the benefits of being part of a common project and to foster a sense of belonging.

Externally, the bank launched its first global advertising campaign for the whole Group in international financial media. We believe institutional advertising is essential to reinforce and cement global positioning. The bank's corporate message has always focused on attributes such as capital strength, financial soundness and a geographically diversified business model, but also customer proximity, trust and commitment.

It was also time to put together a plan to raise the awareness of the brand worldwide and the Group opted for a corporate strategy to assure a consistent and international positioning. We decided to have a corporate sponsorship platform instead of running it individually from the different countries. At that time, the Group thought global corporate sponsorships, which can be exploited locally in its different markets, would enable it to

(1) generate synergies and efficiency;
(2) have better control of the brand and its international expansion;
(3) reach out to diverse audiences, especially young people, with non-financial communication codes.

Regarding sponsorship, it is widely recognised that there are two sports that generate enthusiasm worldwide, F1 and football. Santander first sponsored the McLaren Formula 1 team and later began a long-lasting partnership with Scuderia Ferrari, which proved to be extremely successful. The average return on investment of the sponsorship turned out to be 5 to 1: we created value in communication. In Latin America, the bank became a key sponsor of the Libertadores football competition.

Santander's broad strategy bore fruit: in 2010, Banco Santander was included for the first time in the Interbrand ranking, becoming one of the big global brands. This was a breakthrough in the history of the bank, but it was just a starting point. Santander's aim since then has been to escalate its position in this ranking to become one of the top brands in the world. Today, it is the leading international retail brand by the prestigious Brand Finance Global 500 ranking published by The Banker magazine.

Challenges to the Strategy

The financial crisis, the worst in almost a century, proved the strength of the Santander model. Santander was among the very few banks to continue to pay dividends to its shareholders throughout the crisis period and to avoid a single quarter of losses. Moreover, the crisis offered the Group the opportunity to increase its presence in some of its key markets. Santander was perceived as a strong, trustworthy brand thanks to the recurrence of its results and the soundness of its balance sheet.

However, the financial crisis and its aftermath broadly changed the industry's landscape and posed a huge challenge in terms of business trends, regulation, consumer preferences and, of course, reputation. Banks around the world have to respond to unprecedented emerging difficulties in the economic, financial and regulatory environment, where there are increasingly strict frameworks for action. Moreover, they have to provide differential value to the main target audiences in an environment where there is a lack of trust in banks and where customer behaviours are rapidly changing as a result of the digital revolution.

In 2014, following the appointment of Ana Botín as the Group's executive chairman, Santander carried out an in-depth review of its priorities in view of the changes the industry was facing. Strengthening its culture, adapting and updating it to the needs of its customers and of the communities where the Group operates emerged as one of them. It became clear to the bank and its top management that in order to succeed, it was key to pursue a cultural transformation that required it to focus not only on the nature of the business Santander conducts, but also on the way it actually performs.

As a bank, Santander's purpose is to help people and businesses to prosper. We are convinced that if we fulfil that purpose, it will make us a better bank and the business will also prosper. And it must do it by being Simple, Personal and Fair in everything the bank does and by fostering corporate behaviours which we believe respond to the needs of all our stakeholders: its team members, customers, shareholders and the communities where the bank operates. In line with its local approach, communicating its purpose and the Santander way of doing business is adjusted to local cultures. The bank strives to be Simple, Personal, Fair in the United Kingdom; Easy, Personal, Fair in the United States; Simples, Próximo, Justo in Portugal or Simples, Pessoal, Justo in Brazil.

While the cultural transformation that is underway goes well beyond a communications issue, it is necessarily at the heart of Santander's communications strategy because it clearly requires evolving the way the bank delivers its messages to its stakeholders and, more importantly, the way it listens to them. It is a process that will sit on the Group's solid grounds and track record to help the bank respond to the unprecedented challenges and make Santander thrive.

Juan Manuel Cendoya
Juan Manuel Cendoya is Senior Executive Vice-President of Communications, Corporate Marketing and Research at Banco Santander in Madrid, Spain.

About Banco Santander
Banco Santander is a leading retail and commercial bank, based in Spain, with a meaningful market share in ten core countries in Europe and the Americas. Santander is the largest bank in the eurozone by market capitalisation and among the top banks on a global basis. Founded in 1857, Santander had €1.52 trillion in managed funds, 12,500 branches and 190,000 employees at the close of June 2016. In the first half of 2016, Santander made an underlying profit of €3,28 million.

From a communication perspective, it is supraterritoriality that makes the major difference (see Box 4). It means that we share media and channels that make information available to us in seconds or even fractions of a second. For example, this has important consequences for crisis communication where scholars talk about 'cross-national conflict shifting'.[25] Issues become global but have to be handled locally, without losing the mission and the original context of the organisation as the Danish company Arla experienced. They became involved in the famous cartoon crisis when people in the Middle East started boycotting Arla products because of its Danish roots and they associated those products with the cartoons of the prophet Mohammed published in Denmark.[26]

---

[25] Molleda and Quinn (2004).
[26] Holmström, Falkheimer and Nielsen (2009).

Box 4 Supraterritoriality

1. Transworld simultaneity
    Communication can extend anywhere across the planet at the same time, for example, nearly all of us use the same Apple or Android mobile devices that enable us to simultaneously share experiences, we share social media.
2. Transworld instantaneity
    Communication can move anywhere on the planet in no time, for example, the Internet is instantaneously moving nearly anything across our shared devices and media.

To become and remain excellent in communication in this brave new world of transplanetarity and supraterritoriality is a challenge organisations face in the twenty-first century. What does this mean for excellent communication management? Excellent communication today is globalised communication. This means that there is a deep understanding of the economy and society as globalised. A globalised world makes it necessary to have a global communicative perspective on the organisation and its activities and at the same time acknowledging the local circumstances that the organisation has to deal with. That is a typical hypermodern paradox. The interplay of the five aspects of globalisation (internationalisation, liberalisation, universalisation, Westernisation and globality) and how to handle those communicatively is one of the main practical issues for the profession in the future. Like it or not, strategic communication is (and has always been) undeniably one of the driving forces behind globalisation. The hypermodern paradox of the global and the local is a paradox that has many forms and calls for tailor made communicative solutions in every situation. Keeping the principles of Grunig's public relations theory and its extension of global and specific applications as a base gives the profession a good and workable starting point to help organisations grow in today's globalised world.

References

ARWU. (2016). *Academic Ranking of World Universities*. Retrieved from http://www.shanghairanking.com

Castells, M. (2010). *The Rise of the Network Society* (2nd ed.). Chichester: John Wiley & Sons.

Debeljak, A. (2012). In praise of hybridity: Globalization and the modern Western paradigm. In K. Sriramesh & D. Verčič (Eds.), *Culture and Public Relations: Links and Implications* (pp. 42–53). New York, NY: Routledge.

Fukuyama, F. (1989). The end of history? *The National Interest, 16* (Summer), 3–18.

Fukuyama, F. (1992). *The End of History and the Last Man.* New York, NY: Free Press.

Giddens, A. (1991). *The Consequences of Modernity.* Cambridge: Polity Press.

Grunig, J. E. (Ed.) (1992). *Excellence in Public Relations and Communication Management.* Hillsdale, NJ: Lawrence Erlbaum Associates.

Grunig, L. A., Grunig, J. E., & Dozier, D. M. (2002). *Excellent Public Relations and Effective Organisations: A Study of Communication Management in Three Countries.* Mahwah, NJ: Lawrence Erlbaum Associates.

Holmström, S., Falkheimer, J., & Nielsen, A. G. (2009). Legitimacy and strategic communication in globalization: The cartoon crisis and other legitimacy conflicts. *International Journal of Strategic Communication, 4*(1), 1–18.

Kippenberg, T. (2002). *Leadership Styles.* Oxford, UK: Capstone Publishing.

Levy Jr., M. J. (1996). *Modernisation and the Structure of Society, Volume 2: The Organisational Contexts of Society.* New Brunswick, NJ: Transaction.

Markoff, J. (2016). China wins new bragging rights in supercomputers. *The New York Times,* June 20. Retrieved from http://www.nytimes.com/2016/06/21/technology/china-tops-list-of-fastest-computers-again.html?_r=0

Molleda, J. C., & Quinn, C. (2004). Cross-national conflict shifting: A global public relations dynamics. *Public Relations Review, 30*(1), 1–9.

Peters, T. J., & Waterman, R. H. (1982). *In Search of Excellence: Lessons from America's Best-Run Companies.* New York, NY: Harper & Row.

Scholte, J. A. (2008). Defining globalization. *The World Economy, 31*(1), 1471–1502.

Sriramesh, K., & Verčič, D. (Eds.) (2009). *The Global Public Relations Handbook: Theory, Research, and Practice* (2nd ed.). New York: NY: Routledge.

The Holmes Report. (2016). *Global Top 250 PR Agency Ranking 2016.* Retrieved from http://www.holmesreport.com/ranking-and-data/global-communications-report/2016-pr-agency-rankings/top-250

Verčič, D. (2013). Comparative research in public relations: From European to global research designs. In D. Ingenhoff (Ed.), *Internationale PR-Forschung* (pp. 11–20). Konstanz: UVK.

Verčič, D., & Grunig, J. E. (2000). The origins of public relations theory in economics and strategic management. In D. Moss, D. Verčič, & G. Warnaby (Eds.), *Perspectives on Public Relations Research* (pp. 9–58). London: Routledge.

Verčič, D., Grunig, L. A., & Grunig, J. E. (1996). Global and specific principles of public relations: Evidence from Slovenia. In H. M. Culbertson & N. Chen (Eds.), *International Public Relations: A Comparative Analysis* (pp. 31–65). Mahwah, NJ: Lawrence Erlbaum Associates.

Verčič, D., Zerfass, A., & Wiesenberg, M. (2015). Global public relations and communication management: A European perspective. *Public Relations Review, 41*(5), 785–793.

Welzel, C. (2013). *Freedom Rising. Human Empowerment and the Quest for Emancipation*. Cambridge: Cambridge University Press.

Zerfass, A., Moreno, A., Tench, R., Verčič, D., & Verhoeven, P. (2013). *European Communication Monitor 2013. A Changing Landscape – Managing Crises, Digital Communication and CEO Positioning in Europe. Results of a Survey in 43 Countries*. Brussels: EACD/EUPRERA, Helios Media.

Commandment 2
Mediatised: Media All Around Us

Let's be honest. Successful communication is difficult to achieve, especially when mass media are involved. Today media are almost always involved in the communication process. When the Canadian philosopher Marshall McLuhan described the world as a global village[1] due to media causing its implosion there was no Internet, and the Internet changed everything. McLuhan's basic idea was that societies change when they start using new technologies, including media technology.

The development of that media technology has changed the way organisations communicate considerably in the last decade. Organisations can no longer only rely on the traditional mass media to get their message across and reach their stakeholders. Today they have to actively communicate with publics online and through social media as well. As a result of the changing media landscape some corporations are becoming media producers themselves searching for an audience. Besides advertising, publicity and press relations a whole range of new media practices have emerged; from social media and web care teams to forming alliances with media companies and creating owned media (the new term for corporate publishing) to communicate directly to publics. It has added new touchpoints with audiences, new ways of interaction and speeded up considerably the communication process as well as adding new, active publics.

The ability to cope with the dramatically changing media landscape has consistently been found to be one of the most important strategic issues for the field according to the professionals surveyed in over the ten years of the European

---

[1] McLuhan and Fiore (1968).

© The Author(s) 2017
R. Tench et al., *Communication Excellence*,
DOI 10.1007/978-3-319-48860-8_2

Communication Monitor. Coping with digital evolution and the social web was always high on the list of strategic issues for the profession.[2] Other top challenges identified in the study series are the increasing speed and volume of the information flow and the demand for more transparency and active audiences. Buzzwords in the field today are digitalisation, being always connected and blurring boundaries between advertising and editorial media content. If we take a step back we can summarise all these developments and issues with the term *mediatisation*.[3] The mediatisation of society influences organisations and the way they communicate. Should an organisation with an excellent communication function today be a mediatised organisation? We will argue: yes. That's why the second commandment for excellent communication is: be mediatised. In general that means that excellent communication professionals are aware of the omnipresence of media inside and outside the organisation and the possible effects that has on relationships and reputation. Mediated communication is different from interpersonal communication, has specific characteristics and specific consequences. Let's first take a closer look at the concept of mediatisation.

The Omnipresence of Media

Mediatisation first and foremost means the omnipresence of media in our current hypermodern society. We do not live *with*, but *in* media, is the central message of the book *Media Life* written by communication scholar Mark Deuze from the Netherlands.[4] He describes how people today are surrounded by media and are almost constantly in the presence of media. This omnipresence of media is the first dimension of mediatisation. But there is more to it. Media that are at hand anytime, anywhere also have cultural consequences. Institutions in society, like corporations and other types of organisations, will adapt to this omnipresence of media. They will be influenced by the way media work and by what is important to media. They will start behaving accordingly. News values and news factors are traditionally only important for journalists, yet today are becoming a wider cultural phenomenon.[5] Furthermore these news values and factors are – along with others – connected to entertainment because of the commercialisation of the media world. This contagion of journalism and

---

[2] Zerfass et al. (2016b), pp. 54–57.
[3] See for an overview Hjarvard (2008).
[4] Deuze (2012).
[5] Galtung and Ruge, (1965); Harcup and O'Neill (2001).

entertainment has produced a widespread media logic that is recognisable everywhere in the hypermodern society.[6] For example in the way individuals present themselves on YouTube, Facebook, Twitter and other social media. Many people today from all walks of life know unerringly how to make a good media product and do it. This broad cultural development in the direction of media logic is the second dimension of mediatisation.

Organisations are not only influenced by this mediatisation in their relationships with the traditional media and journalists, but also in their relationships with other people, such as employees, consumers and advocacy groups. Mediatised communication is everywhere, inside and outside the organisation. And communication professionals will be asked how all these media should be used best.

Commandments in Practice: Mediatised

PORSCHE

Corporate Digital Solutions for Modern Media Consumption Habits

With the launch of the *Porsche Newsroom*, the German sportscar manufacturer has moved its public relations activities into the digital age, enabling it to provide transparent information via modern channels. The Internet platform combines social media content with a rich array of editorial material. It thus serves as a corporate blog, an online magazine and a social media hub in one. This approach has many advantages. While the traditional press release continues to play an important role when working with journalists, new channels and target groups are increasingly coming to the fore. The importance of bloggers and social media users for companies is continuously increasing.

---

[6] Altheide and Snow (1979).

Moreover, media professionals are working online more and more. Now they have a central port of call on the Internet, which not only offers them exclusive content but also makes a wide range of additional information, such as press releases, photos and videos, available for download. Fast, up-to-date and comprehensive. The Porsche Newsroom transitions public relations into the new, digital age of corporate communication.[7] This case study explains how companies can adapt to the changes caused by the digital media shift and meet the needs of modern journalism at the same time.

Changes in Communication Regarding Content and Direct Communication

A brand is nothing without content: to enthuse people for your brand, you must use stories. About half of today's corporations focus on content rather than on advertising messages. In the future, quality will outweigh quantity – and this quality has to meet journalistic criteria.

The discrepancy between high theoretical demand and insufficient practical relevance has increased in times of the digital media shift. Digitisation accelerates the convergence of different channels and thus promotes the merging of communication sub-disciplines. While classic media theory dictated a strict separation of the development of advertising content, public relations messages and media strategy, the rise of digital channels like social media requires a much stronger integration. Corporations no longer rely on classic gatekeepers such as journalists – they are capable of communicating directly with end customers. To generate interest and acceptance among users, the distributed content has to support the corporate strategic targets and, at the same time, meet news value criteria from public relations.

The world is changing at a much faster pace than it used to. Business models that are considered highly modern today might lose their relevance tomorrow. Everybody is affected by these kinds of changes. They can either follow the trend or remain unchanged. The question is whether those who remain unchanged continue to achieve economic success.

Communications at Porsche

Dr. Ing. h.c. F. Porsche AG has been part of the Volkswagen Group since 2009. In the fiscal year 2015 Porsche delivered 225,121 vehicles, and its turnover was 21.5 billion Euro. By the end of August 2016, the number of employees had reached a new record, with 26.732 people working at the company. Around 100 communication professionals work for Porsche in the departments of Product and Technical Communications, Politics and External Relations, Event and International Communications, Porsche Museum, Corporate Communications and Corporate Publishing. They all provide input to a central editorial team. Here, messages and topics are created, formatted with a multimedia approach, and spread through the various channels available – externally through the *Porsche Newsroom* (newsroom.porsche.com), social media sites and the customer magazine *Christophorus*, and internally through various media branded with the *Carrera* name.

---

[7] Arweck (2016a).

The Porsche Newsroom as a Primary Contact Point Online
Porsche has been challenged by external changes resulting from the digital media shift – primarily the rise of digital channels like social media. These changes confronted the business with the need to do some rethinking and adapting. The considerations led to the formation of four propositions for future communication:

- Online presence is becoming an increasingly important factor for companies since many journalists carry out research online before contacting media spokespeople.
- As mentioned previously, the well-known gatekeeping approach of traditional media is evolving into new areas.
- Furthermore, teenagers between the ages of 12 and 19 whose media usage is 94 per cent from the Internet are becoming a relevant target group for companies.
- And, last but not least, both bloggers and print journalists alike are facing constant time pressure. This means that companies have to respond to inquiries more quickly than before. After all, most of the journalists' work is carried out online, making mobile functionality, responsiveness and fast loading times an absolute necessity.

Porsche's answer to these propositions has been to define a digital agenda: up-to-date resources are to be provided for traditional media and Porsche also wants to create its own online media. What's more, new multipliers have to be taken seriously.

Porsche promotes a transformation 2.0 to adapt to modern media consumption habits – and the answer is the Porsche Newsroom (the Newsroom) as its own digitised communication channel. By targeting new multipliers like bloggers and social media influencers (SMIs), Porsche refines classic media with up-to-date instruments.

Porsche has established the online newsroom as the corporation's key communication instrument and made it its primary contact point for information search online. The open-source strategy supports accessibility for new media target groups and supplies influencers with company-specific content.[8] The link-up with social media platforms provides users of the Newsroom with a multichannel supplementary offer. Thus, the Newsroom functions as a platform for cross-media interaction and as an interface to provide content and information. The Porsche Newsroom benefits from Twitter due to its rapidity and immediacy. A platform to combine all channels was missing until now. The Porsche Newsroom changes that and minimises research efforts by means of efficient search engine optimisation (SEO) of the content. With its Newsroom and social media platforms, Porsche has facilitated direct and specific contact with (new) target groups as well as stakeholders.[9]

---

[8] Arweck (2016b).
[9] Arweck (2016a).

Content can be distributed among users without being influenced by gate-keepers. The benefits are topicality and outreach. However, the corporate influence on public opinion is reduced. Nevertheless, bidirectional communication and the possibilities for reputation management and branding outweigh the arising challenges. Return channels on social media platforms offer diverse feedback opportunities and allow directly accessible monitoring. The respective Newsroom articles form thematic hubs, which are complemented with additional content and value-adding services such as videos, live streaming, galleries, downloads and links.

The Newsroom facilitates the merging of new media content and classic corporate publishing in order to offer sustainable information for journalists and influencers. The key to successful corporate publishing both internally and externally is good content. Good content provides answers to questions and offers solutions. What's more, good content is also fun. It is intended to entertain and inspire without being deadly serious or even shallow. Moreover, it implies an aspect of service and engages to a high degree. All in all, good content is a great variety of things. However, this variety is meticulously planned and anything but random. The Porsche Newsroom provides insight into this level of variety, with complex technical topics, recent product reports and articles about events – all presented in a contemporary way.

To make this possible, all the departments in public relations, marketing and the Porsche in-house Newsroom work closer together both spatially and thematically. Synergy effects allow in-depth editorial analysis, which makes the Newsroom content a collection of hard facts and news and also provides secondary information from different fields of activities. Additional data, behind-the-scenes material and first-hand information are collected from the departments. This ensures that the density of news and information is considerably boosted by the expertise of employees actively creating Newsroom content.

A Multichannel Platform: Present in the Concept of Every Article
On 15–16 July 2014, Porsche returned to the legendary 24 Hours of Le Mans – the world's most famous long-distance race. The event caused a media sensation worldwide, so it was the ideal moment to launch a new communication channel. Starting on 10 June, Porsche offered pre-race coverage in the Newsroom with exclusive content on Le Mans. The reporting was aimed at motorsport journalists, bloggers and the online community. After the race, the content was expanded to several topics and business activities. The target group was thus broadened to include all representatives of the press. In the introduction phase, Porsche consciously focused on new channels like Twitter and Vine. E-cards on certain articles and short videos posted daily were supposed to raise interest. The content was widely disseminated on social media, and online multipliers were included from the beginning.

Over two years the company published approximately seven articles per week on the front page in different main categories such as Company, Products, Technology, Motorsports, History and Christophorus. The latter includes stories from the eponymous Porsche customer magazine. The coverage on Le Mans 2016 shows how the Newsroom has developed. In the weeks ahead of Le Mans, the Newsroom offered news and pictures about the race strategy, tests, qualifying rounds and the Porsche Racing Team. Furthermore, the latest press releases were publicised online, where they were accessible without registration. The articles and background coverage offered detailed information and a multitude of insights. One day before the race, the Newsroom provided a race forecast in a broadcast press conference.

During the race, social media and live streaming made it possible for information to be disseminated late, directly and immediately as breaking news. The social media stream formed the heart of the Le Mans article. This element was a positive addition to the live coverage from Le Mans. Within seconds, users were offered streaming updates on the race – something a press release could never have achieved in such a short period. Thus, the Newsroom directly addressed a second target group, which seeks to consume information quickly and in a compact form and at a glance. The social stream is a hands-on example of how Porsche managed to adapt its news coverage to modern media consumption habits. It covered the information channels from the racing team, the motorsports department and the Newsroom itself.

Editors also uploaded current press releases to the Newsroom so that users had access to many previous racing hours. The Le Mans article was rounded off by a wide range of additional information and material such as videos, galleries, links and downloads as well as an infographic illustrating the race. The event was accompanied on social media: the rapidly growing Instagram community received first-hand picture material directly posted by a team member on site. The team provided live updates from the pit on Twitter. Therefore, the Le Mans return in combination with the Newsroom coverage has been a big success for the company.

Another example of the diversity of stories and material in the Newsroom is the coverage of the world premiere of the concept study Mission E, the first four-door all-electric vehicle in the company's history. With almost one million page impressions on Twitter, Porsche even reached the Top 10 Hashtags on Twitter Germany – a milestone and another measure of success.

Regarding the world premiere of the new model Porsche Panamera in June 2016, Porsche used the Newsroom as an information channel in the run-up to this major event. A live stream covering the launch was placed in the Newsroom. Afterwards, this video was made available as a recording.

The Newsroom not only provides stories and information but also reflects journalists' views on Porsche. After selected journalists had tested the new Porsche 718 Boxster, for example, Porsche covered the feedback responses from the international press. The Newsroom had announced the article as part of a campaign on Facebook and Twitter. This way, the Porsche Newsroom not only addressed journalists but also the online community.

A Success Story: How the Porsche Newsroom Lives Up to Journalists' Expectations
A survey on the online use of communication professionals and journalists in Germany in 2013 showed that nine out of ten spokespersons address not only journalists with their content.[10] Customers, competitors, other players in the

---

[10] News Aktuell and Faktenkontor (2013). For this study, 452 journalists, 711 professionals working in communication departments and 307 practitioners working in public relations agencies in Germany were surveyed online.

market and the general public have become relevant target groups as well. At the same time, editors and operators of corporate newsrooms often struggle to understand which content and additional material are actually interesting to journalists; what material facilitates their work; and in which way content should be displayed. This primarily includes the supply of graphics: pictures complement stories and support storytelling by playing a major role in the reader's understanding of texts. Since many journalists work under time pressure, they themselves also rely on photographs as part of the information. According to another study, 87 per cent of journalists think it is important or very important to receive press releases that include graphical material.[11]

Besides graphical material, videos and PDF documents increase the feedback on press releases and news. In the earlier survey, 81 per cent of the journalists and 87 per cent of public relations practitioners agree on the benefits of additional material.[12] Social media platforms also have a growing impact. Younger journalists regularly use the platforms for research purposes.[13] Furthermore, a number of influential bloggers and online multipliers are active on Twitter.

The *Porsche Newsroom* lives up to these expectations: the hits increase constantly. Within one year, the number of visits rose by more than 140 per cent. The social media platforms also gained new followers.

One of the indicators of success in the early stage of the Newsroom was the huge growth of the Twitter channel and the rapid increase in range. On the day of 'go live', 10 June 2014, 245 users followed the @PorscheNewsroom account. Within five weeks, the channel exceeded the mark of 1,000 followers. One year after the launch, 104,000 people followed the Newsroom on Twitter. In June 2016, at the time of the 24 Hour Race of Le Mans, the Newsroom had surpassed the milestone of 264,000 followers – and today there are 400,000. Users interact, retweet and respond positively to the content.

Companies have to tell stories in order to raise interest – a variety of stories can be told about Porsche. Storytelling has emerged as a more significant form of representation and content creation. In conclusion, thanks to the *Porsche Newsroom*, journalists and bloggers receive information faster and can use it on different channels, thus generating efficient coverage that spans a range of media. But the general public also has access to the content. The keyword here is open source. In this way, every user can become a distributor. The advantage of adapting this journalistic model in corporate communication is therefore self-evident.

---

[11] News Aktuell (2016). The study is based on a convenient sample of 1,223 journalists across Germany.

[12] News Aktuell and Faktenkontor (2013).

[13] News Aktuell (2016).

Josef Arweck
Dr. Josef Arweck is the Vice President of Communications at Porsche AG in Stuttgart-Zuffenhausen, Germany.

About Porsche
The Dr. Ing. h.c. F. Porsche AG is the most successful manufacturer of luxury sports cars. The company is based in Stuttgart-Zuffenhausen. In the fiscal year 2015 Porsche delivered 225,121 cars to customers. Revenues were 21.5 billion euros, a 25 per cent increase compared to the previous year. The operating results increased by one quarter to 3.4 billion euros. The number of employees (26,732) reached a new record level.

The Great Convergence of Media Importance and Use

Are social media more important for strategic communication today than press and media relations? Is corporate publishing more important than events or online communication? The answer is: not really. There are slight differences between the popularity of various channels and instruments. But overall the past decade has shown a great convergence of media importance and use in the field of communication management in Europe. Today all media are perceived as equally important. Offline and online press and media relations, corporate publishing or owned media, online communication, social media, mobile communication, events, interpersonal and non-verbal communication. They all constitute one big group of media used by professionals. That is a very different situation compared to ten years ago when there were still clear boundaries between the different media types. Press and media relations stood apart from social media and interpersonal and nonverbal and so did events and paid communication. Over the years the importance of online communication and social media increased but it did not fully replace the importance of press and media relations. The gatekeepers of the traditional mass media remain important. This great convergence of media use can be seen in Fig. 5 where the media use by communication professionals over the years is plotted.

Strategic communication today has a diversified mix of media at its disposal. It has to work with the increased amount of touchpoints with all kinds of publics. For communication professionals this is mediatisation in overdrive, or without hyperbole, hypermediatisation!

Perceived importance for addressing stakeholders, gatekeepers and audiences

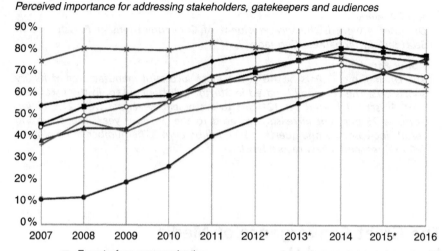

- ■- Face-to-face communication
- ◆- Online communication via websites, e-mail, intranets
- ●- Social media and social networks (Blogs, Twitter, Facebook and the like)
- ▲- Press and media relations with online newspapers/magazines
- ○- Press and media relations with TV and radio stations
- ✳- Press and media relations with print newspapers/magazines
- +- Events

Fig. 5 The great convergence of media and channels rated important for strategic communication through the years 2007–2016[14]

The Three Faces of Mediatisation for Communication Management

Although all media are considered equally important, in practice mediatisation has three different faces for communication professionals in organisations: the classical face of press and media relations with journalists,[15] the new face that goes under the heading of social media or computer-mediated communication (CMC)[16] and the future face of strategic mediatisation where opportunities are taken and

---

[14] Zerfass et al. (2016b), p. 60. Longitudinal analysis 2007–2016 based on 13,709 responses from communication professionals in 43 countries. Q: How important are the following methods in addressing stakeholders, gatekeepers and audiences today? Scale 1 (not important) – 5 (very important). Percentages: frequency based on scale points 4–5. * No data collected in these years; figure shows extrapolated values.

[15] For example, see Ihlen and Pallas (2014).

[16] For example, see Walther (1992).

alliances with media corporations are being built to search for new audiences (see Box 5).[17]

Box 5 Three faces of mediatisation

- The classical face
  Of press and media relations with journalists like newspapers, radio, television and online channels made by journalists.
- The new face
  Going under the heading of computer mediated or social media communication, like blogs, videoblogs, YouTube channels, Facebook, Twitter, Instagram and similar outlets and platforms.
- The future face
  Strategic mediatisation where opportunities are taken and alliances with media corporations are being built to search for new audiences like content marketing, native advertising and brand journalism.

When we look at press and media relations it is clear that online communication with journalists has increased and therefore in tandem the form and speed of media relations has changed. The importance of media relations in both the offline and online world has not changed. When we consider CMC with others and not just journalists, we can see that over the years there is a constant overestimation of the new developments and a slow adaptation to social media. In other words communication professionals are enthusiastic about the new media possibilities but do not know how to implement them immediately in the context of their organisation.

There are also inevitably new questions for practice that emerge in this changing landscape. The main challenge being the new role of employees in the mediatised world. Employees today can exercise more influence through social media on the information flow and the image of organisations than even before. They are a new group of gatekeepers but they are inside the organisation. This new openness and loss of control due to the technological developments of the media is feared by some, but is unstoppable.

When we consider strategic mediatisation the importance of owned media and strategic alliances with media corporations is expected to grow in order to influence public opinion about the organisation. Many communication professionals are thinking about these new forms of strategic mediatisation as a way to go. Let's now take a closer look at these three faces of mediatisation.

---

[17] Zerfass et al. (2016a).

The Classical Face: Press and Media Relations, Still the Top Dog

We know that press and media relations have always been at the heart of public relations. It still is and this key position has not changed in the last decade. There has only been a shift from paper to screen. Handling the offline press has lost importance and handling the online press and TV and radio has gained importance in the last ten years. That is why it is the first face of mediatisation.

These press and media relations distinguish public relations from other communication disciplines. Its importance shows its political dimension. What does this mean? It means that organisations are aware of the public debate and where it touches the organisation and its issues. Organisations monitor the public debate, participate in it and try to influence the opinion climate and the public mood about their organisation and issues that are associated with the organisation. Even in times of social media communication professionals know and recognise the opinion-leading role of journalists. That will stay important since research also shows that having a proactive media policy has been shown to have a positive effect on the media image of corporations.[18] Although the visibility of corporations is low[19] and it is always about the same group of corporations,[20] we know that traditional media generally report positively about companies. Media frames, which are the frameworks in which certain problems are diagnosed, evaluated and prescribed,[21] in newspapers follow corporate frames except when environmental and health issues are involved or financial malpractice.[22] Non-governmental organisations have more influence on newspaper content than corporations[23] and in times of corporate crisis we know that the news media can be of crucial importance for an organisation.[24]

But what are the effects of publicity about organisations on the public? The effects are diverse and paradoxical, as media effects always are. Media attention can be positive, negative or have no effect. News about successes of a company reinforces an already existing positive reputation. Negative news about a company may damage the reputation, but not necessarily so. It can also lead

---

[18] Verhoeven (2016).

[19] Capriotti (2009).

[20] Mizuno et al. (2012).

[21] Entman (1993).

[22] Verhoeven (2016).

[23] Boumans (2016).

[24] Van Der Meer (2016).

to an underdog effect; for example after a negative news story the reputation can become more positive, in other words the public blames the media or other actors for negatively describing an organisation or a sector.[25] For example aviation fans will not change their image of their favourite airline after negative publicity. Sometimes there is an effect on the organisation itself; the organisation changes its own behaviour after being held accountable by the international business press.[26]

The New Face: Co-Production of News

The traditional mass media and its effects are at the root of mediatisation. Today journalists are accompanied by bloggers, videobloggers and other digital thought leaders, for example, on Twitter, but the underlying communication process is the same. Research shows that the process of news production about business is a co-production between corporations and the media.[27] The key word is interdependence. The production of news about organisations is a multi-levelled interdependent process.[28] What do we mean by that? Mutual relationships are present on the individual level of communication professionals and journalists, on the departmental level of communication departments and editorial offices of the media and on the level of society where the flow of information about organisations depends on the professions of public relations and journalism. These networks at different levels result in firm cooperation that is more or less successful.

The co-production of news is influenced by several factors (see Box 6). First by the relationship between public relations professionals and journalists, second by the organisational and societal culture, third by the business sector and fourth by the visibility of communication professionals in the media that can both be negative or positive.[29] Public relations professionals and journalists in Europe acknowledge their mutually dependent relationship and have buried the hatchet.[30] But what about the future?

---

[25] Meijer and Kleinnijenhuis (2006a, 2006b).

[26] Dyck et al. (2008).

[27] Verhoeven (2016).

[28] Van Ruler (2005); Bentele et al. (1997).

[29] Verhoeven (2016).

[30] Neijens and Smit (2006).

Box 6 Co-production of news: four influencing factors

- Relationship between PR professionals and journalists
- Organisational and societal cultures
- Business sector or societal system
- Visibility of PR professionals in the media that can both be negative or positive

The Future Face: The Media as a Partner: Strategic Mediatisation

Next to the function of press and media relations geared towards so-called earned publicity, there has always been a parallel function of corporate publishing. This function is concerned with media that are owned by the organisation and over which the organisation has control. Traditionally corporate publishing is familiar in the form of internal employee and external customer magazines and then other paid information like image ads and co-productions with media. Although the importance of these owned media has not changed in the last decade, under the influence of the changing media landscape and the information and communication technology revolution, this branch of professional communication has diversified and taken on new forms. This third face of mediatisation is referred to as strategic mediatisation and will, according to European communication professionals, gain considerable importance in the future.[31] But what does this strategic mediatisation entail? What is new?

Strategic or reflective mediatisation refers to changes in the media landscape on two levels. First the blurring of lines between advertising and editorial content of the media and secondly the media housing of corporations. This media housing involves the production of media content by organisations themselves instead of by traditional media companies.[32] Corporations, non-profits and governmental organisation have all started creating their own media houses that produce media content and explore media platforms, for example, on YouTube. In this way they can communicate directly to defined audiences and have total control of the content of the information and the way it is presented.

---

[31] Zerfass et al. (2016a).

[32] Macnamara et al. (2016); Verčič and Tkalac Verčič (2016).

Boundaries between journalism, public relations, branding and advertising are breaking down. The key point of strategic mediatisation consists of this process of developing new modes of cooperation with the mass media and also operating as a media producer.

Media Housing of Organisations

The new ways of cooperating with the mass media are labelled in the following new terms: *native advertising, content marketing* and *brand journalism.*[33] *Native advertising* refers to the placement of paid content about an organisation or its products in an editorial media environment. This is another way of working with the media through media content sponsoring and product placement. This new form of advertising is especially suited for online media but is also used in the press and on radio and TV.[34] *Content marketing* is the '21st century corporate publishing'.[35] It is creating and distributing all kinds of content about the organisation in all kinds of self-owned media. The goal is attracting publics, customers and other stakeholders to this content and connecting with them. *Brand journalism* uses journalistic skills to write and report about the corporate or product brands of the organisation. It can be observed in special features and special sections in the media, properly identified and labelled as originating from an organisation.[36] Brand journalism suits the media logic very well in combining information and entertainment. Brand journalism operates in the sunlight, bright and open so everyone can see who the sender of the messages is.[37]

These three new forms of media content can be produced in a strategic alliance with a media organisation or by the organisation itself and published in owned media and on online media platforms. More than half of the European communication professionals think that this new use of owned media to shape public opinion about the organisation and its activities will gain importance in the next few years.[38] Strategic partnerships with mass media are the most likely form it will take with the co-production of content and the offering of joint

---

[33] Verčič and Tkalac Verčič (2016); Zerfass et al. (2016a).

[34] Verčič and Tkalac Verčič (2016).

[35] Macnamara (2014), p. 747.

[36] Dvorkin (2012).

[37] Verčič and Tkalac Verčič (2016).

[38] Zerfass et al. (2015), pp. 16–25.

publications and services to the public. A new practice of media housing that supplements and modifies classical media relations is born.

The Rise of Social Media and CMC

Since 2007 communication professionals in Europe have slowly become accustomed to the new media landscape of Facebook, Twitter and all other forms of social media. The rise of CMC is the third face of mediatisation for strategic communication. What does this mean for organisations and what is the broader context of this new and comprehensive media landscape? It is a new phase in the electronic age where personal and social environments are connected through the new communication technologies. Some call our time the start of a digital era, a new era of communication where the global village is rewired. Rewired into a world with increasingly personalised media use. This new media world has advantages over the old media world like the decentralisation of power and control but it also has a risk of tribalisation. A new media world where you are alone with your personalised medium or locked up in your 'tribe', your own group with no communication with the outside world.[39]

Communication professionals surveyed by the European Communication Monitor knew right from the start that these digital developments were important, especially concerning media, but they consequently overestimated how it would be implemented in organisations and did not adapt very quickly to it. Obviously organisations and professionals could not keep pace with the changing media environment. Why? First of all, like everyone else, they had to get into it. Personal use of social media developed slowly among practitioners, but when it did it helped to increase professional use. Second, age had something to do with it. Younger professionals are more competent in the digital world than older professionals. Although overall the social media skills of communication professionals remain moderate. Third, social media was considered an opportunity but at the same time a threat. The openness it required and the loss of control of the communication process it caused were feared. What to do, for example, with employees who suddenly start speaking publicly about the organisation? Let's take a closer look at CMC and strategic communication.

---

[39] Griffin et al. (2015).

CMC Equals Face-to-Face Communication

CMC has long been considered a lesser form of communication compared to face-to-face communication. The ideal of a rich interpersonal contact in each other's presence could not ever be matched with communication through computers we thought. CMC was considered only useful for instrumental and impersonal communication, simple task information, news and business conversations. Especially the lack of social context cues was a concern. That could easily result in so-called 'flaming'; a process where much more hostile language is used online than would be used in an offline context.[40] Flaming is not only a problem for individuals but also for organisations, as many communication professionals will have experienced, for example, on Twitter when one tweet leads to an enormous flow of shares, new tweets and finally attention by journalists in the newspapers, on radio and on television.

Thanks to the development of media technology in the last decade, online communication today is much richer than before. The increased richness of cues in CMC, for example, through sound, images and real-time connection, makes it possible for users to effectively develop close relationships online. In terms of processing social information CMC has become almost the same as face-to-face communication.[41]

Today online, social media, mobile and face-to-face communication are considered almost equally important by communication professionals. Their importance, but that of interpersonal communication as well, has risen a great deal since 2007 (see Fig. 5). It seems that also organisational communication is heading into the direction of hyper-personal communication that fits the time.[42] For communication management this has an external as well as an internal aspect.

Social Media Use in Strategic Communication

As we saw in the development of media use in the last ten years, social and online media blended in with the traditional mass media (see Fig. 5). Since 2013 there is no growth anymore in the perceived importance of social

---

[40] Griffin et al. (2015).

[41] Walther (2011).

[42] Walther (1996).

media. Analysing the wide range of new media possibilities that European organisations use we see two dimensions. A group of low-profile social media, on the one hand, and a group of high-profile social media, on the other hand. The low-profile group is the most important part of social media use by organisations (see Box 7), showing that many have not yet got used to the new reality of media-rich CMC.

Box 7 Two dimensions of social media use in strategic communication

- Low-profile social media
  Wiki's, social bookmarks, online audio, slide sharing, mobile applications, mash-ups and location-based services
- High-profile social media
  Online videos, weblogs, online communities (social networks), microblogs (e.g. Twitter) and photo sharing

---

In general, communication professionals in Europe know how to deliver messages via social media and they know about social media trends and strategies.[43] Managing online communities and initiating web-based dialogues however is not something they feel themselves capable of. Social media are therefore mainly used as a one-way communication tool and not so much as a possibility to engage with internal and external stakeholders. Social media skills are higher in private companies and agencies compared to joint stock companies, governmental and non-profit organisations. Also consultants and communication professionals working in agencies have a stronger belief in social networks and Twitter then professionals working in departments.

The vast majority of communication professionals in Europe think however that social media influences the perceptions and attitudes about the organisation of external stakeholders and of employees. The most important consequence of the new media landscape is the rise of new gatekeepers.[44] Traditionally journalists were the most important gatekeepers in the public sphere. Journalists in media organisations selected and processed certain events about the organisation and took decisions to publish or not. They decided what events were admitted through the gates of the media on the

---

[43] Zerfass et al. 2016b), pp. 84–89.
[44] Zerfass et al. 2016b), pp. 68–75.

grounds of amongst other things newsworthiness.[45] Today journalists have company. New gatekeepers stood up in the last ten years and joined journalists. For organisations, consumers, bloggers and employees are the most important ones that use social media to express themselves about the organisation, its products or on wider issues. They are commonly known as SMIs (see Box 8).

> **Box 8 Social media influencers (SMIs)**
>
> SMIs can be defined as a 'new type of third party endorsers who shape audience attitudes through blogs, tweets, and the use of other social media'.[46]

The results of the European Communication Monitor show that the majority of organisations in Europe (58.4 per cent) understand that SMIs are important but are still struggling with how to communicate with them. A minority of the organisations know how to monitor them (40.1 per cent) or have specific strategies for communicating with these new opinion leaders (42.9 per cent). Identifying important SMIs is another question. A vast majority of communication professionals identify them by looking at the relevance of the topics or issues covered by the SMI on social media and his or her personal reputation. Other characteristics are the content SMIs share and forward and their position in the social network they represent (see Fig. 6 for an overview). Many communication professionals have not fully grasped the concept of influence and opinion leadership by the SMIs. This major characteristic of mediatisation is a challenge for the profession.

The Rise of the New Gatekeepers

Consumers, bloggers and employees are considered relevant and important as new digital gatekeepers about the organisation on the social web, and therefore take an important position alongside and in addition to journalists.

The active public of interested and involved consumers and interest groups now have their own media as well, just like the organisation has.

---

[45] McQuail (2005).
[46] Freberg et al. (2011), p. 90.

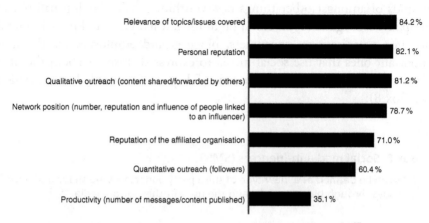

Fig. 6 Important factors for identifying social media influencers[47]

Not much new there, only the speed of information flow and the dynamics of it has changed. This is especially notable in times of crisis for example.[48] The active public now has its own channels and they use them to send their messages quickly and in an unfiltered form.

The most important change however is the rise of the employee as gate-keeper for sharing information about the organisation with the outside world. Employees today can easily bypass the public relations department and blog, tweet or take part in online discussions about the organisation and its issues. This shows the blurring line between internal and external communication. Clear boundaries between the inside and the outside world no longer exist. The social media revolution has put employees in a new communicative role. Although most of them use this new role to share positive experiences about the organisation,[49] organisations are worried about this. The development of social media governance structures gained momentum in 2011 when almost 40 per cent of the European organisations had implemented guidelines for communicating about the organisation on blogs and Twitter.[50] Also tools for monitoring stakeholder communication

---

[47] Zerfass et al. (2016b), p. 73. n^{min} = 2,489 communication professionals across Europe. Q: In your opinion, how important are the following factors for identifying social media influencers which are truly relevant for an organisation? Scale 1 (not important) – 5 (very important). Percentages: frequencies based on scale points 4–5.

[48] Van Der Meer (2016).

[49] Verhoeven (2012).

[50] Zerfass et al. (2011), pp. 90–105.

came into place about that time in one third of the organisations. Training programmes for social media and the development of key performance indicators for measuring social media activities of organisational members lagged behind and are not often implemented yet, but were wished for.

Besides the new gatekeeping role for employees the new media landscape also led to the mediatisation of internal communication. Employees today are, just like any other public, always connected through media to each other but also with the rest of society.

Excellence Linked to Mediatised

Excellent communication today is mediatised communication. This means that there is a deep understanding of the concept of the world as a global village[51] connected by media and that we live in media not with media.[52] Our life and also our organisational life is mediatised, as citizen, employee and as a communication professional. For the profession the mediatisation has three interplaying faces: the independent, free and global press, the owned media of the organisation itself and the hyper-personalised CMC in all its forms. Recognising and acknowledging all these different kinds of media with their specific patterns and ways of working is the ground rule for any communication department which wants to be excellent (see Box 9).

Box 9 What we have learned from excellent departments concerning mediatisation

Excellent communication departments:

- collaborate more intensively with the mass media, especially in producing joint quality content and topical platforms;
- monitor news and public opinion better;
- spread information proactively;
- evaluate media coverage more;
- influence gatekeepers, media agenda and stakeholders more
- are better at sourcing internal media;
- point out the demand for communication and transparency by the mass media;
- are better qualified in the field of social media
- are pioneers in mobile communication.

---

[51] McLuhan and Fiore (1968).
[52] Deuze (2012).

References

Altheide, D. L., & Snow, R. P. (1979). *Media Logic*. Beverly Hills, CA: Sage.

Arweck, J. (2016a). Fallbeispiel Porsche: Ein Social Media Newsroom für Journalisten, Blogger und Online-Multiplikatoren. In C. Moss (Ed.), *Der Newsroom in der Unternehmenskommunikation* (pp. 169–178). Wiesbaden: Springer VS.

Arweck, J. (2016b). *Der Porsche Newsroom: Ein Blick hinter die Kulissen*. Retrieved from http://content-marketing-forum.com/blog/der-porsche-newsroom-ein-blick-hinter-die-kulissen

Bentele, G., Liebert, T., & Seeling, S. (1997). Von der determination zur Intereffikation. Ein integriertes Modell zum Verhältnis von public relations und Journalismus. In G. Bentele & M. Haller (Eds.), *Aktuelle Entstehung von Öffentlichkeit. Akteure – Strukturen – Veränderungen* (pp. 225–250). Konstanz: UVK.

Boumans, J. (2016). *Outsourcing the News? An Empirical Assessment of the Role of Sources and News Agencies in the Contemporary News Landscape*. Amsterdam: Amsterdam School of Communication Research (ASCoR).

Capriotti, P. (2009). Economic and social roles of companies in the mass media: The impact media visibility has on businesses' being recognized as economic and social actors. *Business & Society, 48*(2), 225–242.

Deuze, M. (2012). *Media Life*. Cambridge, MA: Polity Press.

Dvorkin, L. (2012). *Inside Forbes: The Birth of Brand Journalism and Why it's Good News for the News Business*. New York, NY: PARS International Corporation/ Forbes Media.

Dyck, A., Volchkova, N., & Zingales, L. (2008). The corporate governance role of the media: Evidence from Russia. *The Journal of Finance, 63*(3), 1093–1135.

Entman, R. (1993). Framing: Toward clarification of a fractured paradigm. *Journal of Communication, 43*(4), 51–58.

Freberg, K., Graham, K., McGaughey, K., & Freberg, L. A. (2011). Who are the social media influencers? A study of public perceptions of personality. *Public Relations Review, 37*(1), 90–92.

Galtsung, J., & Ruge, M. H. (1965). The structure of foreign news. The presentation of the Congo, Cuba and Cyprus crises in four Norwegian newspapers. *Journal of Peace Research, 2*(1), 64–91.

Griffin, E., Ledbetter, A., & Sparks, G. (2015). *A First Look at Communication Theory*. New York, NY: McGraw Hill.

Harcup, T., & O'Neill, D. (2001). What is news? Galtung and Ruge revisited. *Journalism Studies, 2*(2), 261–280.

Hjarvard, S. (2008). The mediatization of society: A theory of the media as agents of social and cultural change. *Nordicom Review, 29*(2), 105–134.

Ihlen, Ø., & Pallas, J. (2014). Mediatization of corporations. In K. Lundby (Ed.), *Mediatization of Communication* (pp. 423–441). Berlin: De Gruyter Mouton.

Macnamara, J. (2014). Journalism-PR relations revisited: The good news, the bad news, and insights into tomorrow's news.*Public Relations Review*, *40*(5), 739–750.

Macnamara, J., Lwin, M. O., Adi, A., & Zerfass, A. (2016). 'PESO' media strategy shifts to 'SOEP': Opportunities and ethical dilemmas. *Public Relations Review*, *42*(3), 377–385.

McLuhan, M., & Fiore, Q. (1968). *War and Peace in the Global Village*. New York, NY: Bantam Books.

McQuail, D. (2005). *McQuail's Mass Communication Theory* (5th ed.). London: Sage.

Meijer, M. M., & Kleinnijenhuis, J. (2006a). Issue news and corporate reputation: Applying the theories of agenda setting and issue ownership in the field of business communication. *Journal of Communication*, *56*(3), 543–559.

Meijer, M. M., & Kleinnijenhuis, J. (2006b). News and corporate reputation: Empirical findings from the Netherlands. *Public Relations Review*, *32*(4), 341–348.

Mizuno, T., Takei, K., Ohnishi, T., & Watanabe, T. (2012). Temporal and cross correlations in business news. *Progress of Theoretical Physics Supplement*, *194*, 181–192.

Neijens, N., & Smit, E. (2006). Dutch public relations practitioners and journalists: Antagonists no more. *Public Relations Review*, *32*(3), 232–240.

News Aktuell (2016). *Recherche 2016*. Retrieved from https://www.newsaktuell.de/pdf/whitepaper_recherche2016_newsaktuell.pdf

News Aktuell & Faktenkontor (2013). *Social Media Trendmonitor 2013: Kommunikationsprofis, Journalisten und das Social Web*. Retrieved from http://www.newsaktuell.de/pdf/social_media_trendmonitor_2013.pdf

Van Der Meer, G. L. M. (2016). *Communication in Times of Crisis. The Interplay Between the Organization, News Media and the Public*. Amsterdam: Amsterdam School of Communication Research (ASCoR).

Van Ruler, B. (2005). Organizations, media and the public sphere: Ménage a trois. A societal perspective on communication management. *Tijdschrift Voor Communicatiewetenschap*, *33*(1), 72–87.

Verčič, D., & Tkalac Verčič, A. (2016). The new publicity: From reflexive to reflective mediatisation. *Public Relations Review*, *42*(4), 493–498.

Verhoeven, J. (2012). *Medewerkers als merkambassadeurs*. Amsterdam: SWOCC.

Verhoeven, P. (2016). The co-production of business news and its effects: The corporate framing mediated-moderation model. *Public Relations Review*, *42*(4), 509–521.

Walther, J. B. (1992). Interpersonal effects in computer-mediated interaction: A relational perspective. *Communication Research*, *19*(1), 52–90.

Walther, J. B. (1996). Computer-mediated communication: Impersonal, interpersonal, and hyperpersonal interaction. *Communication Research*, *23*(1), 3–43.

Walther, J. B. (2011). Theories of computer-mediated communication and inter-personal behavior. In M. L. Knapp & J. A. Daly (Eds.), *The Handbook of Interpersonal Communication* (pp. 443–479). Thousand Oaks, CA: Sage.

Zerfass, A., Verhoeven, P., Tench, R., Moreno, A., & Verčič, D. (2011). *European Communication Monitor 2011. Empirical Insights into Strategic Communication in Europe. Results of an Empirical Survey in 43 Countries.* Brussels: EACD, EUPRERA.

Zerfass, A., Verčič, D., Verhoeven, P., Moreno, A., & Tench, R. (2015). *European Communication Monitor 2015. Creating Communication Value Through Listening, Messaging and Measurement. Results of a Survey in 41 Countries.* Brussels: EACD/EUPRERA, Helios Media.

Zerfass, A., Verčič, D., & Wiesenberg, M. (2016a). The dawn of a new golden age for media relations? How PR professionals interact with the mass media and use new collaboration practices. *Public Relations Review, 42*(4), 499–508.

Zerfass, A., Verhoeven, P., Moreno, A., Tench, R., & Verčič, D. (2016b). *European Communication Monitor 2016. Exploring Trends in Big Data, Stakeholder Engagement and Strategic Communication. Results of a Survey in 43 Countries.* Brussels: EACD/EUPRERA, Quadriga Media Berlin.

Commandment 3
Reflective: Organisations Reinvent Themselves

Excellent organisations are more open to influences from wider environments than non-excellent organisations. It is precisely this openness that gives them a competitive, strategic advantage. This holds not only for companies, but also for governmental and non-governmental organisations. Survival and success are functions of adaptation, and excellent organisations expose themselves to as many challenges as early as possible, because problematic situations enable and force them to learn. They use insights about shifts in public opinion, megatrends and demands from stakeholders to identify opportunities for growth. Constantly scrutinising and reinventing the organisational profile, policies, products and services is a necessity in today's hypermodern world.

While globalisation promotes openness, organisations need media to reach as far as possible: media are extensions of our nervous system and without them we could experience only as much as we can see, hear, smell or sense personally. The Internet allows a truly global media system connecting all the dots around the globe: mediatised companies listen globally and they present themselves globally – as far as needed. Social media and owned media supplement the traditional mass media. Information is abundant and not spare, and the challenge to be faced is how to make sense in this data affluent world. For this, the ability to reflect is key to contemporary hypermodern organisations. The third commandment for excellence therefore is: *be reflective*. But what does it mean for an organisation to be reflective? And how can communication departments help organisations to be reflective? What is reflective communication management?

© The Author(s) 2017
R. Tench et al., *Communication Excellence*,
DOI 10.1007/978-3-319-48860-8_3

Reflective Communication Management

Strategic management is founded on a very simple idea: that the world is progressively changing due to the use of scientific methods and continuous learning. In engineering and natural sciences, observation and measurement help to understand natural laws, and once they have been deciphered, specialists can apply them to improve human conditions. Organisations can improve ways in which they operate by using the same logic of observation and measurement. By assessing ways in which people behave in organisations, they can become excellent, that is, better than they were in the past, and/or better than their competitors. This is what excellence in management is all about: continuous learning.

Successful organisations are notorious for their bias for action. This was the first attribute that Tom Peters and Robert Waterman, at that time consultants working in the largest management consultancy in the world, McKinsey, discovered and explained in one of the best-selling management books of all times – *In Search of Excellence*.[1] Today's excellence is a follow-up to an older notion of craftsmanship and they both underline the importance of practice – practice makes perfect. Successful organisations are successful because they do something better than other organisations. And at the basis of every successful organisation is experience.[2] But to make success sustainable, organisations have to interact with their environments and stakeholders. They have to reflect on both successes and failures. To that end, all three aspects discussed in the first part of this book are relevant: globalisation is important because it gives organisations the widest possible experience. Media are important because they enable interactions. And reflection is important because it enables learning (Box 10).

Box 10 Reflective organisations: practice makes perfect

- Action
- Interaction
- Reflection
- Learning

---

[1] Peters and Waterman (1982).
[2] Sennett (2008).

Excellence can only be achieved through a process of continuous learning and this can only be done through communication. Through communication people and organisations expose themselves to the world, through communication they interact with the world and through communication they reflect their own identity, values and interests. Organisational learning is a process of continuous, iterative communication with the environment. The organisation should be able to see itself from the perspective of the outside world and learn from that. In a complex hypermodern global society, continuous self-observation and the ability to reflect on the views of others on the organisation is a prerequisite for legitimation of the organisation.[3] Accordingly communication becomes a function of management per se. Combining communication and reflection makes communication management, to put it a bit more abstractly, about 'maximising, optimising, or satisfying the process of meaning creation using informational, persuasive, relational, and discursive interventions to solve managerial problems by coproducing societal (public) legitimation'.[4] This so-called reflective communication management is very important for the success and the future of organisations.

Communication for Successful Organisations

If there is one thing that makes excellent communication departments different from other communication departments, it is their self-understanding: who they are and what they are supposed to do, the way they reflect on themselves and on the world around them. In other words their ability to reflect on themselves and on the position of the organisation in society.

In the European Communication Monitor we asked across Europe about how communicators and their departments help to reach the overall organisational goals of their organisations. These activities can be broken down to outbound and inbound activities.[5] There are two sets of outbound activities: building immaterial assets (brands, reputation, culture) and facilitating organisational processes (influencing customer preferences, motivating employees, generating public attention). And there are two sets of inbound activities: helping to adjust organisational strategies (identifying opportunities, integrating public concerns and collecting customer

---

[3] Holmström (2004, 2009).
[4] Van Ruler and Verčič (2005), p. 263.
[5] Zerfass (2014), pp. 28–32.

feedback) and securing room for manoeuvre (by managing relationships and crises, building and securing legitimacy). Box 11 provides a summary.

Box 11 How communication enables organisational success

Outbound communication

- Facilitates organisational processes and value creation (generates attention, influences customer/stakeholder preferences, motivates employees and members of the organisation)
- Builds immaterial assets (brands, reputation, organisational culture)

Inbound communication

- Helps adjust organisational strategies (identifies opportunities, integrates public concerns, collects customer feedback)
- Secures room for manoeuvre (manages relationships and mitigates crises, builds and secures legitimacy)

To whichever side we look, outbound or inbound, professionals in excellent communication departments are statistically significantly more focused on substantial contributions they can make to their organisations when compared to organisations with non-excellent communication departments (Fig. 7).

Even if organisations are open to their environments (globalised) and interactive (mediatised), they will not be successful if their ears, eyes, noses and skins cannot sense what is critical and important inside and outside organisations. Reflection is thinking about what matters. It is collecting information and making sense out of it. Reflective organisations are able to live in meaningful experiences enriching both their potential for adaptation and their worth.

Excellent Communication Starts at the Top

The most communicative organisations are not those with the best communicators or communication departments, but with a top management that appreciates and understands communication. Without the support and collaboration of the executive board, even the best communicators can do only so much, but not more. This is why excellent communication starts at the top.

Mutual respect and understanding between the top management and top communicators produces synergies that differentiate the best from the rest. As our research shows, professionals in excellent communication departments focus on supporting top management, while non-excellent departments lag behind.

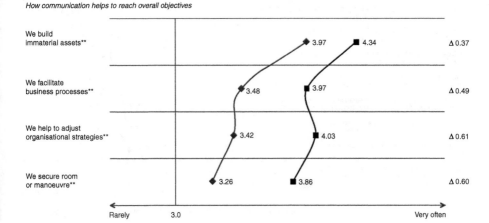

Fig. 7 Excellent organisations use all leverages for supporting goals through communication[6]

Excellent communication departments support top executives by providing information/insights to facilitate decision-making and activities, advise top executives how to handle specific communication challenges and enable top executives to recognise the communication dimensions of their decisions and activities. They enable everybody to communicate (see Fig. 8).

Decisions to globalise, mediatise and reflect can be made only at the top. That is what makes some organisations communicative organisations, being able to understand and use communicative aspects of their behaviour ('Actions speak louder than words!') and behavioural aspects of their communication ('Words matter!'). For communication literate top management communication is not something to be done after actions to explain them, but communication is an act in itself.

As it is impossible for a good top executives to be financially illiterate or to be unable to assemble people to work with him or her, so it becomes harder and harder to imagine a good top executive who is illiterate in the field of communication and public opinion dynamics or insensitive to it. Collecting, nurturing and growing immaterial assets, facilitating organisational processes, adjusting organisational strategies and securing room for manoeuvre are exactly

---

[6] Zerfass et al. (2015), p. 116. n = 1,600 communication professionals working in communication departments across Europe. Q: How do you and your department help to reach the overall goals of your organisation? Scale 1 (rarely) – 5 (very often). Mean values. ** Highly significant differences (Pearson correlation, $p \leq 0.01$). * Significant differences (Pearson correlation, $p \leq 0.05$).

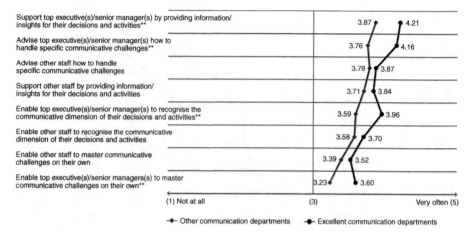

Support top executive(s)/senior manager(s) by providing information/ insights for their decisions and activities** — 3.87 — 4.21

Advise top executive(s)/senior manager(s) how to handle specific communicative challenges** — 3.76 — 4.16

Advise other staff how to handle specific communicative challenges — 3.78 — 3.87

Support other staff by providing information/ insights for their decisions and activities — 3.71 — 3.84

Enable top executive(s)/senior manager(s) to recognise the communicative dimension of their decisions and activities** — 3.59 — 3.96

Enable other staff to recognise the communicative dimension of their decisions and activities — 3.58 — 3.70

Enable other staff to master communicative challenges on their own — 3.39 — 3.52

Enable top executive(s)/senior managers(s) to master communicative challenges on their own** — 3.23 — 3.60

(1) Not at all   (3)   Very often (5)

→ Other communication departments   → Excellent communication departments

Fig. 8 Excellent organisations enable everybody to communicate[7]

the core responsibilities of a top management job. In that sense communication is a top management function. Professional communicators and communication departments are just specialised and institutionalised expressions of that responsibility – just as other core management functions are helping to fulfil other tasks, like finance, operations, human resources, etc.

Communication professionals in excellent communication departments also argue with top management about communication differently than their colleagues in non-excellent departments. They are much more focused on what matters, like explaining positive effects of good reputation, organisational culture or brands, illustrating the benefits of listening to stakeholders and identifying opportunities, and demonstrating positive economic benefits (effects on sales or employee motivation) as can be seen in (Fig. 9).

Communication professionals in excellent departments understand the value of time and attention: to get the attention of other managers and to get their time, they speak the language executives understand. It is in management language that they frame communication, the need for it and its benefits. Without attention and appreciation to behavioural aspects of communication and communicative aspects of organisational behaviour communication planning is in vain. Communication is not something organisations do, communication is what organisations are. In other words,

---

[7] Zerfass et al. (2016), p. 124. n^{min} = 1,066 communication professionals working in communication departments across Europe. Q: When you coach, advise or enable executives/senior managers or other members of your organisation/client, how often do you practice the following activities? Scale 1 (not at all) – 5 (very often). **Highly significant differences (Pearson correlation, $p \leq 0.01$).

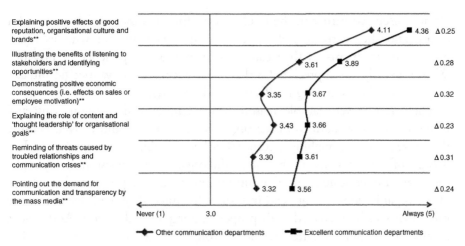

Fig. 9 Explaining the value of communication[8]

communication constitutes organisations. It calls organisations into being, without communication there is no organisation (Box 12).[9]

Box 12 Goal orientation: what have we learned from excellent organisations?

Excellent organisations ensure that communicators

- focus on organisational goals;
- work in or with the top management;
- use management language when interacting with top executives and business partners.

Action, Interaction, Learning

There is an old saying that organisations can make or buy things, but there are some things that cannot be bought exactly as they are needed. One can buy experience, but it is impossible to buy specific experiences. As we have

---

[8] Zerfass et al. (2015), p. 117. $n = 1,601$ communication professionals working in communication departments across Europe. Q: How do you usually argue for the relevance of strategic communication when addressing top executives and (internal) clients? Scale 1 (never) – 5 (always). Mean values. **Highly significant differences for all items (Pearson correlation, $p \leq 0.01$).

[9] See for example McPhee and Zaug (2000); Taylor and Van Every (2000).

already discussed earlier in the book, successful organisations have a bias for action and they actively seek experience and they interact with as many diverse environments as they can to gain as much experience as possible. What is usually not appreciated is that experiences are always specific and can be generalised only through reflection and learning.

There is one very simple reason why organisational re-engineering and turnarounds are so hard to make: organisations survived and thrived because they were good at something, because they had valuable (past) experiences. It is because of these experiences that successful organisations invest in their people, they train and educate them. Communicators who have profound knowledge of the organisations, sectors and industries in which they work have intrinsic value that can be increased with proper training and education. And that is exactly what differentiates excellent from non-excellent communication departments: they invest more in the skills and knowledge of their people. Interestingly, the biggest (100 per cent) difference in how much they invest in education, is in the field of technical and management knowledge (see Fig. 10).

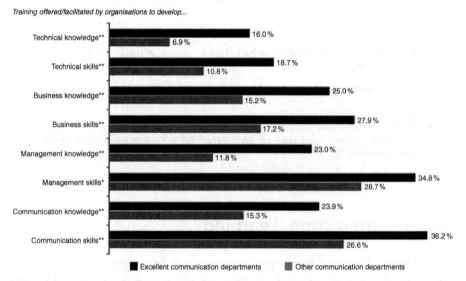

Training offered/facilitated by organisations to develop...

Fig. 10 Excellent organisations invest more in personnel development[10]

---

[10] Zerfass et al. (2016), p. 125. n^{min} = 1,431 communication professionals working in communication departments across Europe. Q: Thinking of yourself, your current capabilities and your future development, which of the following skills and knowledge areas do you believe are in need of developing? My organisation offers/facilitates training. *Significant differences (chi-square test, $p \leq 0.05$). **Highly significant differences (chi-square test, $p \leq 0.01$).

This is an interesting finding, as often an unusual performance in communication is explained by the availability of communication technicians and communication managers in organisations. Technicians are described as producing messages and means of communication and managers are planning, organising and evaluating communication activities. Yet, as Fig. 10 shows, the difference – at least in the sphere of personnel development – is not between technicians and managers, it is between well-educated and trained and less educated and trained practitioners. One can speculate that reflective organisations have both better communication technicians and better managers. Act, interact, reflect, learn is a series that makes excellence possible.

Commandments in Practice: Reflective

PRIME ⬛ RESEARCH

How Top Companies Reflect Their Environment

The world's leading organisations are hungry for data. They are eager to collect and analyse as much information about the 'outside world' as is possible, and manageable. These companies have a genuine interest in understanding the perception of different publics overall and in comparison to key competitors. They seek information about old and emerging issues and key societal changes. Before the Internet became ubiquitous, this task required substantial energy and resources. In the current phase of digital transformation, the methods and tools used to understand these environmental trends had to be reinvented.

The new digital era can be characterised by two fundamental developments: (1) all media and information is online, (2) most information is accessible via mobile devices which are becoming supercomputers through cloud technology. This has a major impact on the communication environment of every organisation and communication department:

- Information is spreading at an unprecedented speed 24/7 – there is no 'night-time' or 'weekend pause'.
- The flow of information is global – markets or language barriers no longer exist.
- The traditional (media) channels are accompanied by new social and often visual media channels – adding a new level of volume and complexity to the communication environment.

How are leading communications departments managing these new digital challenges?
Through a digital (listening) platform (often called 'newsroom') which is providing real-time information and insights 24/7. These new tools have four core functions:

- informing the audience with relevant news about the organisation, the competitive environment and the society in general;
- detecting new and emerging trends and top influencers while tracking the dynamics of current issues;
- enabling (communication) management to navigate in challenging times and in crises;
- benchmarking the success and effectiveness of activities and communication programmes – across different (earned, paid and owned) channels.

Together with partners in the United States like GE, eBay and McDonald's and partners in Europe like Daimler, DHL and Airbus, PRIME Research developed the i.Suite to cope with the new inbound and outbound requirements of modern communication departments. The i.Suite is a cloud-based software solution for smartphones and desktops giving real-time access to all relevant news channels and sources – from traditional media like print, radio and TV to digital, online channels and all social media sources like blogs, forums, Facebook, YouTube and others – on a 24/7 basis. The basic technology behind this 'big data' solution is a highly sophisticated natural language processing system that categorises and analyses the content and sentiment of thousands of documents per second – making millions of documents available for insights about the changing environment.

These i.Suite solutions are global systems, capable of covering 90+ markets with 60+ languages. A built-in professional version of an automated, real-time translation tool (Google Translate) allows users to follow news in markets without knowledge of the language (i.e. Chinese or Russian). In addition, different media channels like print, online, radio and TV and social media are no longer handled in isolated silos. They are now fed into one fully integrated system. This is also true for audio-visual content, where the i.Suite leverages modern speech-to-text technology.

This integrated approach has multiple advantages, underscored by the fact that all content – social and traditional – is analysed with one standardised methodology, providing consistent cross-media metrics (i.e. about the relevance and impact of different messages, stories and issues). This makes it is possible to analyse the dynamics of news and issues across all channels. For example, the i.Suite can provide detailed information about the resonance of digital news in social channels (i.e. how often the news has been shared, liked or commented). In addition, the system has the ability to identify news that has been picked up by search engines like Google News thus boosting the reach and impact of the story.

Transforming Communications Functions for Key Organisations

In 2012, GE had over 10 providers for media monitoring and analysis across its expansive network of regions, business units and functions. In a Six Sigma project with PRIME, these individual and segmented services were integrated into one comprehensive solution: the GE media insight suite. 'Some people were listening or measuring, others not . . . but everyone was doing it differently. We've adopted PRIME Research across our companies' varied businesses and regions for one consistent and efficient take on monitoring and measurement.', said Gary Sheffer,

Vice-President Communication and Public Affairs, GE Corporate. This new standardised approach comparing 'apples with apples' provides the new insight platform for all corporate news functions until today, constantly updated and further developed in line with the increasing digital transformation of the media system.

When designing the 'MasterCard Conversation Suite' one organisational target was of particular importance: to change the culture of the company from a business-to-business 'broadcasting company' into a consumer-oriented 'listening organisation'. To visualise this commitment, MasterCard, in partnership with PRIME, installed the Conversation Suite – a large, dynamic display in the heart of MasterCard's headquarters in New York. The big screen display of all incoming news, posts and tweets, analysed in real time, is accompanied by a 'social media corner' offering engagement opportunities for all employees passing by. The attached 'insight alley' provides meeting opportunities for market intelligence and decision-making. To this day, the i.Suite serves as an award-winning physical and digital space used to reinforce the role of PR and communications in generating insights to inform strategic business decisions across the organisation.

Communication has a growing role in different management functions, and the PRIME i.Suite is supporting this trend. All corporate functions, including marketing, finance, procurement and HR, have the ability to design their own sub-suite, which is tailor-made to focus on the most relevant media, publics and stakeholder groups. This new digital information environment therefore leads to a closer cooperation between different corporate functions.

So, with new tools and technologies, large global organisations are able to navigate the new, dynamic, digital communication environment. These platforms and the intelligence behind it offer the opportunity to extend the 'senses' of every organisation – into different publics, stakeholder groups, regions and markets. With this advantage, however, comes complexity; there are more channels and sources, increasing amounts of content, and infinite interactions between new and old opinion leaders. Alongside the opportunity offered by this big data environment there is a need for simplification and distilled, actionable insights. The i.Suite reduces the complexity, ultimately helping CCOs and management from leading organisations make informed, data-based decisions.

Rainer Mathes
Dr. Rainer Mathes is the founder and President of PRIME Research with headquarters in Mainz, Germany.

About PRIME Research
With nine international offices on four continents, PRIME Research employs more than 400 software developers, linguists, analysts, project managers and consultants to conduct communication research in more than 60 languages around the world. The firm integrates, analyses and evaluates media performance across all channels – social, digital, print and broadcast – to deliver actionable insights and strategic guidance for better communications, marketing and business results. Since 1987, PRIME Research has been a trusted partner of more than 500 international top brands and blue chip corporations and is a recognised global leader in its field.

Play Hard, Enjoy More

Communicators in excellent organisations work more than their colleagues in non-excellent organisations, but they also enjoy it more – they report statistically significant higher levels of satisfaction with their job. Hard work, including overtime, with associated higher job satisfaction can be interpreted as a side effect of the bias for action: getting work done and done well is more important than working hours. And excellent results make actors satisfied with themselves. Figure 11 shows how much more communicators in excellent organisations work in comparison to those in non-excellent organisations.

The patterns of satisfaction between excellent and non-excellent communicators are similar, but differences in values are statistically significant. Overall, on average, communicators are satisfied with their job, but those in excellent communication departments are much more. Communicators enjoy interesting and manifold tasks, but even more in excellent departments. Superiors and (internal) clients value their work, but more in excellent departments. Their job has a high status, and again this is more often true for those working in excellent departments.

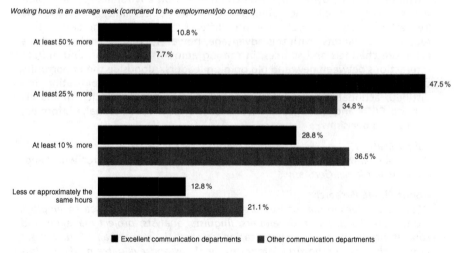

Working hours in an average week (compared to the employment/job contract)

At least 50% more — 10.8% / 7.7%

At least 25% more — 47.5% / 34.8%

At least 10% more — 28.8% / 36.5%

Less or approximately the same hours — 12.8% / 21.1%

■ Excellent communication departments   ■ Other communication departments

Fig. 11 Excellent organisations require more overtime work in communications[11]

[11] Zerfass et al. (2014), p. 144. n = 2,090 communication professionals working in communication departments across Europe. Q: How many hours do you work in an average week, compared to the hours required by your work contract (with or without financial compensation)? Highly significant correlations for all items (Kendall rank correlation, $p \leq 0.01$, τ = –0.121).

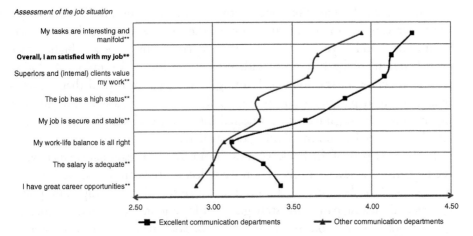

Assessment of the job situation

My tasks are interesting and manifold**

Overall, I am satisfied with my job**

Superiors and (internal) clients value my work**

The job has a high status**

My job is secure and stable**

My work-life balance is all right

The salary is adequate**

I have great career opportunities**

2.50   3.00   3.50   4.00   4.50

━■━ Excellent communication departments   ━▲━ Other communication departments

Fig. 12 Excellent organisations provide a satisfying job environment[12]

Interestingly, although communicators in excellent communication departments report more overtime work, the difference in work-life balance is practically the same for both groups – this is the only item in our empirical research where no statistically significant difference showed up. Communicators in excellent communication departments report that their salaries are more adequate than those in non-excellent departments, and they have significantly better career opportunities than their colleagues in non-excellent departments (Fig. 12).

Excellent organisations are more globalised, more open to the world and they are more mediatised, and more interactive with their environments. Openness and interaction enable reflection which stimulates learning. In such a setting, communication departments envision their work differently and communicators learn more, work more and also have greater enjoyment in what they do (Box 13).

Box 13 Working conditions: what have we learned from excellent organisations?

Excellent organisations ensure that communicators

- learn and train more;
- work more;
- enjoy their work more.

---

[12] Zerfass et al. (2014), p. 145. n = 2,090 communication professionals working in communication departments across Europe. Q: How do you feel about your actual job situation? Scale 1 (strongly disagree) – 5 (totally agree). Mean values. **Highly significant differences (Kendall rank correlation, $p \leq 0.01$).

Excellence is a self-reinforcing concept: the more you practice, the better you get; the better you are, the more you enjoy it; the more you enjoy, the more you want to do – and so you start again with practice, but this time at a higher level, even better than the first time, with even more fun and stamina. Ambition stands on action, interaction and learning. It is an upward spiral that connects organisations, departments and professionals. Global, mediatised and reflective organisations are organisations connected into the world which nurtures influential and reflective communication departments.

In the next part of the book we move from the organisational perspective to the departmental level. In this section we reflect on the communication department's need to be integrated into the processes of leadership and power (embedded); taking part in the strategic planning and in the evaluation processes of the whole organisation (strategised) and consider the invaluable and essential contribution of research and the growing importance of big data (datafied).

References

Holmström, S. (2004). The reflective paradigm. In B. Van Ruler & D. Verčič (Eds.), *Public Relations in Europe, a Nation-by-Nation Introduction of Public Relations Theory* (pp. 121–134). Berlin: de Gruyter.

Holmström, S. (2009). On Luhmann. In Ø. Ihlen, B. Van Ruler, & M. Fredriksson (Eds.), *Public Relations and Social Theory. Key Figures and Concepts* (pp. 187–211). New York, NY: Routledge.

McPhee, R. D., & Zaug, P. (2000). The communicative constitution of organisations: A framework for explanation. *Electronic Journal of Communication, 10.* Retrieved from http://www.cios.org/EJCPUBLIC/010/1/01017.html

Peters, T. J., & Waterman, R. H. (1982). *In Search of Excellence: Lessons from America's Best-Run Companies.* New York, NY: Harper & Row.

Sennett, R. (2008). *The Craftsman.* New Haven, CT: Yale University Press.

Taylor, J. R., & Van Every, E. J. (2000). *The Emergent Organisation: Communication as its Site and Surface.* Mahwah, NJ: Lawrence Erlbaum Associates.

Van Ruler, B., & Verčič, D. (2005). Reflective communication management: Future ways for public relations research. In P. J. Kalbfleisch (Ed.), *Communication Yearbook 29* (pp. 239–273). Mahwah, NJ: Lawrence Erlbaum Associates.

Zerfass, A. (2014). Unternehmensführung und Kommunikationsmanagement: Strategie, Management und Controlling. In A. Zerfass & M. Piwinger (Eds.), *Handbuch Unternehmenskommunikation* (2nd ed.) (pp. 21–79). Wiesbaden: Springer Gabler.

Zerfass, A., Tench, R., Verčič, D., Verhoeven, P., & Moreno, A. (2014). *European Communication Monitor 2014. Excellence in Strategic Communication – Key Issues,*

Leadership, Gender and Mobile Media. Results of a Survey in 42 Countries. Brussels: EACD/EUPRERA, Helios Media.

Zerfass, A., Verčič, D., Verhoeven, P., Moreno, A., & Tench, R. (2015). *European Communication Monitor 2015. Creating Communication Value Through Listening, Messaging and Measurement. Results of a Survey in 41 Countries.* Brussels: EACD/ EUPRERA, Helios Media.

Zerfass, A., Verhoeven, P., Moreno, A., Tench, R., & Verčič, D. (2016). *European Communication Monitor 2016. Exploring Trends In Big Data, Stakeholder Engagement and Strategic Communication Results of a Survey in 43 Countries.* Brussels: EACD/EUPRERA, Quadriga Media Berlin.

Part II

Influential Departments

This second part of the book looks at the departmental level or the communication function inside the organisation. The three commandments (chapters) in this section reflect the communication department's need to be integrated into the processes of leadership and power (embedded); work with and founded on the basis of research (datafied) and take part in the strategic planning and in the evaluation processes of the whole organisation (strategised). How to be influential is the key question in this part of the book. How can communication professionals support the organisation in an excellent way.

Three commandments are applicable here: be *embedded*, be *datafied* and be *strategised*.

The first commandment is be *embedded*. Communications departments have to be completely embedded into their organisations and with their environment. An embedded situation involves leadership, influence and a prominent position in relation with other functions of the organisation. To encounter the hypermodern complexity of an organisation and its contexts, organisational leaders need to be able to be 'sensemakers' for their organisation. In this context the softer aspects of management, like communication, become just as important as the traditional management skills. In this new environment communication acquires a central role, for example, with coaching and enabling organisational leaders to communicate. Communication managers have to lead effective communication departments that help the organisation to be excellent. The conceptualisation of excellence in public relations is very much dependent on the influence the communication department has in the organisation. Influence means power and points to political dynamics among people within an organisational structure, both in the hierarchical positions and in the relations with other functions. Being embedded means to be influential both vertically (formal), and horizontally (informal) in the organisation.

Our second commandment is be *datafied*. To be able to be more strategic and to explain the value of communication data and good research are a prerequisite. In our age of 'big data' the communication department cannot simply disregard the process of measurement and evaluation of its own activities and of the whole organisation. Today datafication or digitalisation are integrated in every dimension of our lives, changing our world and our ways of living and working. Digitalisation has changed almost all forms of human labour and particularly those associated with cognitive processes. This is also true for communication. Excellent communication departments are forerunners therefore in research and measurement and have an awareness that big data is important for communication as well.

Our third commandment is be *strategised*. The communication profession is moving from a tactical or operational level towards a strategic level. Nevertheless, communication differs from other functions because of the complexity of its activities. Despite this complexity, strategised departments are better able to explain the value of communication and to link communication to business goals and strategies than non-strategised departments.

Commandment 4

Embedded: Influence Through Communicative Leadership

In the previous chapters we have seen how communication helps the organisation to be related to the dynamic of the world. To make this happen communication departments need also to be completely *embedded* into the organisation they work for. That is the fourth commandment in this book: excellent communication departments are embedded in the organisation they work for and the organisation is effectively embedded in the societal, cultural and social spaces they are part of (see Box 14). A prerequisite for being embedded is effective *leadership*. Communication professionals have to show *leadership* to be able to become embedded in the organisation and the organisation has to show leadership to become embedded in its surroundings.

Today, leadership is a much debated concept and the subject of many books, conferences and seminars. In this debate scientific insights, from psychology to management science, compete with many non-scientific and even spiritual ideas about leadership. The lack of leadership is often seen as the big problem of our time.[1] But what is a leader and what is the role of a leader? Is leadership an authentic characteristic of a person or is it a role taken up by a person that is attributed with the leadership by his or her environment? What kind of leadership style is effective and does that vary in different cultures or European regions?

---

[1] Aascher (2016), in a special edition of *De Gids* about leadership.

© The Author(s) 2017
R. Tench et al., *Communication Excellence*,
DOI 10.1007/978-3-319-48860-8_4

> **Box 14 Embedded organisations[2]**
>
> *Embedded* companies aim at more than just having a business impact. Beyond their short-term financial performance, their ambitions and actions are driven by another overarching target: to shape a broader and lasting specific world of their own. Their success comes from being simultaneously the architects and the epicentres of new societal, cultural and social spaces: the ultimate benchmarks and common denominators of all involved. We call this process 'marking a territory'.

In this ever-changing, global and competitive world, the leaders in organisations should be able to embrace uncertainty in order to create new opportunities. Leaders applying a communicative approach within the organisation can increase theirs and their organisation's effectiveness and make it easier to take decisions. What does this mean for communication professionals? We will argue, based on the European Communication Monitor research, that communication executives face a threefold leadership challenge:

1. To help organisational leaders to be communicative
2. To support overall goals of the organisation through strategic communication, which includes messaging as well as listening
3. To lead the communication department

For targeting these three related goals excellent communication departments design their leadership styles with an appreciation of the corporate culture, with a need to be influential in the executive board (C-suite) or other decision committees and to maintain fluid relations with other functions inside the organisation. In other words they have the capacity to cross borders and boundaries.

Help Organisational Leaders to be Communicative

The 'Panama Papers' created quite a storm. The material came to light in 2015 making public thousands of bank accounts belonging to public figures and highly reputable companies who were utilising well-known tax havens. The release of information from the papers not only opened the debate about

---

[2] Thoening and Waldman (2007), n.p.

cases of corruption and the legitimacy of tax havens. It also brought to the discussion table that not only rigorous legal systems, but ethics, moral and cultural aspects influence the evaluation that societies make of organisations and their leaders.

Until the twenty-first century the value of companies was mainly measured by their profitability and tangible assets generated – products, buildings, equipment, property, etc. Today, intangible assets – such as brand, reputation, culture, etc. – also contribute substantially to the value of a company. In this context new forms of ethical and sustainable measurement exist such as Sustainalytics, Dow Jones for Sustainability, Standard & Poor's 500, OEKOM, Vigeo, FTSE4Good, GS Sustain (Goldman Sachs), RobecoSAM, Ethical Investment Research Services (EIRIS), Tomorrows Value Rating or STOXX Global ESG Leaders Index. Nowadays, the complexity of the markets evaluating business models is clearly illustrated by a breadth of indices that go further than tangible assets. Markets do not measure companies only based on hard values, such as revenues, profits, number of employees and other indicators of size, but based on all the constituent parts that can provide trust for consumers, shareholders and other enabling stakeholders like lawmakers and public administrators; or legitimisers like public opinion.

In view of this broader perspective, organisational leaders face an increasingly complex world where change and uncertainly are an everyday occurrence. To encounter this new complexity, they also need updated competences. The soft aspects of management must be additional to the traditional management skills and it is in this environment where communication acquires a central role.[3] This was recently exemplified in the Volkswagen diesel emissions scandal, DieselGate. The company was blamed for using deceptive software to hide the limits of emissions on Volkswagen cars worldwide. 'Our company was dishonest . . . we have totally screwed up' was the frank statement by Michael Horn, then Chief Executive and President of Volkswagen of America, when he first appeared before the media on 21 September 2015. This came after a whole weekend of speculation and finger pointing as the controversial issue was alive and active in debates on social media and produced little initial comment or response from the company. The scandal pushed the Volkswagen Group €3.5 billion into the red, making this its first quarterly loss in 15 years. The crisis also had repercussions for the overall management structure of the company with key resignations from figures such as CEO Martin Winterkorn, and a subsequent reduction in the number of

---

[3] Mintzberg (2004); Dahlgaard-Park and Dahlgaard (2007).

executive managers with half the number reporting directly to the new CEO, Matthias Müller. The crisis was based on management issues, on deviations of the rules and established processes and it was all rather hard for the media and general public to believe that just two rogue engineers had, apparently, been entirely to blame and should take sole responsibility. The Volkswagen case damaged the group itself but also put into question the German car industry and the whole automotive industry worldwide. It also focused the spotlight on the regulations and policies of macro institutions such as the European Union, but above all it demonstrated that for today's leaders the importance of solid ethical values and responsibility is impossible to ignore. As Harvard neuroscientist Howard Gardner stated: bad people can never become excellent professionals.[4] Being responsible and transparent in your communication to society is a key priority of global companies to avoid severe damage to their reputation.

These anecdotes show that new appropriate leadership is necessary, leadership that fits the demands of society and public opinion. This new appropriate leadership can be labelled as communicative leadership, reflective and responsive to developments and looking outside the organisation. Helping organisational leaders to lead communicatively is one of the most important tasks of communication departments. Not only outside the organisation but also inside the organisation in communication with employees (Box 15).

Box 15 Communication for leadership

Communication departments help top executives and organisational members to communicate appropriately

---

To deal with the continuous changes and the overload of information, leaders are sensemakers for their organisation. Dennis Gioia and Kumar Chittipeddi describe this process in three cognitive ways as sensemaking, sensegiving and sensenegotiating[5]: they give meaning to experiences and events, they gain followers and support for that meaning and they negotiate collective understanding to make decisions (see Box 16).

---

[4] Amiguet (2016).
[5] Gioia and Chittipeddi (1991).

Box 16 Leaders as sensemakers

1. *Sensemaking:* To give meaning to experiences and events.
2. *Sensegiving:* To gain followers' support. In order to achieve this aim, leaders can use rituals, metaphors, storytelling, rewards.
3. *Sensenegotiating:* Attempting to negotiate some collective understanding so as to make decisions.

But what happens when the CEO or other top executives stop making sense with their public statements? There is one thing worse than an organisational leader who does not comment formally on behalf of the organisation and that is an organisational leader who does not understand the basic principles of communication and public opinion. Today leadership training therefore is not only about presentation skills but also about building relationships and links between communication, management and activities of the organisation from a strategic framing approach. Organisational leaders have to communicate complex phenomena such as values, norms, visions and overall goals and organisational identity through a wide set of instruments both within and outside the organisation.[6] Therefore it is a very important action for the future to train managers to act as communicators, namely to have leaders that hold communication competences. Three quarters of European communication professionals identify this organisational need and nearly one-third see a challenge in re-establishing the lost societal credibility of management.[7]

Today stakeholders demand more and more information in a transparent way and because of this communication practitioners must work hard with leaders throughout the whole organisation. They are increasingly responsible for positioning organisational leaders both internally and externally. Communicators also have the important task of training and developing the specific communication skills of CEOs and other top executives. Profiling leaders is a major part of CEO communication. Data from the European Communication Monitor show that effective communication is very important for great leadership. The vast majority of communication professionals (83.3 per cent) support this view. The communication department is a key partner to effectively lead internal stakeholders, to position CEOs and other executives as effective leaders and to help them to achieve leading positions for the organisation both in their markets and the

---

[6] Falkheimer (2014).

[7] Zerfass et al. (2009).

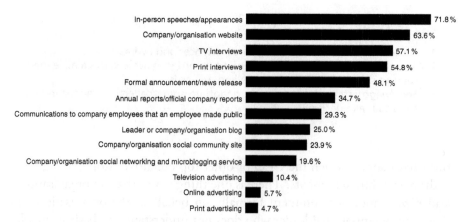

Fig. 13 Impact of communication activities on public opinion about leadership[8]

public sphere. A mix of different approaches and instruments is necessary to make this happen, where personal communication is seen as most important for organisations being perceived as leaders (see Fig. 13).

Supporting Overall Organisational Goals with Communication

Besides helping organisational leaders to communicate effectively the second aspect of leadership for communication departments is to support overall goals of the organisation through strategic communication.

Achieving power for the communication department in an organisation is also connected to leadership. Communication leaders, it is argued, are crucial for taking strategic and effective decisions in organisations and defining the strategic decision-making capability as a dimension of leadership referring:

> to the extent to which public relations leaders understand external socio-political environments and internal organizational structures, processes and practices, and are able to translate relevant knowledge into effective advocacy and become involved with strategic decision-making processes in the organization[9]

---

[8] Zerfass et al. (2014), p. 75. n = 2,777 communication professionals across Europe. Q: When stakeholders form a view on the leadership of a company/organisation, which five (5) communications activities have the greatest impact on their opinion? Top 10. Max. 5 picks per respondent.

[9] Meng (2012), p. 337.

Communication departments play a key role in the construction of meaning, identity and legitimation for their organisation. They do this through the management of intangible assets, giving advice to executives and other members of the organisation and through the coordination of each act of communication. Because of the task of producing communication content, public relations and strategic communication has a privileged position to create and recreate the organisation, the stakeholders and themselves through communication. Paradoxically, despite this important role in the construction of meaning and discourse, communication practitioners have traditionally had difficulties with gaining access to the decision-making position in their organisations.[10]

Commandments in Practice: Embedded

Enhancing Reputation Through Empowering Employees and Leadership to Communicate

We are gradually moving into an era of "no management". Because I believe that many employees are capable, willing and enthusiastic if they are able to organise work themselves', says Hans Koeleman, the Director of Corporate Communications and Corporate Social Responsibility for KPN Royal Dutch Telecom. 'Managing reputation of companies is not done by official "Reputation Managers", whatever that may be. It's done by our people, every day, and it's done by empowering them to communicate freely and actively, though also responsibly.'

This year in February KPN received an award from the International Reputation Institute for its reputation in the Netherlands. KPN started to formulate clear reputation goals in 2010 which are part of the Long-Term Incentive bonus scheme for the top management of KPN. This clearly motivated the board to improve reputation of the company and after all these years we have achieved it, with the second best reputation in the European telecom sector after Swisscom.

One of our core beliefs in reputation management is 'We communicate transparently, openly and honestly'. Total clarity for our customers became the

---

[10] Moreno et al. (2014b).

norm. And if you really want to be open then you have to start from the inside. You have to empower your employees to communicate. Therefore we have built a very open communication environment in which our people are totally free to communicate, whenever they want and wherever they are. Our leaders are strongly advised to be visible too (and that's not optional!) and communicate also in an open manner. Only then can we expect our people to do the same and to take responsibility for their actions.

The platform we have developed and use is called *TEAM KPN*, which reflects our main effort to work and perform as a team in our company. A recent benchmark showed that TEAM KPN is Europe's best and we also a received an Intranet Award in Berlin for TEAM KPN. But more important is the way the employees recognise the platform and the way they participate with it. In 2015, 13,772 employees generated two million views, 4735 blogs, 35,129 responses and 118,679 likes. Almost 100 per cent of our employees are active on the platform. Even the staff in the stores, call centres and our field engineers are connected. By creating so much communicational traffic we have not only boosted the possibility for dialogue in the company but also the pride of our people.

Since it all starts with a clear purpose for internal communication, the strategic alignment monitor from the Reputation Institute is a valuable tool. We monitor very closely if our people really understand the strategy, are capable to perform to it and are really doing the right things. The strategic alignment monitor conveys to us very clearly if we are communicating effectively with our employees. A positive side effect is the impact on the efficiency for the Corporate Communications Department. We now only need to produce the more official corporate news and board messaging and then drive the further development of the platform and monitor what's going on. Most of the content is produced by our people and particularly the senior management. And we are able to see very easily and factually how effective each senior manager is in creating an open dialogue with his or her staff. Even among our board members we have had a talent contest and the winner for the most active and effective blogger of the company was our CEO. But you don't have to be the CEO to be effective. One of the most famous bloggers is one of our engineers who regularly highlights his experiences with customers.

Another, and maybe even more important aspect of modern internal communications, is that much of this information we share internally is external at the same time. More than 30,000 followers of our KPN Twitter account follow us because they want to read about interesting elements on the whereabouts and new technologies of our company. Once the information is posted on TEAM KPN, the colleagues share this information via social media platforms, like Facebook, LinkedIn or Twitter. Logically they like to share stuff about the company they work for and about which they are proud. When the Rijksmuseum held an astonishing exhibition of Rembrandt's art (The Late Works), KPN got as many visitors on the special online environment as there were visitors in the museum; over 500,000. When SAIL Amsterdam was organised in 2015 we managed to create the most effective social media event of the year because of our fixed mobile infrastructure and our KPN Social Media boat, we were able to attract lots of dignitaries and celebrities. Both of these projects were supported by the sharing activity of our own internal community.

New leadership and new communication starts with open and honest communication. The times for leadership to play hide and seek are in the past. If you expect employees to take responsibility for their actions, you have to be there as a manager and communicate yourself in an open manner. Codes of conduct are nonsense (although we have one too); it's in the everyday communications where we make the difference. Be open whether as the company CEO, as the corporate communications department and as senior managers and facilitate your employees in every way to communicate internally and externally. Welcome to the new world.

Hans Koeleman
Hans Koeleman is Director of Corporate Communications and Corporate Social Responsibility for KPN Royal Dutch Telecom in the Hague, the Netherlands. He is also regional coordinator for the European Association of Communication Directors in the Netherlands.

About KPN Royal Dutch Telecom
KPN Royal Dutch Telecom is the largest telecom and IT service provider in the Netherlands and a leading supplier of ICT services internationally. The company serves a large number of diverse customer groups in the Netherlands and abroad with a wide range of products and services under various brands: from prepaid call services in the United States to interactive HD television in the Netherlands. KPN Royal Dutch Telecom has more than 18,000 people working for the company.

Advisory and Executive Influence of Communication Professionals

Power can be seen as an individual attribute, although it can also be considered as departmental.[11] Functions can achieve power in the organisational structure vertically by achieving higher internal responsibility, influence and position. Influence can be seen as actual power. We could state that if power is the capacity to influence in order to get things done or achieving desired results, influence is the realisation or actual use of this capacity.[12] Influence points to the hierarchical dimension of power, which refers to the political dynamics among people within an organisational structure. It is also identified as vertical power in an organisational context. Power holders compete for influencing organisational decisions, resource allocations and interpretations. These ongoing conflicts produce the organisational structure. The internal structural chart of the organisation formally represents this

---

[11] Berger (2005); Smith and Place (2013), Smudde and Courtright (2010).
[12] Pfeffer (1977); Pfeffer (1992).

Advisory influence

How seriously senior managers take the recommendations of communication professionals.

Executive influence

How likely it is that communication representatives will be invited to senior-level meetings dealing with organisational strategic planning.

Fig. 14 Executive and advisory influence

hierarchical dimension, but power can also flux through informal mechanisms sometimes rejecting or bypassing the formal systems such as organisational structure.

The concept of a dominant coalition in an organisation, a group of powerful and influential people, reflects a power perspective. Derina Holzhausen and Rosina Voto suggest that membership of the dominant coalition is not required for the communication department to be influential, but other sources of power can be achieved through relationship building.[13] Indeed most professionals do not describe influence in communication management as just having a seat at the table, but being listened to and having access to diverse decision makers and executive-level committees (Fig. 14).[14]

In the Comparative Excellence Framework, as explained in the introduction chapter, the concept of influence rather than power is used. Influence is conceptualised in two dimensions (see Fig. 14): advisory influence (that is the perception of how seriously senior managers take the recommendations of communication professionals) and executive influence (that is the perception of how likely it is that communication representatives will be invited to senior-level meetings dealing with organisational strategic planning). Although both ways of influence mean that communication professionals have power, the executive influence indicates the most complete level of influence because communicators play a more active role in organisational planning and decision-making.

---

[13] Holtzhausen and Voto (2002).
[14] Reber and Berger (2006); Neill (2015).

How influential are communication professionals in European organisations? The influence of communication departments has continued to increase in the last decade, with advisory influence currently overtaking executive influence. This means that until 2014 communication managers' advice was taken more and more seriously, but the departments still did not always have access to the strategic decision-making table. Nevertheless, the distance between these two ways of influence is disappearing. The most recent results from the European Communication Monitor 2016 assign advisory influence to 76.1 per cent of communication practitioners. Executive influence is reported by 75.1 per cent of them.[15] Therefore the gap is closing.

Who's the Most Influential?

Not surprisingly, not every professional reports the same level of influence. Who are the most influential communication managers in Europe? According to the analysis of the European Communication Monitor male practitioners with more experience and higher positions in the department report more influence.[16] Professionals with a better alignment in the organisation, meaning that they report to the highest management levels and sit on the board, perceive their influence as higher than professional who are less aligned.

Today the majority of top-level communication managers report directly to the CEO or highest executive (president, managing director) in the organisation, although only about a quarter of them actually sit on the board. Reporting lines do not differ significantly between various types of organisation, but they do between regions. In Northern European countries, nearly a quarter of top-level communicators sit on the board, in contrast with Southern Europe where only a fifth of them have the same alignment. Results from the European Communication Monitor show that 57.6 per cent of the departments are aligned, 26.6 per cent strongly aligned and only 15.8 per cent are still weakly aligned.[17] This means that some chief communication officers are not members of the executive board and do not report directly to the top executive of the organisation.

---

[15] Zerfass et al. (2016), p. 111.
[16] Zerfass et al. (2012), p. 60.
[17] Zerfass et al. (2016), p. 13.

The more senior the communication practitioner's position the higher the influence of the communication department is perceived to be. The formal position is closely related to the influence of communication managers on the business strategy of the organisation. Also there is a relation between sitting on the board and perceived influence on the management of the organisation; practitioners on the board perceive a higher influence than practitioners that are not on the board.

Communication departments are more influential in joint stock companies than in other types of organisations. 47.8 per cent of communication departments in that group of organisations are very influential in comparison with 42.5 per cent of governmental organisations and NGOs.[18] Private companies have the least influential communication departments. More than 60 per cent of communication departments in private companies do not have a lot of influence, which includes not taking communication advice seriously and not being invited to strategic planning meetings. Yet the problem does not remain only in this type of organisation. In overall terms, the majority of organisations do not have highly influential communication departments. This means that they cannot reach excellence because influence is a clear prerequisite for excellent communication departments (Box 17).

Box 17 What we have learned about influence in excellent communication departments

The European Communication Monitor shows that excellent communication departments are the most influential:

1. Top communication managers or chief communication officers are more frequently members of the executive board or report directly to the CEO or top decision-maker.
2. Excellent communication departments report the highest levels of advisory and executive influence when comparing with non-excellent communication departments.
3. Moreover, the gap between advisory and executive influence in these excellent departments is visibly reduced. Excellent communication departments are taken more seriously and at the same time they also participate more in strategic decisions of their organisation.

---

[18] Zerfass et al. (2016), p. 112.

Embeddedness of Communication Departments

We have talked about the vertical power of communication departments, the power to reach the top of the organisation, but how are the relationships between communication and other functions in the organisation? In other words how embedded are communication departments in Europe?

The building of alliances with other departments in organisations is explained by the so-called theory of strategic contingencies.[19] This theory explains that strategic alliances, both internal and external, are key to achieve organisational goals. In the horizontal direction, departments related through the working of these strategic contingencies phenomena tend to achieve more power. In *The Hunger Games*, the successful film franchise, there was a fictional, staged arena that is a good analogy for understanding the factors of these strategic contingencies. In the 'game' there was demand for high-level skills to be successful, in actual fact to survive. Katniss, the main character, has exceptional skills through her upbringing and life experience, which enable her to hunt and survive in the forest. At a certain point in the game she occupies a prominent position in the net of competitors. She becomes essential for others to survive, effectively because of her skills in hunting. This makes her successful in even the most difficult situation. Such unique skills, like hunting in the case of *The Hunger Games*, can also become very contingent in an organisation. When a company has an important issue to solve, for example, if it is going public, individuals and departments that are key to the flow of information and provide scarce skills, for example, the finance department, gain organisational power at that point in time. In the same vein it is frequently acknowledged that communication departments become more powerful when an organisation has to face a crisis, especially when it is one in the eye of the media. This means that media relations skills of the communication department entail a set of specific skills and compe-tences that other functions clearly identify with those of the communica-tion's department. And those skills are needed.

The European Communication Monitor has measured the horizontal power achieved by communication departments in organisations with cate-gories originally suggested by Jeffrey Pfeffer, a professor of organisational behaviour at Stanford University and one of today's most influential manage-ment thinkers (see Box 18).[20] According to him there are five sources of

---

[19] Hickson et al. (1971).

[20] Pfeffer (1992).

horizontal power for a department. Besides the example of irreplaceability in *The Hunger Games* case, dependency, financial resources, centrality and uncertainty are the other four sources of horizontal power.

Box 18 Five sources of horizontal power for organisational departments

1. Dependency
2. Financial resources
3. Centrality
4. Irreplaceability
5. Coping with uncertainty

Not all the five factors of horizontal power score highly for communication departments in Europe. On a five-point scale the level of dependency on the communication department in the organisation is rated just near to three, the same as generating financial and immaterial assets for the organisation.[21] Irreplaceability of the communication department is higher, although only anticipating situations and conflicting issues, together with the importance of the role communication departments play in overall performance of the organisation, reach a score of four. These last two aspects of horizontal power together seem to strengthen the internal position of communication departments because they are also related.

Regarding the connections between formal and horizontal power the results show that the horizontal power of communication departments is stronger when the top communication manager has broader responsibilities. Communication managers with responsibility for at least three fields or stakeholders score higher on all five of Pfeffer's dimensions than communication managers that are only responsible for media relations and/or internal communication.

So in the horizontal direction, departments make strategic alliances to get the required skills and the access to information to try to achieve power. Therefore, the question is who does the communication department relate to in the organisation? A longitudinal analysis of the European Communication Monitor shows that ties between functions have not been strengthened during a period of five years (see Fig. 15).

---

[21] Zerfass et al. (2011), p. 56.

The communication department works always closely with the ...

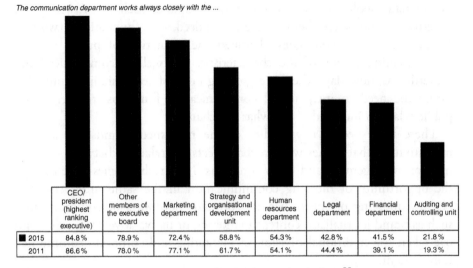

	CEO/ president (highest ranking executive)	Other members of the executive board	Marketing department	Strategy and organisational development unit	Human resources department	Legal department	Financial department	Auditing and controlling unit
■ 2015	84.8%	78.9%	72.4%	58.8%	54.3%	42.8%	41.5%	21.8%
2011	86.6%	78.0%	77.1%	61.7%	54.1%	44.4%	39.1%	19.3%

Fig. 15 Integrating communication by horizontal relations[22]

Working relationships are especially close with the CEO and other members of the executive board. Next to them, on the overall organisation structure, marketing is clearly the department with whom the communication function has the closest working relationship. There are also close relations with strategy and organisational development units. Relations with human resources, legal and financial departments are less frequent. At the other end of the scale, relations with auditing and controlling units are the weakest.

Not every organisation establishes horizontal relations in the same way. For instance, there are differences between the importance of collaboration with marketing in commercial organisations in contrast with governmental and also with non-profits. The same can be said for the higher relations with legal, financial and human resources departments in joint stock companies. Collaboration is stronger in publicly traded (joint stock) and private companies, and weaker in non-profit and governmental organisations overall.[23]

Why is it important to have intra-organisational collaboration? Traditionally in the field of strategic communication there was an axiom of the necessity to

---

[22] Zerfass et al. (2015), p. 30. n = 1,601 (2015) and n = 1,450 (2011) communication professionals working in communication departments across Europe. Q: How closely does the communication function in your organisation work with the … Scale 1 (never) – 5 (always). Percentages: frequency based on scale points 4–5.

[23] Zerfass et al. (2015), p. 31.

differentiate public relations from other disciplines such as marketing and advertising, and keep them separated. Indeed, the foundational work of James Grunig and colleagues identified the separation of public relations and marketing as one of the characteristics of excellent communication.[24] Nevertheless, nowadays, there is a growing body of academic literature advocating the need to integrate all communication functions, marketing and public relations included.[25] So, what has changed?

There is a special, new reality of the new media landscape and the mediatisation that comes with it, that affects the relations between communication management and other functions. New technologies have brought the opportunity of merging communication in the same interfaces. This physical merging of spaces has also brought new ways of communicating such as brand journalism, content marketing or native advertising, that have overtaken the traditional division of marketing and corporate communication content.

Recent studies identified a strong convergence of stakeholder priorities, goals and instruments when interviewing public relations and marketing professionals about their branding activities, as well as a high level of structural integration and collaboration, although there are also underlying conflicts, discrepancies and contradictory perceptions. The new scenario of convergence brings new proposals for integrating communication and conceptualising all organisational communication activities such as strategic communication to the forefront.[26]

Convincingly 85.6 per cent of respondents of the European Communication Monitor believed that there was an overall need to integrate communication activities, which affects all functions.[27] Professionals in Europe seem to have embraced the new concept strategies as important for the future, and not just as a passing fad. But the challenging point is who will achieve internal, departmental power from these new content strategies?

Nearly two-thirds of respondents report that corporate communication is gaining in importance as it has a long tradition of handling content, while nearly half of respondents (64.0 per cent) also see marketing gaining in importance (45.2 per cent) as a consequence of the same processes. Marketing, brand, consumer and online communicators are more in favour

---

[24] Grunig et al. (2002).
[25] For example, Zerfass (2008).
[26] Hallahan et al. (2007); Holtzhausen and Zerfass (2015).
[27] Zerfass et al. (2015), p. 28.

of emerging concepts like content strategy, content marketing or native advertising than media relations or strategy and coordination people.[28] There seems to be a defensive and conservative tendency at work here involving 'traditional' public relations functions (e.g. media relations).

Instead of using the integration of communication functions as an opportunity, also to organise an umbrella under which communications from marketing departments could migrate and feel welcome, many seem to be trying to preserve their turf in what is a diminishing territory. Media are not what they used to be and the demarcation line between news and advertising is becoming fuzzy. There is no way that the lines between advertising/marketing and publicity/public relations could stay untouched. The question is not if different communications functions will integrate; the question is how and with what effect. Collaboration is key. Only a combination of consistent goals, intelligent structures, transparent processes, a supportive culture and leaders who support integration will make this happen (Box 19).

Box 19 What we have learned about organisational integration from excellent communication departments

Excellent communication departments collaborate more intensively with all other organisational functions:

1. They always work more closely with the CEO and with other members of the executive board.
2. They always work more closely with the marketing department.
3. They always work more closely with strategy and organisational development and with auditing and controlling units.
4. They always work more closely with human resources, financial and legal departments.

Leading the Communication Department

In order to be able to face the future communication professionals also have to show effective leadership in managing the communication department. That is the third leadership challenge communication professionals face (Box 20).

---

[28] Zerfass et al. (2015), pp. 32, 36.

> **Box 20 Leadership for communication**
>
> Communication managers lead effective communication departments that help the organisation to reach its goals

It is easy to talk about 'good leadership' but it is often more difficult to define. We see this across business disciplines as managers search for the essence of effective leadership. Our empirical surveys over the past ten years have also focused on this question. What does great leadership look like in effective communication departments? How do communication managers lead? And how do they adapt to the organisation's needs when leading the communication function?

Leadership directly or indirectly determines structures, culture, power distribution and communication at different levels of the organisation. Research in leadership has been developed from a conception based on the 'traits' of the leader to more sophisticated approaches that focus on behaviours and styles of leadership, skills, group work and management, situational approaches and contingency models. All these approaches have produced an extended corpus of knowledge in diverse scientific disciplines. But, between all of them, the transformational approach has been the most strongly supported and accepted approach in the last few decades. Transformational leadership means that leaders develop a vision that appeals to ideals and values of the followers. Despite the current – and plentiful – scientific literature in the field of management about leadership, just a few studies have focused on leadership in strategic communication and public relations.

The latest cross-cultural research about leadership in communication management by Bruce Berger and Juan Meng evaluates a leadership model that includes seven dimensions and integrates abilities, personal traits, behaviours and cultural and structural factors.[29] The seven dimensions are self-dynamics, team collaboration, ethical orientation, relationship-building skills, strategic decision-making capability, communication knowledge management and organisational culture and structure (see Box 21).

---

[29] Berger and Meng (2014).

Box 21 Seven principles of leadership in communication management

1. Self-dynamics
2. Team collaboration
3. Ethical orientation
4. Relationship-building skills
5. Strategic decision-making capability
6. Communication knowledge management
7. Organisational culture and structure

Characteristics of a Good Communication Leader

In general, today's most in demand professional is one with characteristics such as enthusiasm, energy or passion, trustworthiness and flexibility. All of these characteristics are necessary due to the fact that, among the numerous tasks of communication professionals, one of the most important is to develop and nurture relationships.[30] Furthermore, many organisations agree that leaders must have strategic decision-making capability, problem-solving ability and communication knowledge and expertise if they want to reach excellence.[31] In addition, Bruce Berger and Juan Meng affirm that leaders in the communication sector on a daily basis must manage a vast quantity of data that develop rapidly (see also Commandment 5, Datafied).[32] Hence, in defining effective leadership we must include the capacity of determining what is most relevant, evaluating that information in a strategic and tactical way and identifying valuable opportunities to create internal and external engagement.

Despite these general characteristics for the field of communication management, these studies also underline important cultural and national differences.[33] Leadership is contingent and must be adapted to geographic cultures, but also to the culture and subcultures of and around each organisation. Despite the characteristics of the leader him/herself, leadership can be understood as a complex process with participation by a considerable number of individuals. Leaders cannot be leaders without followers, leadership is a co-creative process. In this sense, to determine how excellent

---

[30] Meng and Berger (2013).

[31] Meng et al. (2012).

[32] Berger and Meng (2014).

[33] Moreno et al. (2014a).

communication departments must be led requires understanding of what leadership styles can be best adopted for communication functions.

The European Communication Monitor researched the styles of leadership in European communication departments.[34] The leadership questions were based on previous research by Kelly Werder and Derina Holzhausen from the United States.[35] These authors reviewed management literature about leadership styles and concluded that in the field of communication practitioners enact three main leadership styles: transactional, transformational and inclusive.

The transactional leadership style draws on authority and reminds followers of common standards. The transformational style develops a vision and appeal to followers' ideals and values. Finally the inclusive style identifies challenges and involves followers in shared decision-making and stimulates them to participate in the process (see Fig. 16).

Transactional and transformational leadership styles have been compared in many studies, highlighting transformational leadership as the most effective style because it creates higher levels of satisfaction in followers. This style appeals to followers' ideals and values so that they work with more motivation and commitment to the organisation; meanwhile the transactional style is more dictatorial and rules are defined. The leadership principles of Bruce Berger and Juan Meng and other recent studies in the public relations field also support the transformational leadership style as the best one for communication departments.[36]

Transactional leadership style — Draws on authority and reminds followers of common standards.

Inclusive leadership style — Identifies challenges and involves followers in shared decision-making and stimulates them in participate process.

Transformational leadership style — Developers ideas and appeals to followers' ideas and values.

Fig. 16 Leadership styles

---

[34] Zerfass et al. (2011), pp. 30–39.
[35] Werder and Holtzhausen (2009).
[36] Berger and Meng (2014); Meng (2014); Jin (2010).

Nevertheless, the European Communication Monitor survey outcomes discovered that inclusive leadership has more support among communication managers. Almost every second respondent reports predominance for the inclusive leadership style, which means that leaders involve followers in shared decision-making.[37] Practitioners in non-profit organisations use significantly different ways of leadership and an inclusive leadership style is even more prevalent in this kind of organisation. This approach matches with a 'power with relations style',[38] which refers to shared power and collaborative decision-making, and is also in line with the symmetric and dialogic approaches to sustainable relationship with stakeholders.

It is essential to outline that leadership styles develop better in some contexts and organisations than in others. The European Communication Monitor shows that the transactional style is more used in governmental organisations and the transformational style is practised more in private companies. In contrast, inclusive leadership is more popular in joint stock companies and non-profit organisations.[39]

So, should joint stock companies practice an inclusive style of leadership and governmental organisations a transactional style? No, not necessarily. Contingencies and context influence the style of leadership and they are a set of complex factors. One factor of influence can be the type of organisation, but we can also find other differences based on the particular culture of the organisation. Leadership and organisational culture also have reciprocal influences on each other. The organisational environment also contributes to how communication fulfils this function. There are positive organisational environments in which communication can flourish because leaders are more accessible and visible for their diverse stakeholders letting relationships build with strong and long-term commitment. The style of leadership has to be developed within the social group of a given organisation. It has to connect, interact with and be part of the culture of the organisation. Previous research shows that communication leaders who demonstrate high levels of ability in collaborating with members and maintaining the core values of public relations as professional standards are more likely to foster an environment of flexible communication. They also foster a supportive organisational culture.[40]

---

[37] Zerfass et al. (2011), p. 37.

[38] Berger (2005).

[39] Zerfass et al. (2011), p. 38.

[40] Meng (2014).

	TRANSACTIONAL LEADERSHIP	TRANSFORMATIONAL LEADERSHIP	INCLUSIVE LEADERSHIP
INTEGRATED CULTURE (participative – proactive)	11.8%	35.9%	52.4%
INTERACTIVE CULTURE (participative – reactive)	20.9%	33.6%	45.5%
ENTREPRENEURIAL CULTURE (non-participative – proactive)	20.8%	49.1%	30.2%
SYSTEMATISED CULTURE (non-participative – reactive)	46.5%	26.9%	26.6%

Fig. 17 Organisational culture and leadership style in communication departments[41]

In the European Communication Monitor we analysed the relationship between leadership and organisational culture based on a classification by Robert Ernest.[42] He established a model of organisational cultures based on two dimensions: (1) orientation to people and (2) answer to the environment (proactive or reactive). From these two dimensions four types of organisational culture are defined:

1. Integrated culture – participative and proactive;
2. Interactive culture – participative and reactive;
3. Entrepreneurial culture – non-participative and proactive; and
4. Systematised culture – non-participative and reactive.

As demonstrated in Fig. 17, the inclusive leadership style is the most common in organisations with an integrated culture, while transformational leadership is the most common in entrepreneurial organisational cultures. Transactional leadership is the most common in a systemised culture (Box 22).

---

[41] Zerfass et al. (2011), p. 41. n = 2,209 communication professionals across Europe. Q: How would you describe the dominant strategy used by leaders in your communication department (or in your consultancy) to achieve common goals? Q: How would you perceive your organisation regarding the following attributes? Significant differences between the three types of culture (chi-square test, $p \leq 0.05$).
[42] Ernest (1985).

> **Box 22 What we have learned about excellent leadership in communication departments**
>
> 1. Excellent leadership in communication points first to contingency and adaptability, to be embedded into the organisation's culture and subculture.
> 2. Today, in Europe as a global region, it points to inclusive styles and integrates cultures.
> 3. Inclusive leadership style positively correlates with job satisfaction and influence of the communication function.

We have seen that being influential is a matter of leadership, power and collaboration. Insofar as the function of communication is actually *embedded* it can bring its value to the organisation. To ensure that the organisation can obtain the maximum benefit of communication, the communication department has to be fully embedded into the organisation: hierarchically and vertically to integrate all communications activities. The communication professional has to be an effective leader to have the needed influence to fulfil its threefold role effectively: by helping organisational leaders to be communicative, supporting overall goals of the organisation through strategic communication and leading the communication department well.

References

Aascher, M. (2016). De rol van de leider. *De Gids*, (3), 3–7.

Amiguet, L. L. (2016). Interview with Howard Gardner, *La Vanguardia*, 11 April 2016. Retrieved from www.lavanguardia.com/lacontra/20160411/401021583313/una-mala-persona-no-llega-nunca-a-ser-buen-profesional.html

Berger, B. K. (2005). Power over, power with, and power to relations: Critical reflections on public relations, the dominant coalition, and activism. *Journal of Public Relations Research*, *17*(1), 5–28

Berger, B. K., & Meng, J. (2014). *Public Relations Leaders as Sensemakers: A Global Study of Leadership in Public Relations and Communication Management.* New York, NY: Routledge.

Dahlgaard-Park, S., & Dahlgaard, J. J. (2007). Excellence – 25 years evolution. *Journal of Management History*, *13*(4), 371–393.

Ernest, R. C. (1985). Corporate cultures and effective planning. *Personnel Administrator*, *30*(3), 49–60.

Falkheimer, J. (2014). The power of strategic communication in organizational development. *International Journal of Quality and Service Sciences*, *6*(2/3), 124–133.

Gioia, D. A., & Chittipeddi, K. (1991). Sensemaking and sensegiving in strategic change initiation. *Strategic Management Journal, 12*(6), 433–448.

Grunig, L. A., Grunig, J. E., & Dozier, D. M. (2002). *Excellent Public Relations and Effective Organizations. A Study of Communication Management in Three Countries.* Mahwah, NJ: Lawrence Erlbaum Associates.

Hallahan, K., Holtzhausen, D., Van Ruler, B., Verčič, D., & Sriramesh, K. (2007). Defining strategic communication. *International Journal of Strategic Communication, 1*(1), 3–35.

Hickson, D. J., Hinings, C. R., Lee, C. A., Schneck, R. E., & Pennings, J. M. (1971). A strategic contingencies' theory of intraorganizational power. *Administrative Science Quarterly, 16*(2), 216–229.

Holtzhausen, D. R., & Voto, R. (2002). Resistance from the margins: The post-modern public relations practitioner as organizational activist. *Journal of Public Relations Research, 14*(1), 57–84.

Holtzhausen, D., & Zerfass, A. (2015). Strategic communication: Opportunities and challenges of the research area. In D. R. Holtzhausen & A. Zerfass (Eds.), *The Routledge Handbook of Strategic Communication* (pp. 3–17). New York, NY: Routledge.

Jin, Y. (2010). Emotional leadership as a key dimension of public relations leadership: A national survey of public relations leaders. *Journal of Public Relations Research, 22*(2), 159–181.

Meng, J. (2012). Strategic leadership in public relations: An integrated conceptual framework. *Public Relations Review, 38*(2), 336–338

Meng, J. (2014). Unpacking the relationship between organizational culture and excellent leadership in public relations: an empirical investigation. *Journal of Communication Management, 18*(4), 363–385.

Meng, J., & Berger, B. (2013). An integrated model of excellent leadership in public relations: Dimensions, measurement, and validation. *Journal of Public Relations Research, 25*(2), 141–167.

Meng, J., Berger, B. K., Gower, K. K., & Heyman, W. C. (2012). A test of excellent leadership in public relations: Key qualities, valuable sources, and distinctive leadership perceptions. *Journal of Public Relations Research, 24*(1), 18–36.

Mintzberg, H. (2004). *Managers, not MBAs: A Hard Look at the Soft Practice of Managing and Management Development.* San Francisco, CA: Berrett-Koehler.

Moreno, A., Navarro Ruiz, C., & Humanes, M. L. (2014a). El liderazgo en relaciones públicas y gestión de comunicación. Análisis cuantitativo de los factores de liderazgo en el sector en España. *Palabra Clave, 17*(3), 946–978.

Moreno, A., Verhoeven, P., Tench, R., & Zerfass, A. (2014b). Increasing power and taking a lead – What are practitioners really doing? Empirical evidence from European communications managers. *Revista Internacional de Relaciones Públicas, 4*(7), 73–94.

Neill, M. S. (2015). Beyond the c-suite: Corporate communications' power and influence. *Journal of Communication Management, 19*(2), 118–132.

Pfeffer, J. (1977). The ambiguity of leadership. *Academy of Management Review*, *2*(1), 104–112.

Pfeffer, J. (1992). *Managing with Power: Politics and Influence in Organizations*. Boston, MA: Harvard Business School Press.

Reber, B. H., & Berger, B. K. (2006). Finding influence: Examining the role of influence in public relations practice. *Journal of Communication Management*, *10*(3), 235–249.

Smith, B. G., & Place, K. R. (2013). Integrating power? Evaluating public relations influence in an integrated communication structure. *Journal of Public Relations Research*, *25*(2), 168–187.

Smudde, P. M., & Courtright, J. L. (2010). Public relations and power. In R. L. Heath (Ed.), *The SAGE Handbook of Public Relations* (pp. 177–189). Thousand Oaks, CA: Sage.

Thoening, J., & Waldman, C. (2007). *The Marking Enterprise. Business Success and Societal Embedding*. New York, NY: Palgrave Macmillan.

Werder, K. P., & Holtzhausen, D. (2009). An analysis of the influence of public relations department leadership style on public relations strategy use and effectiveness. *Journal of Public Relations Research*, *21*(4), 404–427.

Zerfass, A. (2008). Corporate communication revisited: Integrating business strategy and strategic communication. In A. Zerfass, B. Van Ruler, & K. Sriramesh (Eds.), *Public Relations Research. European and International Perspectives and Innovations* (pp. 65–96). Wiesbaden: VS Verlag für Sozialwissenschaften.

Zerfass, A., Moreno, A., Tench, R., Verčič, D., & Verhoeven, P. (2009). *European* Communication *Monitor 2009. Trends in Communication Management and* Public *Relations – Results of a Survey in 34 Countries*. Brussels: EUPRERA.

Zerfass, A., Verhoeven, P., Tench, R., Moreno, A., & Verčič, D. (2011). *European Communication Monitor 2011. Empirical Insights into Strategic Communication in Europe. Results of an Empirical Survey in 43 Countries*. Brussels: EACD, EUPRERA.

Zerfass, A., Verčič, D., Verhoeven, P., Moreno, A., & Tench, R. (2012). *European Communication Monitor 2012: Challenges and Competencies for Strategic Communication*. Brussels: EACD/EUPRERA, Helios Media.

Zerfass, A., Tench, R., Verčič, D., Verhoeven, P., & Moreno, A. (2014). *European Communication Monitor 2014. Excellence in Strategic Communication – Key Issues, Leadership, Gender and Mobile Media. Results of a Survey in 42 Countries*. Brussels: EACD/EUPRERA, Helios Media.

Zerfass, A., Verčič, D., Verhoeven, P., Moreno, A., & Tench, R. (2015). *European Communication Monitor 2015. Creating Communication Value Through Listening, Messaging and Measurement. Results of a Survey in 41 Countries*. Brussels: EACD/EUPRERA, Helios Media.

Zerfass, A., Verhoeven, P., Moreno, A., Tench, R., & Verčič, D. (2016). *European Communication Monitor 2016. Exploring Trends in Big Data, Stakeholder Engagement and Strategic Communication. Results of A Survey In 43 Countries*. Brussels: EACD/EUPRERA, Quadriga Media Berlin.

Commandment 5
Datafied: Research, Measure and Evaluate

In a professional environment research is indispensable. Successful strategies depend on research and so does the evaluation of the success of policies and interventions. Additionally the amount of data and information has grown exponentially in the last decades. Today's question revolves around what to do with all this data? How do we analyse and interpret this plethora of information? All professions have to deal with these new phenomena of overwhelmingly available data, but for strategic communication and public relations this is even more important since basically we are in the business of information processing. Good fundamental and applied research is getting more and more important for the high-performing communication professionals. In this scenario it is clear that the field is increasingly becoming *datafied*.

A more central role for data and the analysis and interpretation of it is important for a few reasons. First it is important to make sense of what stakeholders think and say about the organisation and how public opinion about the organisation and its issues develops. The interplay between the traditional media and the new media, especially Twitter, has increased the speed of opinion formation. It is necessary to keep up to date with the way opinions around the organisation develop. Secondly it is important to demonstrate the value of communication to the rest of the organisation. Good research on knowledge, attitudes and behaviour of all kinds of stakeholders is a prerequisite for that. Not only with big data research but also with small data research, more qualitative research with smaller groups of stakeholders to find out

© The Author(s) 2017
R. Tench et al., *Communication Excellence*,
DOI 10.1007/978-3-319-48860-8_5

more about the background of the thoughts people have about the organisation. Both methods of research are important and will remain so. Hence, being datafied is the fifth commandment of excellent communication. Measuring goals and effects with appropriate methods and statistical or qualitative analysis is indispensable for professional strategic communication. It increases the influence and the credibility of the communication department in the organisation together with good embeddedness and strategic insight.

In the European Communication Monitor we regularly ask questions about how communication professionals in Europe measure their activities and what role research plays in the development of their strategies, policies and plans. Let us find out the state of the art of research in communication management in Europe.

Measurement and Evaluation: The Enduring *cri de coeur* of Communication Management

More than 40 years ago, the American public relations theorist James Grunig wrote regretfully about the gap between the awareness of the need of evaluation and the actual failure of the implementation of research and evaluation in the profession, what was later named by British researchers Tom Watson and Paul Noble as Grunig's *cri de coeur* of the profession.[1]

Despite more than four decades of discussions between industry and academics the issue of research and evaluation in communication management has still not been solved.[2] Practitioners recognise the necessity of establishing common standards for measurement and evaluation in the profession, but there does not seem to be much progress in implementing them as recent research continues to re-emphasise.

Recently efforts of diverse associations in the field have tried to create common standards to evaluate communication starting from a joint initiative of communication and controller associations in Germany in 2009 and the

---

[1] Watson, T. and Noble (2014); for the overall discussion on measurement and evaluation, see also Macnamara (2015); Zerfass (2015).
[2] Volk (2016).

first Barcelona Declaration of Measurement Principles in 2010.[3] The Institute for Public Relations (IPR), the Council of PR Firms (CPRF) and the International Association of Measurement and Evaluation of Communication (AMEC) created the Coalition for Public Relations Research Standards in 2011 with the aim of developing standards for measurement and evaluation of public relations and communication management. A year later, in 2012, the Coalition included a total of 11 associations and bodies to work collaboratively on these topics through the Proposed Interim Standards for Metrics. As a result of this cooperation, three important documents were produced as the first stage of social media measurement standards.[4] Apart from this specific field, several task forces from academia and practice are continuously debating overall approaches of communication evaluation. A notable milestone is the integrated measurement framework proposed by AMEC in 2016 that combines many of the previous insights.[5]

Jim Macnamara, a long-time observer of the debate from Australia, summarised four factors that in addition to the lack of budgets and resources have contributed to the enduring *cri du coeur* about measurement and evaluation in communication management[6]: (1) practitioners have deplored and ignored tested theories and models of measurement and evaluation; (2) there has been a poor interaction between practitioners and academics in the social sciences and humanities producing incomplete debates and solutions; (3) a continuing belief (hope) in finding the magic formula for covering all needs and (4) commercial pressures from measurement suppliers who want to promote (and protect) their own particular solutions.

The consequences of this issue are having a major impact on the profession. In Europe three out of four practitioners identified the inability to prove the impact of communication activities on most organisational goals as the major barrier to the further professionalisation of communication.[7]

---

[3] For the German initiative see Zerfass (2010); DPRG and ICV (2011). The Barcelona Declaration of Measurement Principles in 2010 and the revised version 2015 can be found at http://amecorg.com.

[4] Daniels (2012); Digital Analytics Association (2013).

[5] AMEC (2016).

[6] Macnamara (2014).

[7] Zerfass et al. (2012), p. 38.

Commandments in Practice: Datafied

International Committee of the Red Cross

Big Data Analytics Helps Communication to Enhance Proximity and Strengthen Humanitarian Response in War Time

Engaging directly with those affected by, as well as those who are party to, armed conflict and other situations of violence which we call war is critical to the *modus operandi* of the International Committee of the Red Cross (ICRC). To do this the ICRC believes it is essential to have a physical presence in contexts affected by war as this proximity enables both an ability to understand the humanitarian impact on, and thus respond to the needs of, populations affected, as well as to engage on humanitarian law and principles with those who can influence or who are directly participating in the hostilities.

Maintaining or gaining physical proximity to the men, women and children affected by war and the increasing number of armed actors – both State and non-State – is an enormous challenge. Whilst not underestimating the importance of securing physical proximity, the ICRC is increasingly leveraging advances in connectivity, technology and data analytics to complement its ability to read the humanitarian environment or conflict dynamics and to reach – engage with and potentially influence – affected populations and armed actors. Simply put, leveraging virtual proximity to complement or enhance physical proximity in a context affected by war. This recognises that access to mobile phones and the Internet generally continues to function even in war zones, thus can enhance the humanitarian response including, for example, through 'information as aid' and community engagement and increasingly the use of big data analytics.

Big data analytics now enable us to automatically analyse mass data sets to obtain actionable information that due to its velocity, volume and complexity can't be analysed through traditional methods of analysis. Through engaging with different companies and specialists in big data analytics, the ICRC communication department has been testing how to best leverage publicly sourced information to complement its reading of the humanitarian environment, to develop 'influence' maps and to engage with specific actors where physical proximity is restricted. With this objective, in one pilot project, the ICRC worked with computer scientists to analyse more than 10 million Tweets on key terms linked to humanitarian concerns on a specific war context. The aim was to develop influence maps of actors and communities of influence linked to a non-State actor group and to analyse the content of the Tweets and interesting 'communities' linked to geographic locations and concepts. This contributed to the development of a 'virtual' engagement strategy to complement attempts to engage more directly in the specific context and enabled the ICRC to identify social media influencers who could potentially be contacted to work towards improved access.

Recognising that the aggregation of publicly sourced information may include detailed communication of individuals, the ICRC pays particular attention to the risks in relation to the use of big data, to ensure nobody's privacy is harmed and individuals are not put at risk. The ICRC applies its *Professional Standards for Protection Work in Armed Conflict and Other Situations of Violence* as well as its *Rules on Personal Data Protection* which it has developed.

In addition, and because of its purely humanitarian mandate, the ICRC is careful with which companies and specialists it works. It is a rule not to use confidential information that is collected in the course of activities and to not share externally the results of big data analyses – they are managed internally with discretion and/or confidentiality dependent on the content.

As technologies advance, become more secure and affordable (and this is evolving daily), it will be increasingly feasible to analyse data in real time and ultimately to provide even greater insights to help the ICRC read its operating environment, to support development of strategies and to inform decision-making. For those who may wonder why the ICRC is piloting big data capabilities, it is important to recognise that in a world where one in four people now use social networks, there are opportunities to leverage what can be referred to as *digital proximity networking*. This can enhance the ICRC's engagement with affected populations, its ability to influence, strengthen its two-way communication and help enhancing proximity and access (physical and virtual) to beneficiaries and armed actors. These are prerequisites for the ICRC's capacity to deliver a humanitarian response to those affected by war, that is, to act in the service of humanity.

Charlotte Lindsey Curtet
Charlotte Lindsey Curtet is the Director of Communication and Information Management at the International Committee of the Red Cross (ICRC), Geneva, Switzerland.

About the International Committee of the Red Cross
The IRCR is an impartial, neutral and independent organisation whose exclusively humanitarian mission is to protect the lives and dignity of victims of armed conflict and other situations of violence and to provide them with assistance. Established in 1863, the ICRC operates worldwide and employs about 14,500 people in more than 80 countries. The ICRC is funded mainly by voluntary donations from governments and from national Red Cross and Red Crescent Societies.

Evaluation: The Alpha and Omega of Strategy

One of the main barriers to the lack of effective evaluation of communication is the conviction that public relations and other forms of strategic communication have a dual nature. On the one hand they are seen as a more creative and artistic field, and on the other, as a management discipline. The humanist and artistic dimension of public relations and advertising, related to the products it produces, has been an argument to justify its activity and that, therefore, it could not be easily measured using traditional business language and metrics over time. As a consequence, various studies have shown that most communication departments continue to use rudimentary measurement technique such as counting press clippings or other simplistic methods to measure quantity. Although discussions and debates about evaluation in public relations or publicity practices have been documented from the nineteenth century onwards, measurement and evaluation have been practised in very basic forms, such as media monitoring, ever since.

Nevertheless, by reviewing the models for communication planning and evaluation three clear conclusions emerge: (1) communication planning is founded on managerial strategic planning models; (2) their roots are from a functionalist perspective of communication and (3) evaluation is compulsory and included in every planning process. These planning models have their roots in the so-called functionalist approaches in public relations theory. These approaches have formed the dominant paradigm of PR in the context of strategic planning and call for a set of matching research methods and tools.

The conception of successful communication in the functionalist approach is defined as certain evidence that the message has moved and has been received by target publics. That means that the focus is on the transfer of information, as opposed to a more global meaning of communication as the creation or restructuring of culture.

The functionalist paradigm of strategic communication founded on systems theory was popularised in seminal textbooks by Scott Cutlip and Allen Center and later by James Grunig and Todd Hunt, followed by an influential journal article by Larry Long and Vince Hazelton.[8] In this approach communication management is understood as a sub-function of management in organisations. Communication management or public relations are seen as a sub-system that controls and integrates other sub-systems through communication. The communication process is working until the system achieves the equilibrium with other systems in the same environment, but this equilibrium is always precarious and dynamic, which makes the process a continuum. It is from this conception that strategic planning models of communication have been developed.

Just like in management planning, the objective is to provide implementation models for planning and implementing communication programmes and campaigns that can detect what works and what does not and to establish predictive models for improving the future. All these communication planning models have one thing in common which is that research and evaluation is the axis of connection and continuity in time. The model coined in the 1970s that has most influenced the current models is probably the frame RACE –*research,*

---

[8] Cutlip and Center (1952); Grunig and Hunt (1984); Long and Hazelton (1987).

action, communication, evaluation – by John Marston.[9] Marston presented this sequence of four steps that began and finished with stages of research for planning a public relations programme. Consequently, evaluation has always been present conceptually in theories of PR and strategic planning.

During the 1990s academia and industry had a high point of interest in evaluation methods for public relations. Models were designed that identified the diverse stages in evaluating communication. Evaluation can run from the tone of a tweet, through ad hoc research on cognition and changes of opinion, attitude and behaviour of targeted audiences, to the measurement of social and political changes generated in the long term. Most of these models still identify stages related to the effects produced by communication products, although some models began introducing other stages linked to the process of communication management itself. An example of this development is the model developed by Jim Macnamara that presents a division of levels graphically represented like a pyramid that include[10]: *inputs, outputs* – products and their production process, scope and primary cognitive effects – and *results* – change of attitude and behaviour. Other authors also take into consideration the evaluation of the process of communication planning itself and its impact in the organisation.[11] Today it is normal that an organisation's priorities are used to contextualise communication measurements in terms of the overall needs of the organisation as a communicator, setting objectives that are achievable and measurable; assessing the activities and processes involved in the campaign, the outputs produced and the outcomes.

To investigate how communication professionals are doing research today the European Communication Monitor selected a standard framework developed by academics, management accountants and communication associations in Germany (see Fig. 18).[12] This framework includes a stage of measurement and evaluation of communication that has received less attention: the outflow level. The outflow level is the stage that allows a direct link with the value that communication brings to the organisation. The model conceptualises evaluation and measurement activities in four clusters: inputs, outputs, outcomes and outflows. While all are important, demonstrating the business value of

---

[9] Marston (1963).

[10] Macnamara (1992, 1999, 2002, 2012).

[11] Rossi and Freeman (1993); Cutlip et al. (2000); Kendall (1996).

[12] DPRG and ICV (2011); Watson and Noble (2014).

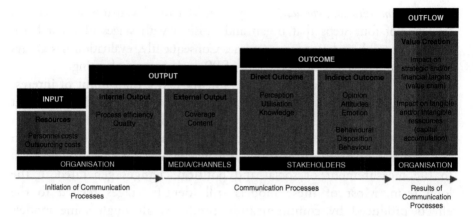

Fig. 18 The overall communication measurement and evaluation process[13]

communication activities is more transparent if done at the outcome and outflow levels, where it is possible to measure and evaluate the impact on the value chain and on capital (tangible and intangible resources of the organisation).

Measurement and Evaluation Stages Implemented in Communication Departments

The European Communication Monitor has researched measurement practices several times. A longitudinal analysis comparing data from 2010 and 2015 shows nearly the same picture. *Output measures* like clippings and media responses, Internet/Intranet usage and the satisfaction of (internal) clients are the most used, followed by *outcome* and *input* measures, with *outflow* measures at the bottom (impact on financial and strategic targets and impact on intangible/tangible resources) (Fig. 19).

Empirical data from our studies corroborates previous research that states that communicators are focused on evaluating media and channels; while they care less about the resources used to initiate communication processes; about the stakeholders addressed by communication activities and, most importantly, about the effects communication has on the achievement of organisational

---

[13] Adjusted from Zerfass et al. (2015), p. 74. Framework originally developed by DPRG and ICV (2011).

Items monitored or measured	2010	2015	Δ
Impact on intangible/tangible resources (i.e. economic brand value)	24.9%	35.6%	10.7%
Impact on financial/strategic targets (i.e. with scorecards, strategy maps)	26.2%	39.4%	13.2%
Stakeholder atitudes and behaviour change	40.9%	45.8%	4.9%
Understanding of key messages	52.4%	53.6%	1.2%
Clippings and media response	82.0%	82.4%	0.4%
Internet/Intranet usage	72.2%	68.9%	–3.3%
Satisfaction of internal clients	55.5%	57.5%	2.0%
Process quality (internal workflow)	26.0%	38.6%	12.6%
Financial costs for projects	46.7%	67.8%	21.1%
Personnel costs for projects	25.7%	44.9%	19.2%

■ Input   ■ Output   ■ Outcome   ■ Outflow

Fig. 19 Measurement practices in communication departments[14]

goals.[15] The biggest increases between 2010 and 2015 are in the areas that have been previously ignored: input measurements (evaluating financial and personnel costs for projects) and outflow measurements (impact on financial/ strategic assets and impact on intangible/tangible resources).

It is positive and interesting to note that one in three communication departments measures the impact of communication on intangible or tangible resources. Yet it is only one in three that measures the impact of communication. The inconsistency between what communicators are pretending to do and how they explain their tasks to top management, on the one hand, and the levels of monitoring and measurement of the same activities, on the other, may help explain why 'linking business strategy and communication' remains consistently the most important issue for communication management over many years.[16]

Evaluating the effectiveness of communication activities but not being able to prove the contribution to organisational goals or how communication has

[14] Zerfass et al. (2015), p. 73. n^{min} = 1,496 communication professionals working in communication departments across Europe. Q: Which items are monitored or measured by your organisation to assess the effectiveness of communication management/public relations? Scale 1 (do not use at all) – 5 (use continuously). Zerfass, Tench, Verhoeven, Verčič & Moreno, 2010. n = 1,533. Q: Which items do you monitor or measure to assess the effectiveness of public relations/communication management? Scale 1 (never) – 5 (always). Percentages: frequency based on scale points 4–5. Gaps might partly be attributed to variations in the questionnaire instrument.

[15] Wright et al. (2009); Michaelson and Stacks (2011).

[16] Zerfass et al. (2016), p. 56.

supported this process is problematic. An important attribute of excellence as identified by the European Communication Monitor is the ability to explain the economic value of communication to top executives. Practitioners have often used methods that have largely proven unreliable an invalid such as the Advertising Value Equivalent and the inappropriate use of the term return on investment (ROI) of communication. Since the turn of the century, a new upturn of attention to evaluation in the communication industry focused on this ROI. The concept of ROI has been propagated by a number of evaluation companies for providing the economic value of communication activities. ROI is described as the proportion of financial profit resulting from an activity against its actual costs. Applied to communication activities, the most important aspects of ROI therefore are the financial assessment of the resources used for communication, a standardised financial valuation of the results achieved by communication and the definition of ROI in financial terms, resulting in the expression of ROI of communication in the ratio of financial profit results from a communication activity against its actual cost (Box 23).

Box 23 ROI of communication

The ratio of financial profit achieved by a communication activity against its actual cost

---

The European Communication Monitor researched this topic and found that almost every second practitioner in Europe claims to use ROI when planning or evaluating communication programmes and activities.[17] Nevertheless, what we found is that the vast majority of communication professionals think that ROI can be expressed in the achievement of communication objectives or be used to demonstrate the non-financial value of communication. This approach is obviously wrong. Using the concept of ROI as loosely as many professionals do can damage the credibility and the reputation of the communication field.[18]

Perhaps research can be seen as the main problem area for communication management today, but there is a cause for hope. The analysis of the European Communication Monitor identifies nearly a quarter of communication departments in Europe are excellent at communication and shine for their ability to explain the value of communication. Moreover, these departments are clearly

---

[17] Zerfass et al. (2011), pp. 64–71.
[18] Watson and Zerfass (2011).

superior on the use of all stages of measurement. Differences are more pronounced exactly in the more controversial areas: outcomes and outflows.[19]

For communication to actually contribute to value creation three preconditions have been proposed: (1) structural positioning in the organisation of the communication function, (2) personal competencies being met for communication staff and (3) recognition of the communication function at the executive (board) level.[20]

Using Results of Evaluation Research

You cannot evaluate what you cannot measure and you cannot improve what you cannot evaluate. But when, despite all the barriers and bias, communication departments measure and evaluate, the question is: how do they use it to make improvements? What do communication departments use evaluation for? The European Communication Monitor delved into this question and found that communication departments do not take full advantage of their evaluation activities.[21] There is a low percentage of communication departments using measuring data for leading communication teams or steering agencies and service providers. Slightly more are using these insights for processes to reflect goals and direct communication strategies or planning new activities. The value of data for managing strategic communication seems to be overseen by many professionals today. Moreover, only 59.5 per cent of the communication departments use measurement insights to explain the value of communication to top executives.

Excellent communication departments use measurement insights more frequently for managing all their activities including explaining the value or reflecting goals and strategies (see Fig. 20).

These results point to what Jim Macnamara calls 'a conflation of measurement and evaluation which fails to recognise their disturbingly different processes'.[22] Indeed, measurement can be used to evaluate and identify value of implemented activities of communication, but also must produce insights that can inform the future and connects with the organisational strategies (Box 24).

---

[19] Zerfass et al. (2015), p. 121.
[20] Zerfass and Volk (2018).
[21] Zerfass et al. (2015), pp. 76–77; Zerfass et al. (2017).
[22] Macnamara (2015), p. 379.

Box 24 What we learned about communication measurement from excellent departments

1. Excellent communication departments use more measurement to be better equipped to demonstrate the value of communication.
2. Excellent communication departments implement outcomes as a level of measurement.
3. Excellent communication departments implement outflow as a level of measurement more often.
4. Excellent communication departments use insights from measurement and evaluation for managing all their activities.

Big Data and Automatisation: the Last Straw on Communication Evaluation

The first stages of research and evaluation involve data collection and analysis. These data do not need to be all collected by the organisation itself, but they can also come from other information sources to triangulate and contextualise the results. It is in this context of collecting data that a new and 'big' reality has emerged in the profession in the last few years: the use of big data.[23]

Since the beginning of the twenty-first century and the arrival of the Internet, different forms of data collection have emerged. Moreover with the development of social media there is an abundance of user-generated content from different platforms that has been further enhanced by the mobile revolution, which has made it possible to access information everywhere. Indeed, a single social media post can gather a large volume of real-time feedback and opinions from customers and diverse stakeholders whose opinions and activities the organisation is most interested in. Today big data is at the heart of nearly every digital activity and organisations are trying to find the usefulness of this large volume of data to create and capture value for business and societies.

Datafication or digitalisation and big data analytics are changing our world and our ways of working, in every dimension of life. Digitalisation has changed almost all forms of human labour and particularly those associated with cognitive processes. We are even promoting the 'datafication of people and their relationships' for instance through the datafication of 'like' sentiments of over one billion users of Facebook.[24]

---

[23] Weiner and Kochhar (2016); Zerfass et al. (2016), pp. 16–41.
[24] Mayer-Schönberger and Cukier (2013).

Measurement data and reports are used for...

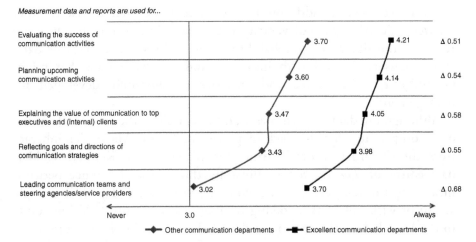

Fig. 20 Use of measurement insights in communication departments[25]

Big data and big data analytics are terms that have been used to describe
the data sets and analytical techniques in applications that are so large (from
terabytes to exabytes) and complex (from sensor to social media data) that
require advanced and unique data storage, management analysis and visua-
lisation technologies.[26]

The description of big data has been popularised through the so-called Vs.
Most authors define big data based on three Vs: volume, velocity and variety
and widely accepted definitions are based on these three characteristics.[27]
Volume points to the amount of data and its granular nature. This nature
can vary from tens of terabytes to hundreds of petabytes for an organisation.
Velocity refers to the speed of data. Information the organisation receives and
needs to act upon in real time defines the velocity characteristic of big data.
Variety refers to the structural heterogeneity in a data set. In this regard, data
can be classified between structured – tabular data found in spreadsheets or
relational databases –, unstructured – that is, text, images, audio and video
which sometimes lack the structural organisation required by machines for
analysis – and semi-structured.

---

[25] Zerfass et al. (2015), p. 123. n = 1,601 communication professionals working in communication
departments across Europe. Q: How are insights from communication measurement used in your
organisation? Scale 1 (never) – 5 (always). Mean values. ** Highly significant differences for all items
(Pearson correlation, $p \leq 0.01$).

[26] Chen et al. (2012).

[27] TechAmerica Foundation's Federal Big Data Commission (2012); Davenport (2014).

More recently, in addition to the three basic characteristics other Vs were added[28]; whereof veracity is the most important one. Veracity refers to the degree of unreliability inherent in some sources of data. It is necessary to deal with imprecise and uncertain data that might be addressed using tools and analytics appropriately developed for management.

Although big data is often messy and incomplete, the sheer scale of the data compensates for this lack of precision. Viktor Mayer-Schönberger from the Oxford Internet Institute and his co-author Kenneth Cukier, data editor of *The Economist*, illustrate this as the difference between measuring the temperature in a vineyard just once a day with a single sensor or with 100 sensors taking readings every minute.[29] Value points to the knowledge inherent in the data and data mining is the automated extraction of patterns from massive information databases and data streams.

Following these characteristics, the European Communication Monitor offered a definition of big data in its questionnaire, including the four Vs (volume, variety, velocity, veracity) and has found little understanding of a comprehensive concept among practitioners.[30] It is not surprising when the discussion about big data – how to acquire and use data from various sources to inform decision-making and deliver better products or services – has only very recently entered the realm of PR and strategic communication. The study reveals that three out of four communication professionals in Europe indeed believe that big data will change their profession. Almost one quarter state that this is one of the most important issues for communication management in the near future. Nevertheless, only 59.3 per cent of the respondents have given close attention or attention to the debate about big data. Big data might change the communication function dramatically as digitisation and big data analytics are clearly impacting the knowledge labour market (Box 25).

How can big data support organisations and more specifically communication functions?[31]

---

[28] Gandomi and Haider (2015).

[29] Mayer-Schönberger, V., and Cukier, K (2013).

[30] Zerfass et al. (2016), pp. 16–33.

[31] Weiner and Kochhar (2016).

Box 25 Big data and the human touch

Organisations must learn and recognise that data alone does not answer 'why' or explain inferred insights. Uncovering insights of big data require a human element and critical thinking to create meaning.

Organisations have access to a diverse range of data, which provide different levels or grades of control and includes: internal, shared and external data streams. All of these sources produce a great amount of data in diverse areas and functions that provide opportunities for data collection and analysis. Shared data streams are produced by third parties like retailers and are accessible to other organisations. External data is harvested from outside sources like social media conversations, news, omnibus surveys, and academic studies, as well as public sector and demographic data.

Big data has come into action in business because of the need to create real-time intelligence from the high volume of available data that continues to increase every minute given the exponential use of mobile devices all over the world. But big data is about the 'what', not the 'why'.[32] Obviously the importance of big data is the value that can be created to improve an organisation's performance. The availability of large volumes of data improves decision-making processes by basing decisions on data that is collected at an unparalleled rate and can therefore increment the variables that are considered for making predictions. By using big data organisations try to improve strategies and tactics with the explicit aim of helping to achieve their objectives.

More than ever communication functions have access to an amazing quantity of information from stakeholders that are willing to express themselves. They also produce and have access to a great range of data from social media, news releases, etc., but much of the data generated for them comes through research based on the measurement of output, outcome or outflow. This means that big data today has helped with the previously discussed 'problem child' for communication of measurement, but it has still not managed to fill in the cracks. Why? Because the data provided ends up strengthening the same areas of output and outcomes where evaluation practices in strategic communication have already been applied. On the other hand some believe that big data might allow practitioners to improve their traditional functions but also

---

[32] Mayer-Schönberger and Cukier (2013).

to improve the whole process of strategic planning and also the opportunities for measurement and evaluation in order to demonstrate the contribution of communication to the business bottom line. In fact, one of the key benefits of analysing with big data is prediction in the form of probabilities.

Big data is here to stay and its application cannot be slowed down let alone reversed. 'The more an institution or industry relies on information as its core product, the greater and more complete the change will be'.[33]

Connecting with the beginning of this section focused on the departmental level of communication, we stated that the value of the company today was more and more based on intangibles. What does datafication mean in this context? Facebook's flotation valuation was US$104 billion in 2011, yet in pure financial/accounting terms, the company was worth just US$6.3 billion. This massive discrepancy is due to the perceived value of its information. Facebook has over 2.1 trillion pieces of 'monetisable' content. The flotation price valued every customer to have a book value of $100.[34] Recent research states that merely using Facebook 'likes' allows us to model and predict a number of personal attributes including sexual orientation, ethnicity, religious and political views, personality traits, intelligence, happiness, use of addictive substances, parental separation, age and gender.[35]

With this transformational context in mind it is clear the excellent communication departments are in a better position than ever. They produce and manage a huge volume of data on the relationship with stakeholders of organisations. Therefore, datafication can position them in a level of value and influence that has so far never been seen before. But what is the actual implementation and use of big data in communication departments?

Based on the European Communication Monitor 2016 survey only 21.2 per cent of communication departments and agencies had implemented big data activities until then. Another 16.8 per cent were planning to do so before the end of that year. Not surprisingly, joint stock companies and agencies are leading the movement, while governmental organisations and non-profits are significantly lagging behind.[36]

About half the organisations who have implemented big data activities in communication use analytics for planning purposes, for example, to inform

---

[33] Shirky (2008).

[34] Mayer-Schönberger, V., and Cukier, K (2013).

[35] Tufekci (2014).

[36] Zerfass et al. (2016), pp. 24–25; for a more detailed discussion see Wiesenberg, Zerfass and Moreno (2017).

future campaigns; fewer rely on big data for communication measurement or for guiding day-to-day actions, for example, by automatically generating content for specific publics.[37]

Actually big data has opened a door to real-time content texting and automatisation based on algorithms. Search engines like Google and e-commerce platforms such as Amazon display advertisements and products based on previous search behaviour. Facebook uses auto-moderation functions to identify inappropriate postings on brand pages, which has a direct impact on the public discourse in crisis situations (Box 26).[38]

> **Box 26 Algorithms**
>
> Algorithms are 'an exact prescription, defining a computational process, leading from various initial data to the desired result'.[39]

Modern algorithms are dynamic in a sense that they are able to adapt to multiple situations. As such, the outcome of an automated communication process, for example, the content presented to a user in a specific situation on a particular device, is not known in advance, but generated in the course of the interaction.

However, empirical insights from our survey across Europe show a large gap between the perceived importance and today's implementation of algorithms in strategic communication.[40] Moreover, a passive and supportive use of algorithms is preferred. Three out of four respondents agree that communication activities should be adapted to the external algorithms of search engines or social media platforms. But only 29.2 per cent state that their communication department or agency uses such approaches. Both figures are surprisingly low as search engine optimisation (SEO) and content production aligned to the selection criteria of multipliers are nothing new at all. Two-thirds of the communication professionals believe that algorithms are important to support decision-making or content distribution. Again, the implementation rates are much lower. Interestingly, only a minority thinks that active applications of algorithms are important, for example, for automatically adapting content or creating content.

---

[37] Zerfass et al. (2016), pp. 37.
[38] Collister (2015).
[39] Markov (1954), p. 1.
[40] Zerfass et al. (2016), pp. 34–41.

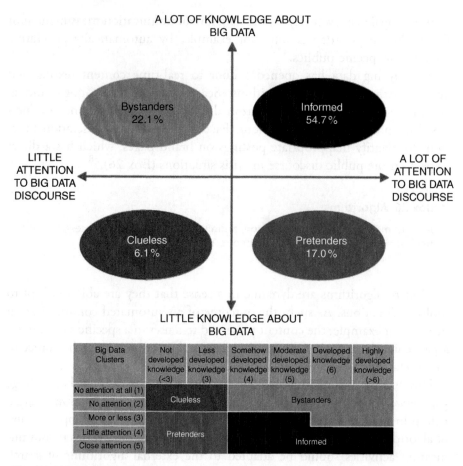

Fig. 21 How different types of communication professionals deal with the big data challenge[41]

A correlation analysis proves that organisations who have implemented big data analytics to guide day-to-day actions use algorithms of all kind more often than other organisations. Both trends – big data and algorithms – are clearly intertwined. The rising importance claimed for both might lead to a situation where we see increasing auto-communication. This might look

---

[41] Zerfass et al. (2016), p. 30. n = 2,710 communication professionals across Europe. Cluster analysis based on two questions (attention given to the debate on big data, ranging from no attention at all to close attention/knowledge about big data definitions) identified four different groups of respondents.

promising at first glance as it helps to be faster and more efficient, despite challenges for the profession.

So, we must ask ourselves what are the reasons for the limited penetration of big data and its derivative uses in the field of strategic communication? On the one hand, the communication profession lacks analytical skills to make sense of big data and time to study such data. These limitations were confirmed by nearly half of the respondents. Moreover, statistical analyses confirmed that there is a highly significant correlation between the knowledge and awareness of big data among communication professionals and big data activities of their organisations. However, a cluster analysis of respondents shows that 54.7 per cent of the practitioners can be classified as informed, meaning they give attention to big data discourse and have a lot of knowledge in the field. Ironically, an alarming lack of skills and knowledge hinders public relations and communication professionals – who tend to define themselves as information experts – from profiting from the massive amount of structured and unstructured data available for public communication today (Fig. 21).[42]

Excellent communication departments are pioneers in big data. They are more engaged in these new challenges for the profession and most of them are both attentive and knowledgeable about the topic. Moreover, big data analytics are used more intensively in excellent departments to plan overall strategies, justify activities and guide day-to-day action (Box 27).[43]

Box 27 What we have learned about big data from excellent communication departments

1. Excellent communication departments are more attentive and knowledgeable to big data.
2. Excellent communication departments are more sophisticated and effective in implementing big data analytics.

Cri du coeur or Crocodile Tears?

Measurement and evaluation enable communication practitioners to demonstrate the value of their activities to their organisation, connecting with organisational objectives. If the main challenge of the profession is the

---

[42] Zerfass et al. (2016), pp. 16–33.
[43] Zerfass et al. (2016), pp. 117–119.

linkage of communication with corporate objectives and strategies, evaluation is revealed as the missing link.

And there is a paradox. If evaluation has always been central to strategic planning models of public relations, why then today when communication departments have access to high volumes of data is evaluation not more solidly implemented? What is the missing link and why does theory not match with practice?

We can summarise the main reasons or barriers to the implementation of more effective measurement and evaluation in communication management as:

(1) Limited resources. Industry has traditionally blamed the lack of resources: budget, time, standards, etc. Although some voices argue that big data reduces costs for collecting information and evaluation activities, others found the same barriers or that they were even higher than before.

(2) Low credibility. Communication departments have lost credibility by presenting measures that were perceived more as a post-hoc self-justification of their work. Today it is still the case that a lot of CEOs and senior executives see evaluative communication practices as self-justification and post-rationalisation of their activities.

(3) Misunderstanding of concepts, methods, instruments and stages of measurement and confusion between measurement, evaluation and insights. Usually organisational priorities are used to contextualise measurements in terms of the overall needs of the communicator, setting objectives that are achievable and measurable; assessing the activities and processes involved in the campaign, the outputs produced and the outcomes.

(4) Reductionism in research methodologies. Some scholars also point to the reductionism of scientific quantitative research that reduces the world to a collection of certain types of observable and measurable data and the questioning of these approaches to studying human communication. In this perspective, qualitative research also has to be included as well as diverse techniques from critical analysis, market analysis, etc.

(5) Reductionism in communication models. Communication evaluation is frequently based on communication perspectives of control and outdated views of one-way communication processes led by organisations. These perspectives of communication are in crisis today and many academics and practitioners think that strategic communication is changing its purpose from influencing stakeholders into conversations with stakeholders. Big data is in a lot of respects the ideal of the early communication models of effects: today individuals are generating

their own data voluntarily as well as widely on diverse topics,[44] but this conception contrasts with more dialogic and symmetric perspectives of communication. The Theory of Public Relations by James Grunig and colleagues, for instance, pointed to a more complex explanation of the value of public relations. For an organisation to be effective, it needs to not only produce a ROI or cognitive effect for the audiences of messages regarding corporate intangibles such as reputation, brand, image or identity, but it must also behave in ways that solves the problems and satisfies the goals of stakeholders as well as management.[45]

(6) Reductionism in management models based on rationality and predictability. In spite of capabilities in forecasting, prediction and environmental monitoring which are regarded as best practices, there is increasing talk about the collapse of the planning dream. Today organisations face a more and more unforeseeable, complex environment and cannot predict or manage the future.[46]

(7) Lack of competence and expertise in measurement and evaluation in today's communication departments. This is a major challenge. Big data has not come to solve the problem, but instead can be seen perhaps to upgrade it. In general terms, a deep knowledge is needed to manage the three perspectives of business decision-making: descriptive, predictive and prescriptive analytics in order to actually achieve organisational goals.[47] A lack of skills, knowledge and expertise of communication professional in understanding and managing information is a critical failing for the future of the industry. Competency frameworks have changed. The written word has been overtaken by a need to manage and understand complex information in the form of big data. Therefore, this requires communicators who not only have command of the written word but also the numerical skills to manage and interpret big data. This has implications for training, education and future professional development of the communications practitioner as we will see in the next section of this book focused on the level of individual practitioners.

If evaluation has largely been the missing link between communication and organisational goals and strategies, it seems that the introduction of big data

---

[44] Tufekci (2014).

[45] Grunig (2006).

[46] Taleb (2010).

[47] Chen et al. (2012).

and automatisation are the tipping point. Despite all the barriers and the incremental growth of obstacles and challenges, it is clear that to be influential, communication departments need to demonstrate their contribution to the organisation, be able to demonstrate value by measuring what they do and be able to establish clear links between communication activities and organisational goals through value links. Also measurement has to be turned into evaluation and to insights not only to self-reflection of communication programmes, but to inform future business strategy.

References

AMEC. (2016). *Integrated Evaluation Framework*. Retrieved from http://www.ame corg.com/amecframework/

Chen, H., Chiang, R. H., & Storey, V. C. (2012). Business intelligence and analytics: From big data to big impact. *MIS Quarterly, 36*(4), 1165–1188.

Collister, S. (2015). Algorithmic public relations: Materiality, technology and power in a post-hegemonic world. In J. L'Etang, D. McKie, N. Snow, & J. Xifra (Eds.), *The Routledge Handbook of Critical Public Relations* (pp. 360-371). New York, NY: Routledge.

Cutlip, S. M., & Center, A. H. (1952). *Effective Public Relations*. Englewood Cliffs, NJ: Prentice Hall.

Cutlip, S. M., Center, A. H., & Broom, G. M. (2000). *Effective Public Relations* (8th ed.). Upper Saddle River, NJ: Prentice Hall.

Daniels, M.(2012). *ROI in PR Measurement: Developing a Practical Strategy. Presentation at the First Asia PR Pacific Summit on Measurement*. Hong Kong, March 2012. Retrieved from http://amecorg.com/images/public/downloads/apac/Workshop_B.pdf

Davenport, T. (2014). *Big Data at Work: Dispelling the Myths, Uncovering the Opportunities*. Cambridge, MA: Harvard Business School Press.

Digital Analytics Association (2013). *Social Media Standards Definitions: Reach and Impressions*. Retrieved from http://www.smmstandards.com/wp-content/uploads/2013/03/SMM-Standard-Definitions_DAA_v4.pdf

DPRG, & ICV (2011). *Position Paper Communication Controlling – How to Maximize and Demonstrate the Value Creation through Communication*. Berlin and Gauting, Germany: DPRG, ICV.

Gandomi, A., & Haider, M. (2015). Beyond the hype: Big data concepts, methods, and analytics. *International Journal of Information Management, 35*(2), 137–144

Grunig, J. E. (2006). Furnishing the edifice: Ongoing research on public relations as a strategic management function. *Journal of Public Relations Research, 18*(2), 151–176

Grunig, J. E., & Hunt, T. (1984). *Managing Public Relations*. New York, NY: Holt, Rinehart and Winston.

Kendall, R. (1996). *Public Relations Campaign Strategies Planning for Implementation: Longman*. New York, NY: HarperCollins.

Long, L. W., & Hazelton, V. (1987). Public relations: A theoretical and practical response. *Public Relations Review, 13*(2), 3–13.

Macnamara, J. (1992). Evaluation: The Achilles heel of the public relations profession. *International Public Relations Review, 15*(4), 17–31.

Macnamara, J. (1999). Research in public relations: A review of the use of evaluation and formative research. *Asia Pacific Public Relations Journal, 1*(2), 107–134.

Macnamara, J. (2002). Research and evaluation. In C. Tymson & P. Lazar (Eds.), *The New Australian and New Zealand Public Relations Manual* (pp. 100–134). Sydney: Tymson Communications.

Macnamara, J. (2012). *Public Relations: Theories, Practices, Critiques*. Sydney: Pearson.

Macnamara, J. (2014). *The Development of International Standards for Measurement and Evaluation of Public Relations and Corporate Communication: A Review*. Report for the Australian Centre for Public Communication. Sydney: University of Technology Sydney.

Macnamara, J. (2015). Breaking the measurement and evaluation deadlock: A new approach and model. *Journal of Communication Management, 19*(4), 371–387.

Markov, A. A. Translated by Jacques J. Schorr-Kon and PST staff (1954). *Theory of Algorithms*. Moscow: Academy of Sciences of the USSR.

Marston, J. E. (1963). *The Nature of Public Relations*. New York, NY: McGraw-Hill.

Mayer-Schönberger, V., & Cukier, K (2013). *Big Data: A Revolution That Will Transform How We Live, Work and Think*. Boston, MA: Houghton Mifflin Harcourt.

Michaelson, D., & Stacks, D. (2011). Standardization in public relations measurement and evaluation. *Public Relations Journal, 5*(2), 1–22.

Rossi, P. H., & Freeman, H. E. (1993). Program monitoring for evaluation and management. In P. H. Rossi & H. E. Freeman (Eds.), *Evaluation: A Systematic Approach* (pp. 163–213). Newbury Park, CA: Sage.

Shirky, C. (2008). *Here Comes Everybody: The Power of Organizing Without Organizations*. New York, NY: The Penguin Press.

Taleb, H. M. (2010). Gender and leadership styles in single-sex academic institutions. *International Journal of Educational Management, 24*(4), 287–302.

TechAmerica Foundation's Federal Big Data Commission. (2012). *Demystifying Big Data: A Practical Guide to Transforming the Business of Government*. Retrieved from http://www.techamerica.org/Docs/fileManager.cfm?f=techamerica-bigdatareport-final.pdf

Tufekci, Z. (2014). Engineering the public: Big data, surveillance and computational politics. *First Monday, 19*(7), 1–16.

Volk, S. C. (2016). A systematic review of 40 years of public relations evaluation and measurement research: Looking into the past, the present, and the future. *Public Relations Review*. Doi: 10.1016/j.pubrev.2016.07.003.

Watson, T., & Noble, P. (2014). *Evaluating Public Relations: A Best Practice Guide to Public Relations Planning, Research and Evaluation* (3rd ed.). London: Kogan Page.

Watson, T., & Zerfass, A. (2011). Return on investment in public relations. A critique of concepts used by practitioners from communication and management sciences perspectives. *PRism*, *8*(1), 1–14.

Weiner, M., & Kochhar, S. (2016). *Irreversible: The Public Relations Big Data Revolution*[IPR Whitepaper]. Gainesville, FL: Institute for Public Relations.

Wiesenberg, M., Zerfass, A., & Moreno, A. (2017). Big Data and Automation in Strategic Communication. *International Journal of Strategic Communication, 11*(2).

Wright, D., Gaunt, R., Leggetter, B., Daniels, M., & Zerfass, A. (2009). *Global Survey of Communications Measurement 2009 – Final Report*. London: AMEC.

Zerfass, A. (2010). Assuring rationality and transparency in corporate communications. Theoretical foundations and empirical findings on communication controlling and communication performance management. In M. D. Dodd & K. Yamamura (Eds.), *Ethical Issues for Public Relations Practice in a Multicultural World, 13th International Public Relations Research Conference* (pp. 947–966). Gainesville, FL: Institute for Public Relations.

Zerfass, A. (2015). Kommunikations-Controlling: Steuerung und Wertschöpfung. In R. Fröhlich, P. Szyszka, & G. Bentele (Eds.), *Handbuch der Public Relations* (3rd ed., pp. 715–738). Wiesbaden: Springer VS.

Zerfass, A., Tench, R., Verhoeven, P., Verčič, D., & Moreno, A. (2010). *European Communication Monitor 2010. Status Quo and Challenges for Public Relations in Europe*. Results of an Empirical Survey in 46 Countries. Brussels: EACD, EUPRERA.

Zerfass, A., Verčič, D., Verhoeven, P., Moreno, A., & Tench, R. (2012). *European Communication Monitor 2012: Challenges and Competencies for Strategic Communication*. Brussels: EACD/EUPRERA, Helios Media.

Zerfass, A., Verčič, D., Verhoeven, P., Moreno, A., & Tench, R. (2015). *European Communication Monitor 2015. Creating Communication Value Through Listening, Messaging and Measurement. Results of a Survey in 41 Countries*. Brussels: EACD/ EUPRERA, Helios Media.

Zerfass, A., Verčič, D., & Volk, S. C. (2017). Communication Evaluation and Measurement: Skills, Practices and Utilization in European Organizations. *Corporate Communications – An International Journal, 22*(1), 2–18.

Zerfass, A., Verhoeven, P., Moreno, A., Tench, R., & Verčič, D. (2016). *European Communication Monitor 2016. Exploring Trends in Big Data, Stakeholder Engagement and Strategic Communication. Results Of A Survey In 43 Countries*. Brussels: EACD/EUPRERA, Quadriga Media Berlin.

Zerfass, A., Verhoeven, P., Tench, R., Moreno, A., & Verčič, D. (2011). *European Communication Monitor 2011. Empirical Insights into Strategic Communication in Europe. Results of an Empirical Survey in 43 Countries*. Brussels: EACD/EUPRERA.

Zerfass, A., & Volk, S. (2018). Aligning and linking communication with organizational goals. Manuscript to be published. In M. J. Canel & V. Luoma-Aho (Eds.), *Handbook of Public Sector Communication*. Chichester, UK: Wiley Blackwell.

Commandment 6

Strategised: Informed, Anticipatory and Trusted

You hear the language of strategy in all walks of modern life: in sport, politics, travel, dieting, personal finance, economics and, of course, business. Everybody it seems wants to be strategic today. And, especially, inside contemporary organisations. Business, government, non-profit and non-governmental organisations alike, they all have strategies and nothing moves and no plans are made without one. We have strategies for the long term, for the short term and for every aspect of the organisation ranging from customer services, human resources and, of course, communication. In public relations and communication strategy has become the watchword as well. Strategic communication is even proposed as the overarching term and concept for all communication activities of an organisation, including all subfields.[1]

But what does being strategic really mean? Does the word still have resonance now that everybody is using it? Or is it just another buzzword that you need to trot out in order to be in tune with the rest of the organisation? We argue both Yes and No. 'Being strategic' is frequently used in organisations whether appropriately or not. But it is undoubtedly an essential ingredient for success; for successful organisations and for successful communication activities from press relations, internal communication to campaigning. But what precisely is strategy and what does the concept mean for communication professionals? Does it help or hinder them? Or is it better to abandon the term altogether?

---

[1] Mahoney (2011).

© The Author(s) 2017
R. Tench et al., *Communication Excellence*,
DOI 10.1007/978-3-319-48860-8_6

One of the biggest issues in the field of communication is the ability of communication departments to be involved in the strategic decision-making of the organisation. If they are involved then evidence suggests communication can help the organisation more effectively. But key to getting this engagement is understanding how communication professionals can be best prepared to enable them to take part in the decision-making at the top of the organisation. It is essential to understand what they need in order to do that. First and foremost they have to work strategically themselves. The communication policies and plans need to be strategic and not merely instrumental. Secondly they have to be aligned to the overall strategies of the organisation. It is, after all, linking communication strategies with corporate strategies that are still the most pressing issue for communication management and the most important challenge for the profession in Europe.[2] *Being strategic* is the sixth commandment of this book. Excellent communication departments are strategic communication departments.

Communication as Strategised Work

'Be more strategic!' Good advice, but is it easy to deliver? As we have suggested, strategy is an overused phrase that we all hear in business and in life all the time, but do we really know what it means? Communication practitioners often refer to the term 'strategic communication' but do they really know what it means and do they deliver on the reality of the expectation? Within the field of practice the discipline endeavours to line up with other management specialisms by adhering to the strategy mantra and we expect the communication profession to develop communication policies and plans that are strategic.

The term strategic actually comes from the military: it means to choose a strategic plan to fight the enemy. Many of us can identify with this analogy from our experiences playing the old board games of *Stratego* and *Risk* or in the more contemporary context through the plethora of computer war games and simulations. To put it in simple abstract terms, strategy is the choice a person or organisation makes for navigating a map to reach an endpoint from a given starting point.[3] How to get from point A to B is the basic strategic question. But even then, what makes a plan really strategic? The German

---

[2] Steyn (2007); Verčič et al. (2014).
[3] Kuypers (1973).

philosopher Jürgen Habermas can help and in his theory of communicative action he distinguishes several models for human conduct or action. He distinguishes instrumental action and strategic action. A lot of actions in organisations (or in life in general) are instrumental: we do what we do in our usual settings, without thinking too much about it. Instrumental action becomes strategic when the action of another actor, the opponent, is acknowledged in our plan of action. Strategic action anticipates the reactions of others that oppose you when you do something or are planning to do something. To cite Habermas, strategic is 'when there can enter into the agent's calculation of success the anticipation of decisions of at least one goal-directed actor'.[4] The idea of strategy has also been elaborated upon in decision-making and game theory in economics, in the social sciences and especially in social psychology.

Mainly in the world of the economy and the state this strategic action is very well developed. Habermas calls this the system world.[5] Here acting in a reflex (instrumental) way has been replaced by reflective action[6]: thinking and planning before you act (strategic). This system world has developed its own logic and communicates with so-called generalised media: money in the economy and a monopoly on violence for the state.[7] Obviously many communication practitioners are part of this system world and are asked to develop strategies in the context of the economy or the state. Following this line of thinking strategic communication means communication that anticipates the reactions of other actors to the plans the organisation has made.

The system world, with its instrumental and strategic action, constantly runs into problems with what Habermas calls the 'lifeworld', our daily life where we interact with other people. In the 'lifeworld' other models of action are normal, normative action (action in accordance with norms of the group we are part of), dramaturgical action (action where we present our personality to the outside world) and communicative action (action directed at reaching understanding with other people). It is here that the main and constant conflict that communication professionals are asked to solve strategically is when our own strategic logic contrasts with the lifeworld of the people the system is dealing with.[8]

---

[4] Habermas (1981), p. 85.
[5] Habermas (1981).
[6] Holmström et al. (2009).
[7] Habermas (1981).
[8] Habermas (1981).

To summarise strategic means in the most basic sense of the word to take the counter moves of others into account in organisational and communication policies and plans. There is a lot of literature and studies on the possibilities of adapting strategic planning models to communication management in order to evolve the profession from a tactical (or instrumental) level to a strategic level.[9] Taking on a managerial (strategic) role instead of a technician (instrumental) role has been an important issue for the field.[10]

From Instrumental to Strategic Communication

But how does this aspiration of wanting to be strategic meet with reality? We know from the European Communication Monitor that the picture is an improving one. Today, communication professionals across Europe say their activities are strategised. Almost 85 per cent of the European organisations surveyed have implemented an overall communication strategy or strategies.[11] This means that they have a strategic plan for defining communication goals, stakeholders, key instruments and media for the organisation as a whole or for specific products or services, or specific issues or persons such as the CEO and other executives (Fig. 22).

There are clear differences between countries though, with Portugal taking the lead in having overall communication strategies for organisations and Croatia the lowest levels of communication strategy implementation. Northern European countries show a more homogeneous picture with oscillations between the 80 and 90 per cent having an overall strategy. Surprisingly, some Central European countries such as Germany are below the average (see Fig. 22 for an overview).

Another part of strategic communication is messaging strategies. Message strategies are fundamental for defining topics and storyline for target audiences and for reaching stakeholders. More than three-quarters of the European organisations have those kinds of strategies, which also include processes to integrate content and design.

The question regarding the overall communication strategies is: What happens in organisations that do not implement an overall strategy? Are

---

[9] Gregory (2010); Grunig and Hunt (1984); Van Ruler and Verčič (2005); Vos (1996).
[10] Grunig et al. (2002).
[11] Zerfass et al. (2015), pp. 52–56.

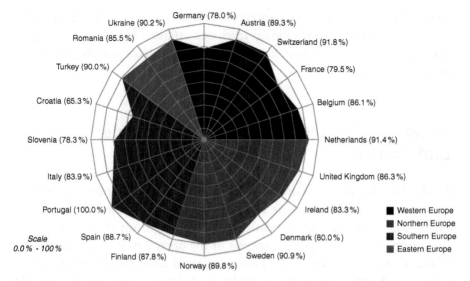

Fig. 22 Country by country implementation of overall communication strategies[12]

they only doing operational and instrumental work and focused only on the short term? Despite the positive responses in parts, the evidence suggests there is still clear room for improvement in being more strategised and consequently moving towards the exemplified departments reflecting *excellence* in the organisational, departmental and personal qualities. Excellent communication departments implement all kinds of formal strategies and they have an overall strategy for communication (see Box 28).

Box 28 What we have learned from excellent communication departments about strategies

Excellent communication functions are strategised:

- They implement all kind of formal strategies.
- They implement overall communication strategies.

---

[12] Zerfass et al. (2015), p. 56. n = 1,330 communication professionals from 20 European countries working in communication departments. Q: Does your organisation have one or more of the following strategies? Item: overall communication strategy or strategies (defining communication goals, stakeholders, key instruments, etc. for the organisation or for specific products/services, persons; etc.). Percentages: based on agreement.

In the literature there is evidence of the communication profession developing from a tactical or operational level to a strategic level. This managerial function of communication has been conceptualised through professional roles[13] and tasks.[14]

What Are Strategic Communication Roles and Tasks?

In the last decade the European Communication Monitor has used the conceptualisations of strategic roles that have been developed for strategic communication and public relations.[15] They focus on the orientation of practitioners to the corporate strategy of the organisation and describe four kinds of strategic roles. These four roles are distributed along two axes: a vertical one referring to the capacity to help business strategy and the horizontal one referring to the capacity to support business goals with managing communication. This schema leads to four types of communication roles (see Fig. 23). First there is the so-called *strategic facilitator*. That is the role that most helps to define strategies and also supports goals. The second most important role for strategic use of communication is the *business adviser*'s role. This role also significantly helps to define strategies but it does not support the business goals with managing communication. The third role is that of the *operational supporter*. In this role the professional strongly contributes to supporting the organisational goals through communication but doesn't intervene in the defining of business strategies. The fourth and last role is the *isolated expert* role that does not contribute to either defining business strategy or to supporting the realisation of business goals by managing communication.[16]

Professionals playing the strategic facilitator role have more influence with the top management of organisations than professionals in the other roles. This influence has two dimensions. The first one is advisory

---

[13] Grunig and Hunt (1984); Van Ruler et al. (2000); Verčič, Van Ruler, Bütschi and Flodin (2002); Tench and Moreno (2015); Dozier and Broom (2006); Van Ruler and Verčič (2004; 2005).

[14] BVC (Dutch Professional Association for Communication) 2002; Logeion (2012).

[15] Lurati and Eppler (2006); Zerfass (2008).

[16] Zerfass et al. (2009), pp. 10, 28–33.

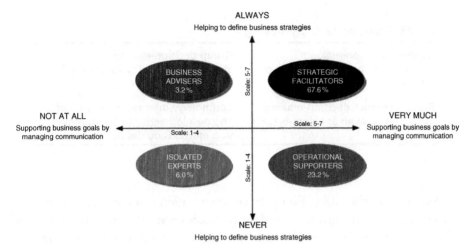

Fig. 23 Strategic roles of communication professionals[17]

influence, being the perception of how seriously senior managers take the recommendations of communication professionals. The second one is executive influence; that is, the perception of how likely it is that the communication representatives will be invited to senior-level meetings dealing with organisational strategic planning. Strategic facilitators are more successful in influencing the management of the organisation.

We also looked at the style of decision-making of these strategic facilitators. Kelly Werder and Derina Holtzhausen developed a classification of styles of decision-making.[18] They proposed four styles of decision-making for public relations practitioners: (1) rational decision-making, when decisions are based on evaluation and all possible information; (2) group-decision-making, when shared responsibility for group decisions is preferred; (3) risk-acceptance decision-making, when risk is taken as an opportunity; and (4) technology-oriented decision-making, when the development of new communication methods guides decisions (see Box 29). No relation was found between the strategic facilitator role enacted by practitioners and a specific style of decision-making. We can therefore conclude that decision-making style does not have an influence on the impact communication professionals have on the management of the organisation.

---

[17] Zerfass et al. (2011), p. 41. n = 2,209 communication professionals across Europe. Q: In your daily work, how much do you focus on supporting business goals by planning and executing communication? (1 = not at all; 7 = very much) / ... do you feel responsible for helping to define business strategies? (1 = never; 7 = always).

[18] Werder and Holtzhausen (2009).

Box 29 Types of decision-making

Rational decision-making Decisions are based on evaluation and all possible information	**Group decision-making** Shared responsibility for group decisions is preferred
Risk-acceptance decision-making When risk is taken as an opportunity	**Technology-oriented decision-making** The development of new communication methods guides decisions

---

Independent of their roles, European communication managers are not attracted to risk-taking in organisations and every professional role tends to use rational decision-making. They are also more inclined towards group decision-making.

The Three Specific Tasks of Communication

The communication function of an organisation embraces a set of specific messaging and listening tasks, which are necessary to reach overall goals. The function can be regarded as institutionalised,[19] meaning that the function is more or less embedded in the organisation. Almost all organisations today have some kind of communication structures installed, whether this is a single person responsible for communication or one or more departments for specific communication tasks. Communication departments and professionals are often responsible for strategies, governance and routine activities, while other members of the organisation communicate in the light of their specific roles.

Communication differs from other functions (e.g. finance, human resources, and logistics) because it includes three aspects. Communication is a *performance function* where activities are realised, for example, by writing articles, press releases or Facebook posts, organising events or listening to stakeholders. Communication is a *management function* when such activities are disposed and aligned, for example, by positioning a company or brand, planning campaigns and leading specialised communication teams. Last but not least, communication is also a *second-order management function* as described by Howard Nothhaft,[20] which influences the management

---

[19] Tench et al. (2009).
[20] Nothhaft (2010).

behaviour of top executives and their peers by confronting them with public opinion, critical issues and alternative views about the organisation.

This variety of tasks is a challenge for communication professionals and their role as 'sensemakers' and 'sensenegotiators' for organisations.[21] Adding to the traditional distinction of operational communication and managing communication, Betteke van Ruler and Dejan Verčič suggested that professionals could bring in reflective capacities to align organisations and their stakeholders.[22] They can also advise and enable top executives and other members of the organisation in the field of media and communication. Coaching, training and consulting are relevant because employees act more and more often as 'active agents in the communication area of a company'.[23] Reflective communication management is the realisation of strategic communication.

Empirical data from the European Communication Monitor show that all of these role requirements from reflective communication management are relevant in practice.[24] In a typical week, communicators spend more than one-third of their productive time at work for operational communication (e.g. talking to colleagues and media, writing texts, monitoring and organising events). Managing activities related to planning, organising, leading staff, evaluating strategies, justifying spending and preparing for crises takes also about one-third of their time. Almost 20 per cent of the time is used for reflective communication management like aligning communication between the organisation and its stakeholders. Coaching, training and enabling members of the organisation or (internal) clients take almost 20 per cent as well. The latter area has risen slightly over the years, which has suggested that coaching has become more important.

European communicators employ different practices of coaching, advising or enabling when they support either senior managers or other staff. The most important activity when working with executives is delivering insights for decision-making (agreed by more than two-thirds of the respondents), followed by advice on how to handle concrete challenges in communication (also two-thirds of the respondents). Less than half of the communicators state that they enable their executives to master communicative challenges on their own. Co-workers and other staff most often receive hands-on advice about communication tasks.

---

[21] Berger and Meng (2014).
[22] Van Ruler and Verčič (2005).
[23] Mazzei (2014).
[24] Zerfass et al. (2016), pp. 42–53.

Not surprisingly, the needs of executives and traditional ways of support are shaping the majority of activities in the field. However, enabling others to reflect and communicate themselves has clearly become an important part of the practice today. It reflects the growing need to deal with multiple voices in strategic communication.[25]

There is a relationship between the tasks employed by communicators and their hierarchical position and the job description they have. Media relations professionals, for example, spend logically nearly half of their time on operational work. Looking at the different types of department we can see that excellent departments are better aligned with the top management. Professionals working there spend less time on operational work. They put more effort in coaching and consulting other members of the organisation with a highly significant focus on advising and enabling top executives to communicate. So the picture is far clearer – the top-performing departments really are more strategic. Excellent communication functions spend less time on operational work, more time on coaching and consulting other members of the organisation and they focus on advising and enabling top executives (see Box 30).

Box 30 What we have learned about the strategic impact of communication practitioners from excellent communication departments

Practitioners in excellent communication departments dedicate more time to strategic work:

- They spend less time on operational work.
- They spend more time on coaching and consulting other members of the organisation.
- They focus on advising and enabling top executives.

Linking Communication and Business Strategy: Biggest Issue for the Field

During the ten years of analysis of the profession the European Communication Monitor has asked professionals every year about the main strategic challenges for communication management. Consistently the results show that the challenge of linking communication to corporate

---

[25] Zerfass and Viertmann (2017).

Strategic issues perceived as most important

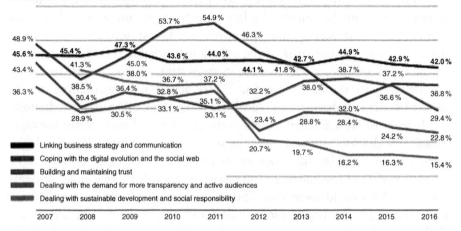

Fig. 24 Development of strategic issues for communication management over the last decade[26]

or business strategies is the most important issue for the field (see Fig. 24). This should be the top priority for the ongoing development of strategic communication and public relations as a professional field. This issue shows that despite growing influence the profession is still fighting to get a place at the decision-making table which is a key determinant to enabling communication to be an active player in the strategic management of the organisation.[27]

Other issues that have also been important during the last decade are the changes that the new media landscape has brought to the professional field. Coping with this media evolution that included the expanding influence of the social web and dealing with the demand for active audiences were issues that peaked at the beginning of the 2010s. Nevertheless, in the years after those practitioners seem to have found an equilibrium and ways to deal with these issues. Firstly because they have acquired competences in the use of new media and because the expectations of these new media have probably reached their upper limits. In other words new media is no longer the new kid in town.

---

[26] Zerfass et al. (2016), p. 56. Longitudinal evaluation 2007–2016 based on 21,273 responses from communication professionals in 43 countries. Q: Please pick those three (3) issues which you believe will be most important for public relations/communication management within the next three years! Percentages: frequency based on selection as top 3 issue.

[27] Cornelissen et al. (2013); Verčič and Grunig (2002).

Analysis over the years shows two gaps regarding perceptions of the importance of media. Firstly the latest media to be incorporated into the media mix set is seen as the one with the fastest forecast expectations. Secondly, over the ten years of the survey it is notable that the significance of all types of new media has been overestimated for future use when compared with traditional media.[28] The actual implementation of new media has actually been much slower than practitioners' earlier predictions.

However we see a different pattern in the experience of another past hot topic. Sustainable development and corporate social responsibility (CSR) was a highly rated issue in 2008, but has progressively lost importance, especially after 2012, when the effect of the financial crisis began to seriously impact some European countries. That could mean that CSR communication is more routinised and institutionalised for organisations today and not a black box anymore.[29] Building and maintaining trust is an issue that can be related to both the media revolution and the crisis for institutions and business as a whole. Nevertheless, it represents instability in how it is perceived with diverse fluctuations over the years, but still taking a top position in the annual rankings.

There are also very interesting differences between countries: 'Linking business strategy and communication' is the hottest issue in Spain, Finland and Ukraine. 'Coping with the digital evolution and the social web' is the top issue in Ireland, Belgium, Romania, Turkey and Croatia; 'Building and maintaining trust' is the top issue in Slovenia and Sweden; while in France the top issue is 'Matching the needs to address more audiences and channels with limited resources'.

It is explicit that the link between communicative and organisational strategies has been the frontrunner and ongoing issue over the years of the empirical study. This linkage between strategies is one of the most important requirements to achieve influence for communication departments, yet at the same time a clear weak spot and Achilles heel for the profession.

Interestingly the European Communication Monitor demonstrates that excellent communication departments stand out because they reflect quite distinct responses to some of these key questions. Strikingly the excellent departments clearly buck the earlier trends and are more concerned about sustainable development and CSR but they are not so worried about the link between communication and corporate strategies. This is probably because they have already found answers to handle these important issues and are comfortable with their response (Box 31).

---

[28] Moreno et al. (2015).
[29] Tench et al. (2014).

> **Box 31 What we have learned from excellent communication departments about strategy and direction**
>
> Communicators working in excellent communication departments seem to be in a better place when facing the key issues than their contemporaries in other communication departments:
>
> - They are less concerned about finding ways to support the business strategy and organisational decision-making and changes, as many have probably already found ways to do so.
> - They are less worried about the challenges emerging from the new media landscape as they are more advanced in this field.
> - They pay more attention to sustainable development and CSR, and positioning their leaders and executives.

The data undoubtedly indicates that excellent communication departments have more success than the less high-performance departments, but linking communication and organisational strategies is still the main challenge even for them. That brings us to a hot issue: why are some communicators better able to link communication and overall strategies and some find this a real challenge? There are several aspects to the answer to these important and long-standing questions for the discipline, which we outline below.

Commandments in Practice: Strategised

Deutsche Post DHL Group

> **Strategic Communications Management: Long-Term Planning and Short-Term Calibration**
>
> Developing a long-term communications strategy was the basis on which Deutsche Post DHL Group decided to take a new approach to corporate communications in 2009. The question at hand was in what communicative currency could the company's products and brands be usefully measured and managed to achieve a ROI for each of its positioning activities. The decision finally fell on the factor of reputation – not least because there is convincing scientific and practical evidence of a positive interaction between a company's reputation and success in the race for capital, customers and employees.
>
> In addition, regression analyses conducted on the basis of comparable reputation surveys showed a high degree of correlation with a set of key reputation

drivers which could also serve both as levers and pressure points for the communications strategy. These were and still are products and services, employer quality (employer of choice), business success, leadership and management, vision and strategy, and corporate responsibility. In the annual strategy-building cycle, the values identified for the reputation drivers cited – both among the general public and in relevant stakeholder groups such as customers, employees, investors and critical NGOs – form the basis for the development and implementation of the global communications plan.

To manage reputation in a targeted way, mismatches between the status quo and the targets to be achieved using the reputation drivers are used to define strategic principles and areas of focus. These also take account of the company's long-term business strategy – Strategy 2015 in a first stage and meanwhile Strategy 2020 – as well as annual planning for the divisions and functional departments. These focal areas, for which Deutsche Post DHL Group has adopted the term 'strategic thrust', are then aligned in an iterative process involving regional and local communicators (those close to the business) and other internal stakeholders, and – more importantly – are supplemented by strategic reputation-building initiatives, with targeted investment of communications resources in the current year.

Strategic projects are always worked on by mixed teams who bring together a range of competencies from the communications function and also act as 'chief coordinator' to ensure the project measures are implemented. Phased implementation of the overall strategy, while staying within the allocated budget, is achieved in parallel to daily communications operations by means of a Technical Implementation Plan (TIP). This is regularly presented to the project management team, both to monitor the status of implementation of individual measures and to apply traffic-light logic to the use of staff and budgetary resources.

Key strategic communications projects designed to build the external reputation of Deutsche Post DHL Group include the *Delivering Tomorrow* publication series on future trends in the logistics industry and their socio-economic impacts, the *DHL Global Connectedness Index* which measures the state of globalisation around the world, the *Deutsche Post Happiness Atlas* – a life satisfaction study on how happy people are in Germany, the DHL advertising campaigns 'The Speed of Yellow' and 'The Power of Global Trade', as well as parallel, customised sponsoring partnerships with the likes of Formula 1 and FC Bayern Munich. For these key projects, in-depth communications plans were implemented to allow both format and content to address the needs of different target groups. These projects range from the Delphi Dialogues (a series of future-focused events), to exchange with opinion leaders on global media partnerships with broadcasters such as CNN, CNBC and Time Inc. Group, to blogger events with opinion leaders from the digital world.

Internal reputation building was driven in a step-by-step approach with such varying measures as the establishment of a readers' council for the employee newspaper, the creation of an extranet for operational employees with no access to a computer in the workplace, the further development of the corporate intranet to produce *myNet*, an interactive digital workplace, and a global employee engagement campaign to implement the Group's Strategy 2015 – under the motto 'Because of you', employees around the world were called upon to submit statements and pictures to explain their contribution in making the strategy a success.

This has resulted in a recognisable boost in the reputation of Deutsche Post DHL Group among its internal and external audiences since systematic reputation management was introduced. Since the first analysis using the TNS Infratest TRI*M Index in 2010, the rating has risen from an initial 74 index points (on a scale up to 100) to 79 index points in 2016. According to TNS Infratest, therefore, Deutsche Post DHL Group tops the reputation rankings in the global logistics industry. Internally, the reputation index rose by 16 points in the same timeframe.

However, elevating strategic communications management to the ranks of a social technology based on the outlined planning system – which would appear eminently feasible via targeted management of aggregates like reputation and the respective driving factors of communicative relations – would mean closing one's eyes to the fundamental complexities of the social interconnections. Following this path would also bring the unavoidable risk of ignoring the new unpredictability of the societal environment. This unpredictability has been described with the acronym VUCA (volatile, uncertain, complex and ambiguous). When transferred to the task of communications management, this new environment gives rise for a new rationale. In addition to strategic planning as a point of reference, there is a need for ongoing tactical calibration of goals. This helps to deliver corporate communications that is not just successful in the short and medium term, but which is also sustainable given that the situation can also change dramatically over night.

Christof E. Ehrhart
Prof. Dr. Christof E. Ehrhart is Executive Vice President and Head of Corporate Communications and Responsibility at Deutsche Post DHL, headquartered in Bonn, Germany. He is also an adjunct professor for international corporate communication at the University of Leipzig.

About Deutsche Post DHL
Deutsche Post DHL Group is the world's leading mail and logistics company. It generated revenues of more than 59 billion euros in 2015. With approximately 500,000 employees in over 220 countries and territories worldwide, the group operates under two brands: Deutsche Post is Europe's leading postal service provider. DHL is uniquely positioned in the world's growth markets, with a comprehensive range of international express, freight transportation, e-commerce and supply chain management services.

Strategic Value of Communication

One perspective and approach to understand the issue of linking communication and business strategy is related to the contribution of communication to the overall corporate or organisational goals. How does communication contribute to the ultimate purpose of the organisation? Part of the answer to this question can be found in the division on communication activities practitioners make between 'inbound activities' and 'outbound activities'.[30] Looking at how communicators and their departments help to reach the overall organisational goals of their organisation it becomes clear that communicators see their major contribution in the outbound activities. These activities entail facilitating business processes (e.g. influencing customer preferences, motivating employees, generating public attention) and building immaterial assets (e.g. brands, reputation, culture).

On the other hand, they pay less attention to the inbound activities such as helping to adjust organisational strategies (e.g. identifying opportunities, integrating public concerns and collecting customer feedback) and securing room for manoeuvre (e.g. by managing relationships and crises, building and securing legitimacy). Communication professionals continue therefore to be more focused on sending messages than on receiving them. The small number of organisations that have genuinely introduced clear listening strategies also underlines this point (Fig. 25).

The overall tendency is clearly a higher distribution of outbound activities at the expense of inbound activities. Nevertheless, excellent

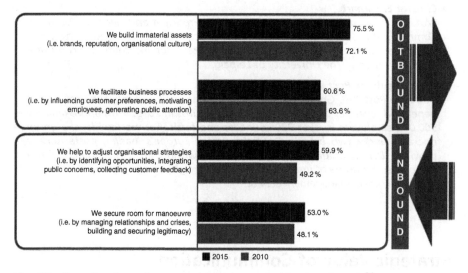

Fig. 25 Contribution of communication to organisational goals[31]

---

[30] Zerfass et al. (2015).

[31] Zerfass et al. (2015), p. 44. n = 2,252 (2015) and n = 1,955 (2010) communication professionals across Europe. Q: How do you and your department help to reach the overall goals of your organisation or your client? Scale 1 (rarely) – 5 (very often). Percentages: frequency based on scale points 4–5.

departments are strongly convinced that both activities contribute to the overall organisational goals. Significant differences are found between the contributions of excellent communication departments through outbound activities compared with non-excellent departments. But the differences from their contributions for inbound activities are even higher when compared (Fig. 26).

A recent qualitative study among chief communication officers in Germany showed that communicators use various strategies to explain what they do and why.[32] The European Communication Monitor took this as a starting point and asked practitioners across Europe how they defend the justification and legitimation of communication in front of CEOs, other executives and internal clients. The results were interesting.[33] The most common way the respondents articulate the relevance of communication is by explaining the positive effects of good reputation, organisational culture and brands. This is followed by illustrating the benefits of listening to stakeholders and identifying opportunities; explaining the role of content and 'thought leadership' for organisational goals. Only slightly

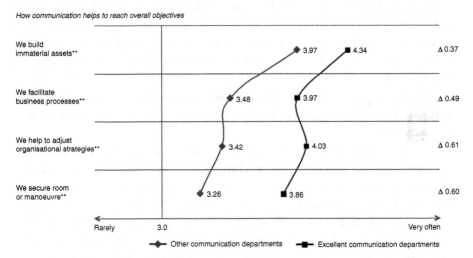

Fig. 26 How excellent departments contribute to overall organisational goals[34]

---

[32] Kiesenbauer and Zerfass (2015).

[33] Zerfass et al. (2015), pp. 48–51.

[34] Zerfass et al. (2015), p. 116. $n = 1,600$ communication professionals working in communication departments across Europe. Q: How do you and your department help to reach the overall goals of your organisation? Scale 1 (rarely) – 5 (very often). Mean values. ** Highly significant differences (Pearson correlation, $p \leq 0.01$). * Significant differences (Pearson correlation, $p \leq 0.05$).

more than half of them claim to demonstrate positive economic consequences of communication activities.

Do practitioners working in governmental organisations and non-profits explain the communication value in the same way as professionals in the private sector?

Clearly not, communicators have to adapt to whoever they work for. In governmental organisations the positive economic effects are considered less important than in the private sector. Instead, government communicators are logically more concerned with demonstrating the importance of the demand for communication and transparency by the mass media. Remarkably they do not focus on the benefits of listening, which seem clearly related to the way they respond to the demand for transparency. This links with a working style called 'in-house journalism' traditionally played by practitioners in governmental organisations. Consultancies are ahead on every argument except for the demand for transparency. Non-profit organisations seem very concerned about the benefits of listening. The private sector gives more weight to economic value and the threat of crisis.

Nevertheless, we can underline geographic differences too. Professionals across countries give preference to different arguments to explain the value of communication. Spanish practitioners, for instance, appeal to economic effects, more often than any other country in Southern, Western and Northern Europe.

On the other hand, listening to stakeholders and identifying opportunities is the second argument used to prove the value of communication to top executives.

An important attribute of excellence as identified by the European Communication Monitor is the ability to explain the value of communication to top executives by using arguments related to economic success and the benefit of listening to stakeholders.[35] While excellent departments use all modes of explanation more intensively, they differentiate most in those two dimensions and in the recollection of threats caused by troubled relationships and crises. This indicates that communication management has to be conceptualised as a strategic discipline, incorporating both messaging and listening, with a clear commitment to demonstrate and evaluate the contribution to overall organisational goals (Box 32).

---

[35] Zerfass et al. (2015), p. 117.

> **Box 32 What we have learned about the value of communication from excellent departments?**
>
> Excellent communication departments are convinced of the value of communication:
>
> - They are strongly convinced of contributing to organisational goals.
> - They contribute using inbound activities more frequently.
> - They use the whole set of arguments for explaining communication value.
> - They are clearly ahead on claiming the economic and listening benefits and the avoidance of threats.

What Does It Mean to be Strategised?

Being a strategised department, beyond the buzz and spin that surrounds the word strategy, first and foremost means that you have an overall communication strategy and policies, combined with specific strategies for specific problems. Strategic means that you take the other into account. Your policies and plans anticipate the reaction of all stakeholders involved. The 'other' can be other organisations, the society or individual members of the public. This strategic action involves having steps in place to counter actions of others and anticipating them without getting into too much conflict.

Strategic departments understand the analytical distinction between the system world that their organisation and some stakeholders are part of and the horizon of individuals that are affected by the organisation: the lifeworld. Assessing and dealing professionally with the on-going conflict between the system and the life world is an important part of strategised communication department. Acting as a strategic facilitator is a prerequisite for that.

Striving for excellence is found to be important for effective communication departments as well. Excellent departments have found a workable way to link communication to the (business) strategy of the organisation, consistently the biggest issue for the field in the last ten years. Explaining the value of communication is the first step to link communication to business or organisational goals. Excellent departments succeed in doing that better than other departments.

Being well embedded in the organisation, able to work with data about the organisation and its environment and being strategic are three main aspects for an excellent communication function. It shows the contours of an effective and successful department that helps the organisation communicatively to reach its goals.

After the societal perspective in the first three chapters of this book and the departmental perspective of the last three chapters, the question remains: What does it take for an individual to be an effective communication professional? In the next part of the book we will describe the individual characteristics necessary for a communication manager: being sagacious (knowledgeable, reflective and shrewd), being linked with people, the media and networks, and being solid (strong, sensitive and savvy).

This second part of the book has explored excellence from the departmental level inside the organisation. The three chapters in this section reflect the communication department's need to be integrated into the processes of leadership and power (embedded); taking part in the strategic planning and in the evaluation processes of the whole organisation (strategised) and working with large and small data and research to understand the environment and support the departmental objectives (datafied). In summary we have explored how to be influential as a department and how communication professionals can manage and lead their departments to support the organisation in an excellent way.

The final section of the book drills down to the core elements that support and deliver 'excellence' at a personal or individual level. The final three chapters therefore discuss the environmental conditions for the high-performing professional communicator and how they can make an individual contribution to wider departmental and organisational communication performance within our excellence framework.

References

Berger, B. K., & Meng, J. (2014). *Public Relations Leaders as Sensemakers: A Global Study of Leadership in Public Relations and Communication Management*. London: Routledge.

BVC (Dutch Professional Association for Communication) (2002). *Job Profile Descriptions in Communication Management* (3rd ed.). The Hague: BVC/VVO.

Cornelissen, J., Bekkum, T. V., & Van Ruler, B. (2013). Corporate communications: A practice-based theoretical conceptualization. *Corporate Reputation Review, 9*(2), 114–133.

Dozier, D. M., & Broom, G. M. (2006). The centrality of practitioner roles to public relations theory. In C. H. Botan & V. Hazleton (Eds.), *Public Relations Theory II* (pp. 137–170). Mahwah, NJ: Lawrence Erlbaum Associates.

Gregory, A. (2010). *Planning and Managing Public Relations Campaigns* (3rd ed.). London: Kogan Page.

Grunig, J. E., & Hunt, T. (1984). *Managing Public Relations*. New York, NY: Holt, Rinehart and Winston.

Grunig, L. A., Grunig, J. E., & Dozier, D. M. (2002). *Excellent Public Relations and Effective Organizations: A Study of Communication Management in Three Countries*. Mahwah, NY: Lawrence Erlbaum Associates.

Habermas, J. (1981). *The Theory of Communicative Action. Volume 1: Reason and the Rationalization of Society*. Boston, MA: Beacon Press.

Holmström, J., Ketokivil, M., & Hameri, A. (2009). Bridging practice and theory: A design science approach. *Decision Sciences, 40*(1), 65–87.

Kiesenbauer, J., & Zerfass, A. (2015). Today's and tomorrow's challenges in public relations: Comparing the views of chief communication officers and next generation leaders. *Public Relations Review, 41*(4), 422–434.

Kuypers, G. (1973). *Grondbegrippen van politiek*. Utrecht, Antwerp: Uitgeverij Het Spectrum.

Logeion (2012). *Beroepsniveauprofielen*. Retrieved from www.logeion.nl/beroepsniveauprofielen.

Lurati, F., & Eppler, M. J. (2006). Communication and management. *Studies in Communication Sciences, 6*(2), 75–98.

Mahoney, J. (2011). Horizons in strategic communication: Theorising a paradigm shift. *International Journal of Strategic Communication, 5*(3), 143–153.

Mazzei, A. (2014). Internal communication for employee enablement: Strategies in American and Italian companies. *Corporate Communications: An International Journal, 19*(1), 82–95.

Moreno, A., Navarro, C., Tench, R., & Zerfass, A. (2015). Does social media usage matter? An analysis of online practices and digital media perceptions of communication practitioners in Europe. *Public Relations Review, 41*(2), 242–253.

Nothhaft, H. (2010). Communication management as a second-order management function: Roles and functions of the communication executive-results from a shadowing study. *Journal of Communication Management, 14*(2), 127–140.

Steyn, B. (2007). Contribution of public relations to organizational strategy formulation. In E. Toth (Ed.), *The Future of Excellence in Public Relations and Communication Management: Challenges for the Next Generation* (pp. 137–172). Mahwah, NJ: Lawrence Erlbaum Associates.

Tench, R., Verhoeven, P., & Zerfass, A. (2009). Institutionalizing strategic communication in Europe – An ideal home or a mad house? Evidence from a survey in 37 countries. *International Journal of Strategic Communication, 3*(2), 147–164.

Tench, R., Sun, W., & Jones, B. (2014). Introduction: CSR communication as an emerging field of study. In R. Tench, W. Sun, & B. Jones (Eds.), *Communicating Corporate Social Responsibility: Perspectives and Practice* (pp. 3–21). Bingley: Emerald.

Tench, R., & Moreno, A. (2015). Mapping communication management competencies for European practitioners: ECOPSI an EU study. *Journal of Communication Management, 19*(1), 39–61.

Van Ruler, B., Verčič, D., Bütschi, G., & Flodin, B. (2000). *The European Body of Knowledge on Public Relations/Communication Management: The Report of the Delphi Research Project 2000.* Ghent, Ljubljana: EUPRERA.

Van Ruler, B., & Verčič, D. (Eds.) (2004). *Public Relations and Communication Management in Europe. A Nation-by-Nation Introduction to Public Relations Theory and Practice.* Berlin: Mouton de Gruyter.

Van Ruler, B., & Verčič, D. (2005). Reflective communication management. Future ways for public relations research. In P. J. Kalbfleisch (Ed.), *Communication Yearbook 29* (pp. 239–274). Mahwah, NJ: Lawrence Erlbaum Associates.

Verčič, D., & Grunig, J. E. (2002). The origins of public relations theory in economics and strategic management. In D. Moss, D. Verčič, & G. Warnaby (Eds.), *Perspectives on Public Relations Research* (pp. 9–58). New York, NY: Routledge.

Verčič, D., Van Ruler, B., Bütschi, G., & Flodin, B. (2002). On the definition of public relations: A European view. *Public Relations Review, 37*(4), 373–387.

Verčič, D., Verhoeven, P., & Zerfass, A. (2014). Key issues of public relations of Europe: Findings from the European Communication Monitor 2007–2014. *Revista Internacional de Relaciones Públicas, 4*(8), 5–26.

Vos, M. F. (1996). *The Corporate Image Concept: A Strategic Approach.* s.l: s.n.

Werder, K. P., & Holtzhausen, D. R. (2009). An analysis of the influence of public relations department leadership style on public relations strategy use and effectiveness. *Journal of Public Relations Research, 21*(4), 404–427.

Zerfass, A. (2008). Corporate communication revisited: Integrating business strategy and strategic communication. In A. Zerfass, B. Van Ruler, & K. Sriramesh (Eds.), *Public Relations Research. European and International Perspectives and Innovations* (pp. 65–96). Wiesbaden: VS Verlag für Sozialwissenschaften.

Zerfass, A., Moreno, A., Tench, R., Verčič, D., & Verhoeven, P. (2009). *European Communication Monitor 2009. Trends in Communication Management and Public Relations – Results of a Survey in 34 Countries.* Brussels: Euprera.

Zerfass, A., Verhoeven, P., Tench, R., Moreno, A., & Verčič, D. (2011). *European Communication Monitor 2011. Empirical Insights into Strategic Communication in Europe. Results of an Empirical Survey in 43 Countries.* Brussels: EACD/EUPRERA.

Zerfass, A., Verčič, D., Verhoeven, P., Moreno, A., & Tench, R. (2015). *European Communication Monitor 2015. Creating Communication Value Through Listening, Messaging and Measurement. Results of a Survey In 41 Countries.* Brussels: EACD/EUPRERA, Helios Media.

Zerfass, A., Verhoeven, P., Moreno, A., Tench, R., & Verčič, D. (2016). *European Communication Monitor 2016. Exploring Trends in Big Data, Stakeholder Engagement and Strategic Communication. Results of a Survey In 43 Countries.* Brussels: EACD/EUPRERA, Quadriga Media Berlin.

Zerfass, A., & Viertmann, C. (2017). Creating business value through corporate communication: a theory-based framework and its practical application. *Journal of Communication Management, 21*(1).

Part III

Ambitious Professionals

This final section of the book drills down to the core elements that support and deliver 'excellence' at a personal or individual level. The final three commandments and chapters therefore select the ingredients that provide the perfect environmental conditions for excellent individual contribution to wider departmental and organisational communication performance. We evaluate the full menu of options that the ten-year European Communication Monitor research has discussed alongside examples from practice. Before discussing in detail each theme and how it improves the communicator's performance, let's focus on the big picture and what has been identified as really making the most difference for the individual. If we are looking for excellence of both an individual and a department the synthesised message from this part of the book focuses on practitioners being *'professional'*, that is, professional in what they do, how they do it and in what kind of working environment they aspire to work in and create. In summary, it's simple and easy to remember the three takeaway items because the best individuals demonstrate these three core elements that we expand on in this section of the book and they are:

Being *sagacious* – as in the definition of this term – involves being knowledgeable, demonstrating reflective wisdom as well as shrewdness and at times applying appropriate mental discernment. We demonstrate these through detailed discussion and evidence in the chapter on educational experience and expectations as well as detailed discussions of the explicit competencies of high-performing communicators. Our next attribute is being *linked* and this includes the importance of relationships as well as in-depth discussions of the vital importance of not only personal and professional networks but also the development and support for the individual and other colleagues through mentoring and mentorship. The third and for the book final commandment in our series of nine is to be *solid*. By this we mean having explicit personal solidity driven by personal, organisational and professional ethics and frameworks as well as exploring issues of pluralism and diversity in the workplace to facilitate and deliver the satisfaction our framework calls for.

Commandment 7
Sagacious: Knowledgeable, Reflective and Shrewd

'What is it you do, exactly?' A frequently asked question of communication professionals by friends over dinner, or colleagues inside the company and, worryingly, sometimes senior managers. Will they ask the same of medical doctors, lawyers or accountants? Probably not. Does it mean that strategic communication and public relations needs more professionalisation? We will argue: yes. Using the ten-year data set from the European Communication Monitor alongside contemporary debates about professionalisation we are able to identify what it means to be a *professional* communicator in Europe today. And which problems practitioners encounter in executing their activities professionally. What are the drivers and opportunities practitioners today and tomorrow need to create and to work in excellent communication environments? What skills do they require? What do communication departments need to do to support the ongoing development of the individual professional?

We talk in this chapter and within the framework of this book about being *Sagacious* – as in the definition of this term – this involves being knowledgeable, demonstrating reflective wisdom, as well as shrewdness and at times applying appropriate mental discernment. We demonstrate these through detailed discussion and evidence in the chapter on educational experience and expectations as well as exploring the explicit competencies of high-performing communicators. Sagacity is a characteristic of an individual professional. It is one of the aspects of an ambitious professional that wants to perform in an excellent way. That is why being sagacious is the seventh commandment for excellent communication.

© The Author(s) 2017
R. Tench et al., *Communication Excellence*,
DOI 10.1007/978-3-319-48860-8_7

Before we go on let's establish the level of education of European professionals today, based on 2016 Monitor results.[1] The good news is they are a well-educated bunch. Today most practitioners (61 per cent) have a master's degree from a university, and even 8 per cent of the respondents have a doctorate. About 26 per cent has a bachelor's degree. The majority of the respondents thinks that a university education is a prerequisite for young people to start working in the field, as is mastering the English language.

These high levels of education have not changed in the last decade, and it suggests that the practice of strategic communication is a real profession. Only 5 per cent of respondents do not have an academic degree. But professionalisation does not stop after getting a degree. In communication management the idea of lifelong learning is very much appreciated and putting effort into your own development is regarded as essential. Let's first look a bit more closely at the concept of professionalisation.

Qualities of Professionalisation

Debates about professionalism and professions are detailed and far-reaching in many books and across numerous disciplines. That is also the case for strategic communication. To start on the same page here let us first take a look at the similar set of qualities that most professions, old and new, have.[2] These are (1) esoteric knowledge – theoretical or technical – not available to the general population; (2) commitment to social values such as health or justice; (3) national organisation to set standards, control membership, and liaise with a wider society; and (4) extra-strong moral commitment to support professional values. Strategic communication and public relations have this same set of qualities. They need to be developed, maintained and fostered. How are practitioners in Europe doing that? In three ways.

Three Dimensions of Professionalisation in Communication Management

Professionalisation in communication management has, according to practitioners in Europe, three dimensions: training the communication team, continuing to develop yourself and engaging in mentoring and networking (see Fig. 27).

---

[1] Zerfass et al. (2016), pp. 13–14.
[2] Cooper (2004), pp. 61–63.

Fig. 27   The three dimensions of professionalisation

These three dimensions of professionalisation contain all kinds of activities. Training the team means training communication skills and management know-how, new communicative tasks and learning to handle communication processes and business models in the organisation. The management of 'high potentials' and succession planning are also part of this keeping the team up to date.

Self-development is personal development and contributing to the much-needed 'academisation' of the field. Developing personal skills, knowledge and competences goes hand in hand with using, understanding and supporting research. This includes investing in an organisation's own research, as is support-ing academic research more generally in the field. Also, supporting the education of future professionals at universities and training institutes belongs to academisa-tion. Building relationships with future professionals through internships and wider employer branding are also activities that contribute to professionalisation. Mentoring and networking involves benchmarking with other organisations as well as sharing best practices with them, for example, at conferences.

Women and young people find professionalisation in all its manifestations more important than men and older professionals. We also found differences in perceived value of professionalisation across different types of profes-sionals. The so-called strategic facilitators think professionalisation, and especially self-development, is more important than do operational suppor-ters and isolated experts (see Commandment 6 and Fig. 23 for an explana-tion of the types of professionals).

A Positioning Problem for Public Relations

The European Communication Monitor shows some ongoing issues in communication management which can both foster and hinder achieve-ments of professionalisation. Why is the public relations profession not as professional as other fields? We found two barriers (1) the low status and reputation of the profession in general and (2) barriers within organisations (see Box 33).

Box 33 Barriers to professionalisation of strategic communication
1. Low status and reputation of the profession
2. Internal barriers

The low status of PR/communication associations and bodies is seen as problematic.[3] The current codes of ethics do not suffice and there is a lack of formal accreditation systems for the field. Most practitioners see advantages of such systems, like those in place in the United Kingdom, Brazil and other countries.[4] They think that the system will improve the reputation of the field but will not help much for developing the quality of the profession. Furthermore a shortage of up-to-date communication training and education is observed and practical experience is more highly valued than specific qualifications in communication/PR. All these elements are hindering the field's professionalisation. The low status of the field is felt by all but young people, with women, team members and more highly educated practitioners worrying more about this than others. Not surprisingly members of a professional association and consultants are also more concerned than others about this positioning problem for public relations. Many argue that other and somehow more advanced concepts like 'corporate communication', 'strategic communication' or 'integrated communication' should be used to create more trust in the profession. But this will be a long way to go.

The second barrier is an internal barrier. This consists of two elements: the lack of understanding of communication practice by top management and the difficulties professionals have in proving the impact of communication on an organisation's goals.[5] Women perceive these internal barriers more than men, and these barriers are also related to the organisational culture. Professionals working in organisations with a so-called interactive or *systemised* culture perceive them more than those working in an organisation with an *integrated* culture (see 'Commandment 4: Embedded:

---

[3] Zerfass et al. (2011), pp. 19–29.
[4] Zerfass et al. (2012), pp. 36–41.
[5] Zerfass et al. (2012), pp. 38.

Influence Through Communicative Leadership' for an explanation of organisational cultures).

Necessary Competencies for Working in Communications

It's a common cliché that, having learned, you never forget how to ride a bike. Cycling is a combination of skills and knowledge that enable most of us to safely and competently navigate the streets from childhood to old age. Therefore competence is a word we use frequently to describe our abilities to do a variety of day-to-day activities. But what does competence mean when we talk about our professional capabilities? Is it simply a case of once learned we never forget? We don't need to maintain and develop the competency? Much is written about competencies for different disciplines and fields, particularly psychology and human resource management.

This debate is also highly relevant for the communications industries as well. Before we get into the specifics for strategic communication and public relations, we take a look at the concept of a competency.

What Is a Competency?

What is clear from studies of skills, knowledge and personal attributes is that they overlap in terminology and that there is a pattern forming about how skills, knowledge and personal attributes lead to broader competencies. Although some studies focused on the skills, knowledge and personal attributes of practitioners, there was no definitive research that brought these elements together in a single study until the ECOPSI research project funded by the European Union.[6] It was conducted by universities from several European countries and Turkey.

The ECOPSI programme took the broad labels provided by prior research and used them to examine four roles in communications: internal communicator, social media expert, crisis communicator and the communication director role. The research observed how these roles are enacted across Europe, and the skills, knowledge and personal

---

[6] Tench et al. (2013a, b); Tench and Moreno (2015).

attributes required, which subsequently contribute to the competencies needed by practitioners to fulfil these roles efficiently. This research helped to define the differences between skills, knowledge, personal attributes and competences for the field of communication management (see Box 34 for the definitions). The research combined qualitative and quantitative research. In-depth interviews with professionals were conducted as well as a survey among professionals as part of the European Communication Monitor.

Box 34 Competencies in communication management – some definitions

- *Knowledge*
  Can be defined as what practitioners are required to know in order to do their job/role effectively.[7]
- *Skills*
  These are the things practitioners must be able to do to perform their job/role effectively.[8] Identifying 'skill' will be a complex process, but a useful definition is: 'goal-directed, well-organised behaviour that is acquired through practice and performed with economy of effort'.[9]
- *Personal attributes*
  Are defined in the literature as separate from competencies. The distinction being that personal attributes can determine how well a competency is performed, and secondly competencies can be taught while personal attributes are modelled or fostered.[10]
- *Competencies*
  Are the sets of behaviours the person can perform. These behaviours are based on the application, combination and potential integration of knowledge and skills.[11]

Researchers Lynn Maud Jeffrey and Margaret Ann Brunton from New Zealand highlight the advantage of studying competencies over roles. They say: 'as . . . roles outline tasks and responsibilities in the job description, in today's dynamic workplace these same roles are likely to change frequently. In contrast, competencies are the underlying foundational abilities that are integral to successfully carrying out the tasks and

---

[7] PRSA (1999, 2006).

[8] Katz and Kahn (1978); Goodman (2006); PRSA Public Relations Society of America (1999, 2006); Gregory (2008).

[9] Proctor and Duttan (1995), p. 18.

[10] Jeffrey and Brunton (2011), p. 69.

[11] Boyatzis (1982); Bartram (2012); Gregory (2008); Jeffrey and Brunton (2011).

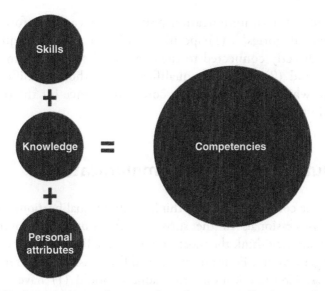

Fig. 28 Skills, knowledge and personal attributes contributing to competencies

responsibilities, and thus remain a stable blueprint for practice over time'.[12] Figure 28 illustrates how skills, knowledge and personal attributes combine to form competencies.[13]

The difficulty in establishing a workable definition of competencies has been discussed in the European Centre for the Development of Vocational Training (CEDEFOP). Their aim was to clarify the concepts of knowledge, skills and competences.[14] Competences provide a link between education (and skills) and job requirements (roles). Three professional competencies can be distinguished. First, 'conceptual competence' which refers to knowledge about an entire domain. Second 'procedural competence' which refers to the application of conceptual competence in a particular situation. Third 'performance competence' which is required to assess problems and select a suitable strategy for solving them.

In communication management competency is usually defined as conceptual competence and performance competence. In other words competencies refer either to the substantive ability to carry out a task or how practitioners should behave in order to perform in the role.

---

[12] Jeffrey and Brunton (2011), p. 61.

[13] Adapted from Tench and Moreno (2015).

[14] Winterton et al. (2005).

Competencies for communication practitioners can therefore be seen as having two categories[15]: (1) specific qualifications – those qualifications which are directly connected to the content of strategic communication as a topic and (2) unspecific qualifications – those qualifications, like leadership, which can be seen as a core competence for the performance of practitioners.

Four Qualifications for Communicators

Following the competence line of thinking about qualifications we asked the European professionals in the survey of the European Communication Monitor what they think the most important qualifications for communication management are. Four groups of qualifications could be retrieved from the answers. Communication professionals should (1) have a social and empathic antenna, (2) be able to produce and deliver effective messages, (3) have research skills and organisational management skills and (4) have knowledge about society (see Box 35).

Box 35 Four necessary qualifications for communication professionals

1. Social and empathic antenna
2. Producing and delivering effective messages
3. Research skills and organisational management skills
4. Knowledge about society

What do they mean? The *social and empathic antenna* has to do with the skill to coach others in their communication or put differently enabling others to communicate. It's also about handling power and coalition building between people inside and outside the organisation. This can mean initiating and moderating dialogues with a cross cultural and cross gender sensitivity. Furthermore it has to do with handing ethical issues and knowing about ethics and with managing projects globally.

In order to be able to *produce and deliver effective messages* it is necessary to have a lot of knowledge about the effects of traditional and new media, about

---

[15] Szyszka (1995).

persuasion concepts and strategies but also about how to manage relation-ships inside and outside the organisation. The actual message production and delivering and presenting messages as a public speaker are also characteristics of this dimension.

Research and organisational management skills concern developing knowl-edge practical understanding about communication technologies and research to be able to perform effect studies as well as forecasting based on data retrieved. Also being able to interpret the data for insights about marketing, consumers and other stakeholders is part of this qualification. The management skills are handling organisational change and development, as well as finances, budgeting and accounting for the communication func-tion of the organisation.

Knowledge about society is about thoroughly understanding the way society and politics work and how this is translated into legal requirements and issues for the organisation. Knowledge about the functioning of organisations in democratic societies and the rule of law are considered important here.

Although there is a high degree of agreement on these qualifications some differences stand out. In general women, professionals working in joint stock companies and strategic advisors consider these four qualifications more important than others in the field.

Commandments in Practice: Sagacious

Communications Playing a Key Part in Cross-Functional Innovation Initiatives

For the past decade or so, Electrolux has been on a journey to reshape the company from a traditional manufacturing and engineering company to become more consumer-focused and innovation-driven. We are well on our way, and with the digital revolution continuing to transform Electrolux and our industry, it is more important than ever to develop our thinking and approach in this area.

This journey is not only affecting how Electrolux does research and develop-ment or designs its products – it is also having a fundamental impact on the role of corporate communications, global marketing and PR. These functions are becoming integral to the innovation process at Electrolux, as we seek to broaden our horizons and build new business in a period of change which we expect will affect the entire value chain and the competitive landscape of the appliance industry. Reflecting current strategies, breaking barriers and building knowledge to shape future markets is a key objective for communications nowadays. There are many questions that need to be answered. We know that a large number of home appliances will become connected in the coming years, but what are the benefits and what are consumers actually looking for in this area? How can we make online services a larger part of our revenue stream? How will we use new technologies like big data, artificial intelligence and machine learning to deliver more value to consumers? What other disruptive developments and opportunities wait around the corner?

Communications and related functions are playing a key part at Electrolux in providing useful answers to these questions, and in developing the solutions. To remain at the forefront of our industry, we have to look beyond the stakeholders traditionally involved in business and product development and build on the tribal knowledge of the entire company, as well as on other potential sources of insight.

Since 2012, Electrolux has operated with the 'Innovation Triangle' as a guiding concept, having teams from R&D, design and marketing collaborate in all product development projects. The marketeers have provided many of the insights and research necessary to ensure a new product will be preferred by consumers. With this integrated strategy in place, it's been a short step to where communications is deeply involved in various external and internal innovation initiatives. The aim is to tap into the collective wisdom of employees, consumers, experts, thought-leaders and other companies.

The first such initiative we introduced on a broader scale was the iJam (innovation jamming), a 72-hour brainstorming session for all of our employees, asking them to draft ideas for products and services on a specific theme and collaborate across functions and business areas to make them even better. The four iJams held since 2012 have generated almost 7,000 ideas, many of which have been integrated in our product portfolio planning. Not just cross-functional in its purpose, the iJam has been cross-functional also in terms of execution, with strategic internal communication one key aspect of the project.

Another project worth mentioning in this context is Electrolux Ideas Lab, a global online-based consumer competition that aims to trigger creativity and out of the box thinking around matters relating to the home and everyday life. Is this project about generating PR, consumer insights or new product ideas? For Electrolux, the first two of these are the main benefits, while useful ideas will be a welcome side effect.

On the other end of the spectrum, the Electrolux Open Innovation organisation is tasked with managing incoming ideas from potential business partners, as well as with scouting the wider market for relevant innovations. Not in any traditional sense a communications activity, Open Innovation is nevertheless an important carrier of corporate messages for Electrolux.

As we can see from the above, communications and business operations are becoming more tightly knit together at Electrolux, with one truly supporting the other and vice versa. It may well be that this is the first step on another transformational journey; one where communications functions broaden the scope of their usefulness beyond stakeholder and leadership communications, to become drivers of new and relevant business development in their own right.

Martin von Arronet
Martin von Arronet is Senior Vice President Corporate Communications for Electrolux in Stockholm, Sweden. He is responsible for corporate communications, public affairs and sustainability affairs.

About Electrolux
Electrolux is a global leader in home appliances and appliances for professional use, selling more than 60 million products to customers in 150 countries every year. The company focuses on innovations that are thoughtfully designed, based on extensive consumer insight.

Advancing a Career in Communication

What do you have to do to advance a career in strategic communication and public relations? What skills and knowledge do you need for boosting such a career? According to the European Communication Monitor, two aspects are important: permanent academic education (prior to the job and on the job) and keeping in touch with the labour market.[16] This last aspect consists not only of moving to a new employer now and then, but also networking among peers and colleagues, job rotation in the same organisation and mentoring by senior colleagues.

Geographically there are regional differences in thinking about career development. In Southern Europe, networking is more important than in Northern Europe. Other marked regional differences are job rotation, which is seen as more important in the East and South as well as specifically in France, Belgium and the Netherlands, and internships, which are less valued in Norway, Sweden and the United Kingdom.

On the more concrete level of skills and knowledge we asked European professionals what skills and knowledge they found important to develop further to advance their career. Their answers showed two groups of skills to be developed once you are working in communications: (1) business and management skills and (2) communication skills (see Box 36).

Box 36 Two areas of professional skills and knowledge development

1. Business and management skills
2. Communicative skills

---

[16] Zerfass et al. (2014), pp. 44–59.

The business and management skills include practical business skills such as budgeting, dealing with invoices, contracts and taxation and knowledge about markets, products and competitors. Management skills like decision-making, planning and organising were considered important and so was knowledge about current affairs, social and political trends, ethics and legal affairs. The older the professional communicator is the less important he or she thinks the further development of these skills are. Women perceive the development of these skills as less important than men anyway and so do unit leaders and team members compared with heads of departments. Juniors value the development of these skills more than seniors, people with a master's degree more than people without an academic degree, joint stock company workers less than consultants which all clearly highlight variance in the assessment of these skills.

The advancement of communication skills includes developing written and oral message production capabilities, building more knowledge about theories and principles of communication, audiences, programme development, as well as campaigning and evaluation research. Here also women perceive developing these skills as less important than their male counterparts do. Unit leaders and team members think it more important than heads of the department, the same goes for junior and mid-career professionals compared to seniors.

Important Management Skills for Career Advancement

Delving deeper into the management skills professionals think are important for career advancement we learn that there are two categories of skills professionals think about: (1) substantive strategic skills and (2) process and procedural skills. What do they mean and how important are they and for whom?

Substantive strategic skills are about the management of information (mainly data analysis), strategic positioning of the organisation and linking communication to business goals. Planning activities like developing communication concepts, tools and activity plans are also part of this area of skills. Does everybody think the same about the importance of these skills? No, they do not.[17] Older professionals think the development of these skills

---

[17] Empirical results on development needs and qualifications are reported in Zerfass et al. (2014), pp. 76–99; Zerfass et al. (2016), pp. 84–97.

is less necessary than young professionals and so do unit leaders, team members and people with other functions compared to heads of departments. Junior and mid-career professionals think it less important than seniors and people with an academic degree think this is more important than people without a degree. Consultants working with agencies consider these skills more important than people working in organisations and people working in an entrepreneurial and systemised culture think this less important than people who are part of integrated cultures.

The second component of management skills, process and procedural, are a combination of bureaucratic and communication skills. Bureaucratic skills include establishing structures and processes like job charts, procedures and workflows, managing human resources, managing financial resources and implementing control systems. Communication skills entail things like managing relationships in shaping the organisation's culture, managing informal networks and building trust. Leading people and groups in the sharing of knowledge and ideas and motivating them are also part of the process and procedural skills that professionals want to develop. Again not everybody thinks the same about the importance of those skills. Women think they are more important than men and so do heads of departments and senior professionals. In non-profit organisations these skills are considered less important than in agencies and the same goes for organisations with interactive, entrepreneurial and systemised cultures compared to integrated cultures.

Mentoring Is Key to Career Development

Mentoring is not a new phenomenon but it is increasingly discussed and applied as a form of career development across management disciplines.[18] It has been acknowledged as one of the key career development and advancement tools in organisations.[19] Also mentorship is recognised as a critical on-the-job training development tool for career success for both men and women.[20]

The greatest problem can be defining when mentoring is taking place. Evaluation of over 200 academic journal articles identifies that most discussion about mentoring is conceptual, anecdotal and empirical rather than

---

[18] Tench et al. (2016).

[19] Simonetti et al. (1999).

[20] Hunt and Michael (1983), p. 483.

theoretical. Their findings also conclude that there is a lack of consensus on definitions for mentoring and mentor; however, researchers continue to examine various facets of mentoring such as types of mentoring, mentoring phases, potential benefits, diversity and alternatives to mentoring.[21] What does that mean for mentoring in communication management?

We found that almost two-thirds of the European professionals consider 'mentoring by senior colleagues' as (very) important and that only a third of respondents had never had a mentor.[22] Almost 20 per cent had searched for a mentor on their own, and about 14 per cent of the PR professionals took part in a mentoring programme offered by their employer. Meanwhile only a few professionals were engaged in an external mentoring programme.

Thinking in a more professional way is the major outcome of mentoring. It has a positive impact on empowerment, career motivation and career progression and on feeling more professional. Professionals who had been both a mentor and mentee are more satisfied in their job, followed by those who had only been mentors and those who had only been mentees. So being a mentor also has a positive impact on their working life. Recent research identified that 10 out of 40 professional PR associations across the world had a mentoring programme. Most were established in the first decade of the twenty-first century, which is relatively late given that mentoring has been recognised as a development tool for young professionals since the 1960s.[23] Mentoring programmes have a strategic value not only for the mentors and the mentees but also for the organisation.

We also found that women are less likely to have a mentor than men. Despite the evidence of success for women in mentoring relationships it is disappointing that fewer women took part in mentoring than men.[24]

Generally professions, including law and accountancy, identify mentoring and networking as essential individual career strategies which help individuals to manage and develop their careers through socialisation.[25] Also from a broader perspective, co-presence, familiarity and face-to-face interactions

---

[21] Friday et al. (2004), p. 629.
[22] Zerfass et al. (2014), pp. 44, 54–59.
[23] Kiesenbauer, Burkert and Zerfass (2015).
[24] Zerfass et al. (2014), p. 55.
[25] Anderson-Gough et al. (2006); Hanlon (1994, 1998).

inherent in mentoring create trust[26] and structures which can stabilise business relationships.[27]

In support of previous research[28] mentoring is seen as important by a clear majority of communication professionals. Interestingly, both the youngest and the oldest or most experienced practitioners name mentoring as one of the top three aspects of career development. Career sponsorship is one of the primary functions fulfilled by a mentor and mentors are usually found at higher organisational levels.[29] Typically, they will discuss options and dilemmas with mentees and advance their careers in organisations through providing sponsorship, coaching, exposure and visibility, protection and challenging work assignments. As sponsors, mentors actively nominate mentees for projects and promotions, publicly advocate them for their abilities and champion their behaviours. As coaches, mentors provide access to information that is available only to higher-level members of the organisation, share career histories, suggest specific strategies to achieve career goals and provide assistance in job-related skills and knowledge.

Mentoring and job satisfaction are mutually related and communication professionals who have been mentors as well as mentees during their career are most satisfied in their job, followed by those who had been mentors and those who had only been mentees. Several positive effects of mentoring are identified. First of all, mentoring makes mentees think and feel more professional. Moreover, mentors convey personal values, work ethics and strategies for achieving career goals. Thinking of the future, tailor-made mentoring programmes for communicators are a valuable approach to develop communication functions in organisations and the profession at large.

What It Means to be Sagacious

We have discussed a range of key issues that help us to understand and frame the role of the 'ideal' professional practitioner in the complex world of the professional communicator in Europe. The findings demonstrate

---

[26] Giddens (1991).
[27] Ouchi (1980).
[28] Allen and Eby (2010).
[29] Seibert et al. (2001).

that the demands and expectations on the individual are immense and intense. How do they respond to the needs of their employer, colleagues, peers and indeed their own aspirations for personal development, which are myriad and potentially conflicting. Individuals are faced with many pressures and challenges. To respond there are many ways and means of accessing information and knowledge as well as guidance to cope with these development challenges.

Being *sagacious* nowadays is necessary for an excellent communication professional. It means being knowledgeable, having reflective wisdom and the ability to judge well. It requires individual understanding about communication processes as well as the effects of communication at a societal, organisational and individual level. This inevitably has a direct impact for you as an individual practitioner as well as your communication peers and other members of the organisation you work in. Educating yourself and others throughout the working life, mentoring the next generation and networking with your peers are effective ways of being and staying sagacious.

We are seeing clear recognition of the value of help from peers through mentoring as well as the direct success and contribution to the individual of engaging in formal and informal networking. When we think of high performance in this context we therefore see pathways to success from the role models of practitioners over the last decade.

Also the field has to acknowledge, recognise and work with the PR professional practice arena as a feminised one. This has implications on how we manage each other, interact and also see the future development of the field. The implications of a feminised profession will emerge in further discussions in later chapters of the book.

In summary the ideal or 'excellent' practitioner will be able to manage the complex, dynamic context and functions of their organisation as they will possess the cognitive, technical, social and communication skills to gain the confidence of colleagues from other sectors and functions. They will facilitate communication within their organisation, as well as with external publics; they will be able to advise senior management using their higher-level skills as well as oversee more detailed hands-on activity (not least because they will have a clear understanding of relevant theories and their value to practice); they will be committed to lifelong learning and continual professional development, as well as being active in the professional body; and they will also educate others about the value of PR and communications and in this way help reinforce the position of public relations and strategic communication as a viable and valued profession. In essence the message to all is clear, 'be professional'.

References

Allen, T. D., & Eby, L. T. (Eds.) (2010). *The Blackwell Handbook of Mentoring: A Multiple Perspectives Approach.* Malden, MA: Blackwell.

Anderson-Gough, F., Grey, C., & Robson, K. (2006). Professionals, networking and the networked professional. In R. Greenwood & R. Suddaby (Eds.), *Professional Service Firms* (pp. 231–256). Bingley: Emerald

Bartram, D. (2012). *The SHL Universal Competency Framework.* Retrieved from http://www.assessmentanalytics.com/wp-content/uploads/2013/08/White-Paper-SHL-Universal-Competency-Framework.pdf

Boyatzis, R. E. (1982). *The Competent Manager: A Model for Effective Performance.* New York, NY: John Wiley & Sons.

Cooper, D. E. (2004). *Ethics for Professionals in a Multicultural World.* Upper Saddle River, NJ: Pearson Education.

Friday, A., Friday, S., & Green, A. (2004). A reconceptualization of mentoring and sponsoring. *Management Decisions, 42*(5), 628–644.

Giddens, A. (1991). *Modernity and Self-Identity.* Cambridge, MA: Polity Press.

Goodman, M. B. (2006). Corporate communication practice and pedagogy at the dawn of the new millennium. *Corporate Communications: An International Journal, 11*(3), 196–213.

Gregory, A. (2008). Competencies of senior communication practitioners in the UK: An initial study. *Public Relations Review, 34*(3), 215–223.

Hanlon, G. (1994). *The Commercialization of Accountancy: Flexible Accumulation and the Transformation of the Service Class.* London: Macmillan.

Hanlon, G. (1998). Professionalism as enterprise: Service class politics and the redefinition of professionalism. *Sociology, 32*(1), 43–63.

Hunt, D., & Michael, C. (1983). Mentorship: A career training and development tool. *Academy of Management Review, 8*(3), 475–485.

Jeffrey, L. M., & Brunton, M. A. (2011). Developing a framework for communication management competencies. *Journal of Vocational Education and Training, 63*(1), 57–75.

Katz, D., & Kahn, R. L. (1978). *The Social Psychology of Organizations* (2nd ed.). New York, NY: John Wiley & Sons.

Kiesenbauer, J., Burkert, A., & Zerfass, A. (2015). Mentoring in public relations: An international study on mentoring programmes of professional associations. In A. Catellani, A. Zerfass, & R. Tench (Eds.), *Communication Ethics in a Connected World* (pp. 367–390). Brussels: P.I.E. Peter Lang.

Ouchi, W. (1980). Markets, bureaucracies and clans. *Administrative Science Quarterly, 25*(1), 129–142.

Proctor, R. W., & Duttan, A. (1995). *Skill Acquisition and Human Performance.* London: Sage.

PRSA Public Relations Society of America (1999). *A Port of Entry.* New York, NY: PRSA.

PRSA Public Relations Society of America (2006). *The Professional Bond.* New York, NY: PRSA.

Seibert, S., Kraimer, M., & Liden, R. (2001). A social capital theory of career success. *Academy of Management Journal, 44*(2), 219–237.

Simonetti, J. L., Arris, S., & Martinez, J. (1999). Through the top with mentoring. *Business Horizons, 42*(6), 56–62.

Szyszka, P. (1995). Öffentlichkeitsarbeit und Kompetenz: Probleme und Perspektiven künftiger Bildungsarbeit. In G. Bentele & P. Szyszka (Eds.), *PR-Ausbildung in Deutschland* (pp. 317–342). Opladen: Westdeutscher Verlag.

Tench, R., Zerfass, A., Verhoeven, P., Verčič, D., Moreno, A., & Okay, A. (2013a). *Communication Management Competencies for European Practitioners.* Leeds: Leeds Metropolitan University.

Tench, R., Zerfass, A., Verhoeven, P., Verčič, D., Moreno, A., & Okay, A. (2013b). *Competencies and Role Requirements of Communication Professionals in Europe. Insights from Quantitative and Qualitative Studies. ECOPSI Research Project.* Leeds: Leeds Metropolitan University.

Tench, R., & Moreno, A. (2015). Mapping communication management competencies for European practitioners: ECOPSI an EU study. *Journal of Communication Management, 19*(1), 39–61.

Tench, R., Laville, L., & Kiesenbauer, J. (2016). Exploring the magic of mentoring; Career planning for the public relations profession. In P. S. Brønn, S. Romenti, & A. Zerfass (Eds.), *The Management Game of Communication* (pp. 205–223). Bingley: Emerald.

Winterton, J., Delamare-Le Deist, F., & Stringfellow, E. (2005). *Typology of Knowledge, Skills and Competences: Clarification of the Concept and Prototype.* Thessaloniki: CEDEFOP.

Zerfass, A., Verhoeven, P., Tench, R., Moreno, A., & Verčič, D. (2011). *European Communication Monitor 2011. Empirical Insights into Strategic Communication in Europe. Results of an Empirical Survey in 43 Countries.* Brussels: EACD/ EUPRERA.

Zerfass, A., Verčič, D., Verhoeven, P., Moreno, A., & Tench, R. (2012). *European Communication Monitor 2012: Challenges and Competencies for Strategic Communication: Results of an Empirical Survey in 42 Countries.* Brussels: EACD/EUPRERA.

Zerfass, A., Tench, R., Verčič, D., Verhoeven, P., & Moreno, A. (2014). *European Communication Monitor 2014. Excellence in Strategic Communication – Key Issues, Leadership, Gender and Mobile Media. Results of a Survey in 42 Countries.* Brussels: EACD, EUPRERA, Helios Media.

Zerfass, A., Verhoeven, P., Moreno, A., Tench, R., & Verčič, D. (2016). *European Communication Monitor 2016. Exploring Trends in Big Data, Stakeholder Engagement and Strategic Communication. Results of a Survey in 43 Countries.* Brussels: EACD/EUPRERA, Quadriga Media Berlin.

Commandment 8
Linked: People, Media and Networks

We all love to be connected. Today we are saturated with opportunities to make friends, meet up with colleagues, find new partners and search for old ones. It is surprising we can keep any relationships as we solicit, pursue, build, relocate and re-establish numerous individual and group relationships. And this is just in our private lives. As communicators we then overlay this with professional work contacts, which spread and grow particularly over social media platforms. But it has always been this way for the professional communicator with a journalistic lineage to the 'contacts' book. So how does this play out in today's world? And, explicitly, in the contemporary communication department? How do the best communicators within these excellent departments manage relationships? In this chapter we explore the challenges of what we discuss as the key criteria of excellence in this eighth commandment: be intricately *linked* both inside and outside the organisation.

Communication Work: From Operations to Coaching

Our findings and discussion over the past decade from the European Communication Monitor have suggested that professional communication, public relations and strategic communication, involves embracing the total life experience of organisations. We not only use communication to orient in time and space (listening), we use it to influence the world around us

© The Author(s) 2017
R. Tench et al., *Communication Excellence*,
DOI 10.1007/978-3-319-48860-8_8

(messaging). Communication is the all-encompassing dynamic both within the organisation and the societies we inhabit: we live in communication, we use communication and we are constituted in and through communication: our identities, images and reputations are communicatively constructed. That makes professional communication different to other management functions such as finance or human resources (HR).

As we have seen in Commandment 6, 'Strategised: Informed, Anticipatory and Trusted', the professional communication function in contemporary organisations exhibits three aspects (performance function, management function and second-order management function).[1] The empirical data from our surveys reveal that these roles, as described on an organisational level, translate into the time an individual communication professional spent on different activities.[2] The majority of time (36.2 per cent, in 2016) is spent on operational communication (talking to colleagues and media representatives, writing texts, organising events, monitoring media). The second largest chunk of time goes into management (planning, organising, leading staff, budgeting).

As part of this leading role within the organisation we note an interesting evolutionary contribution with quite a significant chunk of top practitioners' time spent working with other colleagues in the organisation enabling them to support performance. This supporting role is an interesting broader contribution of the communicator as they go well beyond the performance function of the communicator to support others through coaching, training, consulting and generally and broadly enabling other members of the organisation (see Fig. 29). Communicators, we suggest, are advising and enabling top executives and other members of the organisation in the field of media and communication but other support is provided as communicators act more and more often as 'active agents in the communication area of a company', effectively much broader than just the day-to-day delivery of communication outputs.

Communication: High Tech *and* High Touch

The availability of ten years of data has enabled us to see how things are changing in the way communication professionals in Europe use different communication channels. Analysing 13,709 responses on these issues that we have collected

---

[1] Nothhaft (2010).
[2] Zerfass et al. (2016), pp. 42–50.

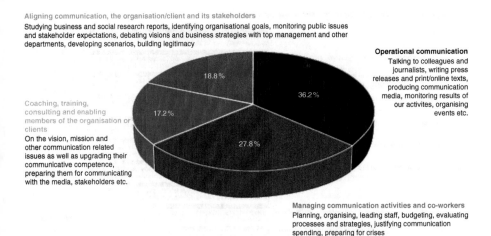

Aligning communication, the organisation/client and its stakeholders
Studying business and social research reports, identifying organisational goals, monitoring public issues and stakeholder expectations, debating visions and business strategies with top management and other departments, developing scenarios, building legitimacy

Operational communication
Talking to colleagues and journalists, writing press releases and print/online texts, producing communication media, monitoring results of our activites, organising events etc.

Coaching, training, consulting and enabling members of the organisation or clients
On the vision, mission and other communication related issues as well as upgrading their communicative competence, preparing them for communicating with the media, stakeholders etc.

Managing communication activities and co-workers
Planning, organising, leading staff, budgeting, evaluating processes and strategies, justifying communication spending, preparing for crises

Fig. 29 How communication professionals spend their productive time at work[3]

since 2007, we can observe how some of them gained and some lost in importance over time. As we saw in Commandment 2, 'Mediatised: Media All Around Us', only a minority of communication professionals rated social media as important between 2007 and 2011. This has clearly changed. Interestingly in this technologically changing landscape is that face-to-face communication is the most relevant instrument today, taking the top position in Europe for the first time in ten years of data. Face-to-face communication is more important in Europe than in the rest of the world, where social media (in Asia Pacific) or online communication (in Latin America) are considered (slightly) more important. In contrast traditional media relations with print media is on the decline in Europe, but not in other parts of the world (see Fig. 30).

It seems clear that contemporary and future professional communication is high tech communication. But, at the same time, as we also see the rising importance of face-to-face communication. Professional communication is emerging not only as high tech communication, it is simultaneously high tech *and* high touch communication. One-to-one communication is surpassing mass media communication in both physical and virtual worlds.

---

[3] Zerfass et al. (2016), p. 44. n = 2,710 communication professionals across Europe. Q: Please think about how you spend most of your time at work. Please divide your productive time spent at work (values should add up to 100 per cent). In a typical week, I spend the following amount of time with . . . figure displays median for each item; values have been rounded based on mean values.

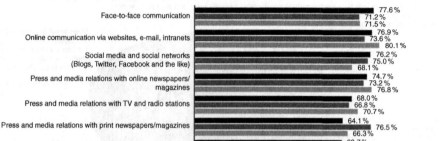

Fig. 30 Relevance of communication channels in Europe, Asia-Pacific and Latin America[4]

Coaching, Advising and Enabling Others to Communicate

Our empirical data also reveal that communicators employ different practices of coaching, advising or enabling when they support either senior managers or other staff.[5] The most important activity when working with executives is delivering insights for decision-making (agreed by 71.9 per cent of the respondents), followed by advice on how to handle concrete challenges in communication (68.7 per cent). Less than half of the communicators state that they enable their executives to master communicative challenges on their own. Co-workers and other staff most often receive hands-on advice about communication tasks (65.2 per cent).

Not surprisingly, the needs of executives and traditional ways of support are shaping the field. However, enabling others to reflect and communicate themselves is clearly an important part of the practice today. It reflects the growing need to deal with multiple voices in strategic communication (Fig. 31).[6]

---

[4] Zerfass et al. (2016), p. 63, n = 2,583 communication professionals across Europe; Macnamara et al. (2015), n = 1,148 communication professionals across Asia-Pacific; Moreno et al. (2015), n = 803 communication professionals across Latin America. Q: How important are the following methods in addressing stakeholders, gatekeepers and audiences today? Scale 1 (not important) – 5 (very important). Percentages: frequency based on scale points 4–5. Overall evaluation based on 4,534 respondents in 84 countries.

[5] Zerfass et al. (2016), pp. 51–53.

[6] Zerfass and Viertmann (2016).

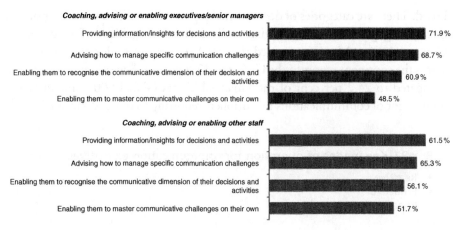

Coaching, advising or enabling executives/senior managers

Providing information/insights for decisions and activities — 71.9%

Advising how to manage specific communication challenges — 68.7%

Enabling them to recognise the communicative dimension of their decision and activities — 60.9%

Enabling them to master communicative challenges on their own — 48.5%

Coaching, advising or enabling other staff

Providing information/insights for decisions and activities — 61.5%

Advising how to manage specific communication challenges — 65.3%

Enabling them to recognise the communicative dimension of their decisions and activities — 56.1%

Enabling them to master communicative challenges on their own — 51.7%

Fig. 31 How communication professionals coach, advise and enable peers and superiors[7]

For communication management the route to professionalisation seems to be linked to boardroom acceptance, 'empowerment legitimacy is dependent on attitudes of senior executives'.[8] This view appears to be embedded in public relations theory: 'degrees of influence are also leading factors in chief executive officer's (CEO's) decision to grant a role within dominant coalition'.[9] It seems the acceptance of communicators has less to do with legislation and established practice and more to do with social capital of the individual: 'Having extended personalised networks of influence is an asset for a career conscious PR practitioner'.[10] In other words, who you know! So being linked is once again underlined.

The skills and attributes that CEOs are looking for in their top communications executives have expanded. Experience in communications is taken for granted, and not considered enough anymore. CEOs want communication executives who are business 'savvy', with a deep understanding of their companies from top to bottom. CEOs also want communications chiefs to be proficient in three key modes of operation – reactive, proactive and interactive (see Box 37). CEOs see their communications chief as a critical part of their team, and across the

---

[7] Zerfass et al. (2016), p. 51. n^{min} = 1,907 communication professionals who spend at least 10 per cent of their time for coaching, training, consulting and enabling. Q: When you coach, advise or enable executives/senior managers or other members of your organisation/client, how often do you practice the following activities? Scale 1 (not at all) – 5 (very often) for both categories. Percentages: frequency based on scale points 4–5.

[8] Johansson and Ottestig (2011), p. 164.

[9] Valentini (2010), p. 158.

[10] Valentini (2010), p. 160.

board. There are categories of decision-making in which CEOs would consider it grossly negligent not to have that individual at the table.[11] The European Communication Monitor revealed that 59.9 per cent of senior communicators across the continent report to the CEO and 17.8 per cent have a seat on the board, compared to 24.2 per cent of the Financial Times Global 500 companies and 45 per cent of communications practitioners reporting to the CEO in the USA.[12]

> **Box 37 Key modes of operation for communication executives**
> - Reactive
> - Proactive
> - Interactive

From these studies it seems that European communication practitioners are better aligned and represented in the organisation than their colleagues in the United States. Our survey data from 2016 show that excellent communication departments are aligned to the executive board with 39.5 per cent acting as members of the executive board and a further 54.5 per cent reporting directly to the CEO or the highest decision maker (see Fig. 32). Research into the CEOs' view on public relations in the United Kingdom indicated that a valued practitioner understands the organisational context, stakeholder requirements, the business model and organisational drivers and has the confidence to challenge. However CEOs recognise they 'under-invest in PR and that if there were the right measures to evaluate its contribution, they would spend more'.[13] While the profession has come a long way in ten years it is still considered a soft discipline, rather than a core discipline for many organisations.

The Communication Practitioner as 'Communicator'

The drive to get on the board of directors is also connected to the desire to be taken seriously. There is some success in this area. For instance all top companies in Europe have corporate communication departments. The question is: how much authority do they have within those companies? Past surveys have suggested that while most reported directly to the chief

---

[11] Arthur W. Page Society (2008).
[12] Arthur W. Page Society (2008).
[13] Gregory (2011), p. 99.

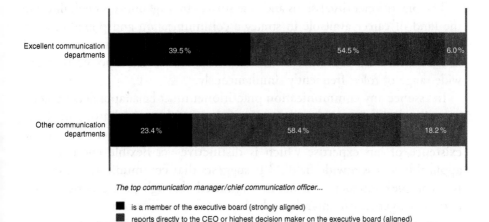

The top communication manager/chief communication officer...

■ is a member of the executive board (strongly aligned)
■ reports directly to the CEO or highest decision maker on the executive board (aligned)
■ does not report directly to the CEO or highest decision maker (weakly aligned)

Fig. 32 Alignment of excellent communication departments to the executive board[14]

executive, many failed to get the attention of the board. Previous evidence from the United Kingdom in the early years of the millennium suggested about a third of communications people sat on their company executive committees and none on the board.[15] The UK's Public Relations Consultants Association's (PRCA) In House Benchmark Report, 2014, however, reported a year-on-year healthy increase of representations at senior management/board level, from 72 per cent to 77 per cent which is a great improvement from the early years of the new millennium.[16] Currently we are seeing improvement across Europe to these figures for those departments operating at the highest level of excellence.

Other evidence suggests a flourishing time ahead for public relations. For example, PR was considered the best return on investment by entrepreneurs in a survey for the *Financial Times* in 2004, and in 2014 Forbes.com reported that 'In today's socially connected world, public relations is more important than ever before'.[17]

---

[14] Zerfass et al. (2016), p. 116. n = 1,504 communication professionals working in communication departments across Europe. Q: Within your organisation, the top communication manager or chief communication officer . . . is a member of the executive board (strongly aligned)/reports directly to the CEO or highest decision maker on the executive board (aligned)/does not report directly to the CEO or highest decision maker (weakly aligned). Highly significant differences (Kendall rank correlation, $p \leq 0.01$, τ = 0.169).

[15] Watson and Sreedharan (2010).

[16] PRCA (2014).

[17] Pozin (2014), p. 1.

The practitioner discussions and case studies throughout this book illustrate the kind of career available in strategic communication and public relations and the richness (and challenge) of the communicator's role at a senior level. As evidence the professional communicator is frequently expected to play a wide range of roles, frequently simultaneously.

In essence any communication practitioner must be adaptable, energetic, versatile, diplomatic and resilient to get along with a mixed group of clients and stakeholder groups. In literature this is sometimes referred to as the existence of 'an expertise which is distinctive yet flexible enough to be applicable across a wide field'.[18] It suggests that communication expertise is a complex interactive structure organised through past experience and current exigencies (demands), which modifies itself through action. This perspective would suggest that there is no one paradigm or template for the role but that it is a dynamic process created through the interface of our past and our interactions with the present.

So, is the communicator a contemporary super(wo)man? Findings from our survey and discussions suggest that some practitioners may exaggerate their contribution, particularly consultants. For example early data showed that 83 per cent of respondents working in consultancies thought that they were used for strategic and/or market insight/experience. However only 41.6 per cent of their clients agreed.[19] As we have seen in Commandment 4, 'Embedded: Influence Through Communicative Leadership', the influence of communication departments has continued to increase in the last decade as perceived by the individual professionals.

Networking for Excellent Communicators

Networking is another one of the buzzwords in professional life. Networking is seen as important and often communication professionals are looked at as experts on it. Networking is communicating. Networks indeed are relevant for communicators both formal (via professional body membership, structured events and invitations to join organised networks) and informal (based on serendipity, irregular meetings, personal and professional activities and relationships). A vast majority of communication practitioners think that networking is important for career progression and

---

[18] Pieczka (2002), pp. 321–322.
[19] Zerfass et al. (2008), pp. 61–62.

personal development.[20] This supports previous claims that 'having extended personalised networks of influence is an asset for a career conscious PR practitioner'.[21] At the same time, networks are also important for reaching business and communication goals of the organisation. There are clearly mixed motives behind many networking activities.

Obviously, networking cannot be reduced to personal interactions in a world shaped by multiple stakeholder relationships, globalisation and mediatisation. Social media offers new opportunities.[22] But concerns about privacy and information security have raised doubts about the suitability of those platforms in professional environments. Communication professionals prefer email as a preferred form of networking followed by social media and face-to-face interactions. However and supporting the literature, different types of networks are being used depending on age and gender. Female communicators identify email as the most prevalent while their male counterparts also use email but have higher responses than their female colleagues for face-to-face and use of the phone. Higher-level, more senior managers prefer face-to-face networking. There are interesting differences in how networking practices are perceived. When compared with the phone and social media, face-to-face is seen as the most professional, trustworthy and productive form by the majority of respondents. Almost everyone supports face-to-face as generating trust in network relationships, which is important and is supported by theoretical discussions of this key benefit of face-to-face networks.[23]

There are regional differences, too. Networking through social media is practised most often in Finland, the United Kingdom, and Norway. Email is more relevant in parts of Eastern and Southern Europe (Russia, Croatia, Spain) as well as in Belgium. Germans are significantly more geared to the phone than peers in other parts of Western and Northern Europe. While only one-tenth of professionals use the phone as their primary networking tool, a clear majority state that using the phone is the most formal and time-efficient form of networking.

What about social media and networking? Facebook is often featured as a key social media tool when reaching out for stakeholders and public debates. However, we determined that other platforms are better suited to professional networking. Business communities such as Linkedin, Xing or Viadeo are rated most important and really stand out as the social networking tools.

---

[20] Zerfass et al. (2014), pp. 60–71.
[21] Valentini (2010), p. 156.
[22] Zerfass et al. (2014), pp. 63–71.
[23] Giddens (1991).

Twitter, blogs, Facebook and Google+ are a different group of networking tools and considered less important than communities. However, there are real age differences between the different tools. For example Facebook is preferred by younger practitioners while those in their 30s are more closely engaged with Twitter as a social media networking platform of choice.

Recent work studied the role of social media in informal mentoring and how social media networking may enable a perceived similarity between protégé and mentor to be more easily achieved.[24] The ease of self-disclosure and the nonintrusive nature of computer-mediated communication may make finding like-minded people more effective. Although their findings related to variables of attitude and self-disclosure to determine behavioural intent they did reveal that seeking a mentor who is similar to oneself in terms of self-disclosure on the Internet may result in overcoming the lack of similarity in the mentoring relationship. As discussed women value social media and social online networks more than men, a point supported by Piet Verhoeven and Noelle Aarts, who stated that 'females value social media significantly more than the males for interactive communication like dialoguing, establishing relationships and exploring digital cultures . . . this could be a way for women to empower themselves and increase their self-perception of effectiveness'.[25]

Commandments in Practice: Linked

Global Communications in a Networked Organisation

KPMG member firms operate in 155 countries around the world and collectively employ more and 174,000 people working in auditing, tax and advisory. All firms commit themselves to a common set of KPMG values and must abide by quality

---

[24] For example, see Lee and Jeong (2014).
[25] Verhoeven and Aarts (2010), n.p.

standards governing how they operate and how they provide services to clients. KPMG International acts as the coordinating entity for this global network of member firms.

The role of Global Communications within such a network is subtly different from a similarly sized corporate business. Perhaps the most obvious difference is that the national heads of communication, located within each member firm, do not report directly to the Head of Global Communications. Their programmes, priorities and budget are set by their respective member firm.

Discussing how he manages the coordinating role for KPMG across so many country contexts, Brian Bannister commented:

> As Head of Global Communications I lead a team of around 40 professionals working across internal and external communications. This small, global, communications team is a very small part of the broader group of communication professionals working within KPMG's 155 member firms.
>
> My role is to develop and implement a global communications plan for KPMG which connects member firms and their plans with our global business strategy. I need to co-ordinate and cajole, to ensure that the sum of all the network's communications adds up to more than the constituent parts. This is an iterative process, it involves lots of dialogue and collective planning, to develop a common communications plan for the wider network.
>
> Ours is a complex, matrixed, organisation. Individuals within the Global Communication Team can support a number of different parts of the business, whether that be a function (such as Audit, Tax or Advisory Services), an industry or sector (such as Cyber) or a specific geography or region.
>
> As global communicators we are charged with supporting the implementation of a globally agreed business plan which has been shaped with significant input from member firms. In practice that means we start from the premise that our global communication priorities are understood and agreed by our member firms. From a global standpoint I need to make sure that this global program is shared with national heads of communication in a way that allows them to connect the global plan with their national communication plans.
>
> To achieve this goal I host an annual planning meeting attended by the majority of these heads of communication to scope out the year ahead. We supplement this yearly meeting with monthly planning calls where we focus on the key campaigns, projects and issues in play for the coming four weeks.
>
> In part Global Communications plays the part of air traffic controller for the various global and national programs coming to market, ensuring that the sequencing is managed to optimise impact and avoiding the risk of competing or conflicting campaigns and messaging going to market at the same time.
>
> One important way we connect the wider KPMG network is through global measurement and monitoring to assess the impact of communications around the world, for example in terms of global media evaluation. The results of this measurement gives national heads of communication the chance to benchmark their media impact with other, similar, member firms and drives a very healthy dialogue and cross-fertilisation of thinking about team structure, priorities and campaign activation.
>
> I began by saying that the role of a global communications function in a professional services network is, in some ways, different from an equivalently sized global

corporation. It may be, however, the focus we have on staying connected is very similar, and the difference might well be more in the way that we set up to achieve that ambition in a more federal, networked, business and organisational model.

Brian Bannister
Brian Bannister is the Global Head of Communications for KPMG International, based in London in the United Kingdom. He is responsible for the network's global profile and communications.

About KPMG International
KPMG is a global network of professional services firms providing Audit, Tax and Advisory services. The company operates in 155 countries and has 174,000 people working in member firms around the world. The independent member firms of the KPMG network are affiliated with KPMG International Cooperative ('KPMG International'), a Swiss entity. Each KPMG firm is a legally distinct and separate entity and describes itself as such.

Relationship Between Agencies and Clients

The use of agencies, consultancies and freelance practitioners is a common practice in communication management. Findings from the monitor survey verify this practice across all types of organisations in Europe.[26] Most of all the communication departments work on an ongoing basis with multiple agencies. In fact only one in five organisations (20.7 per cent) do not work with outside agencies at all, and 13.8 per cent of organisations work on an ongoing basis with a single 'agency of record'. However, communication departments and agencies have very different perceptions of why they work together. While both sides are close on the need to integrate creativity and use additional 'arms and legs', there are wide misperceptions on the side of agencies that they are more often employed for expertise; strategic insight; objective, independent counsel; their ability to understand and explain communication trends and new instruments; and being able to support in explaining communication strategies to top executives.

In summary the agencies are more optimistic about their overall value and contribution to the client organisations when compared with the clients' own responses (see Fig. 33). There are also wide differences in assessing reasons for agency-client conflicts. While clients see the main reason for conflicts originating in the lack of knowledge of the client's business and processes (62.3 per cent), only one in five respondents on the agency side see this as a problem (21.0 per cent).

---

[26] Zerfass et al. (2015), pp. 82–95.

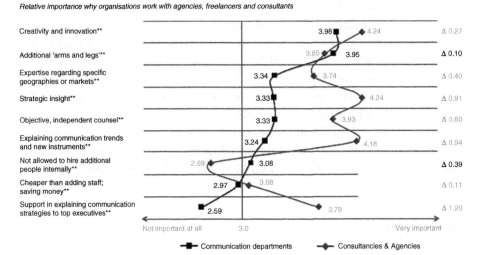

Relative importance why organisations work with agencies, freelancers and consultants

Fig. 33 Reasons for cooperation: different perceptions between clients and agencies[27]

On the other hand, nearly three quarters of agency respondents named unclear objectives and expectations as the main reason for conflicts (73.0 per cent), while only a third of respondents from the client side see this as a major reason (33.3 per cent). Obviously each side blames the other one for conflicts.

How to be Linked

We have discussed in this chapter the characteristics displayed by the high-performance departments and individuals and how they reflect their interconnectedness both inside and outside the organisation and crucially the role that interpersonal relationships play. This 'ideal' excellent communications practitioner will be able to manage the complex, dynamic context and functions of their organisation as they will possess the cognitive, technical, social and communication skills to gain the confidence of colleagues from other sectors and functions. They will facilitate communication within their organisation, as

---

[27] Zerfass et al. (2015), p. 89. n = 1,277 communication professionals working in communication departments and n = 652 communication professionals working in agencies and consultancies. Q: Why does your organisation work with agencies, freelancers and communication consultants? Q: Why does your average client work with agencies, freelancers and communication consultants? Scale 1 (not important at all) – 5 (very important). Mean values. ** Highly significant differences (one-sample t-test, $p \leq 0.01$). * Significant differences (one-sample t-test, $p \leq 0.05$).

well as with external publics; they will be able to advise senior management using their higher-level skills as well as oversee more detailed hands-on activity (not least because they will have a clear understanding of relevant theories and their value to practice); they will be committed to lifelong learning and continual professional development, as well as being active in the professional body; and they will also educate others about the value of strategic communication and in therefore help reinforce the professionalisation of the practice.

These statements and ambitions are not pipe dreams, they are based on the evidence we have observed from those high-performing communication departments and individuals. We just need more communicators to follow suit.

References

Arthur W. Page Society (2008). *The Authentic Enterprise*. New York: Arthur W. Page Society.

Giddens, A. (1991). *Modernity and Self-Identity*. Cambridge, MA: Polity Press.

Gregory, A. (2011). The state of the public relations profession in the UK: A review of the first decade of the twenty-first century. *Corporate Communications: An International Journal*, 16(2), 89–104.

Johansson, C., & Ottestig, A. T. (2011). Communication executives in a changing world: Legitimacy beyond organizational borders. *Journal of Communication Management*, 15(2), 144–164.

Lee, J. S., & Jeong, B. (2014). Having mentors and campus social networks moderates the impact of worries and video gaming on depressive symptoms: A moderated mediation analysis. *BMC Public Health*, 14(1), 426.

Macnamara, J., Lwin, M. O., Adi, A., & Zerfass, A. (2015). *Asia-Pacific Communication Monitor 2015/16. The State of Strategic Communication and Public Relations in a Region of Rapid Growth. Survey Results From 23 Countries*. Hong Kong: APACD.

Moreno, A., Molleda, J. C., Athaydes, A., & Suárez, A. M. (2015). *Latin American Communication Monitor 2015. Excelencia en comunicación estratégica, trabajo en la era digital, social media y profesionalización. Resultados de una encuesta en 18 países*. Brussels: EUPRERA.

Nothhaft, H. (2010). Communication management as a second order management function. Roles and function of the communicative executive: Results from a shadowing study. *Journal of Communication Management*, 14(2), 127–140.

Pieczka, M. (2002). Public relations expertise deconstructed. *Media Culture and Society*, 24(3), 301–323.

Pozin, I. (2014). 5 measurements for PR ROI. *Forbes.com*. Retrieved from http://www.forbes.com/sites/ilyapozin/2014/05/29/5-measurements-for-pr-roi/#4c78d54b1ca2.

PRCA Public Relations Consultants Association (2014). *In House Benchmark Report 2014.* London: PRCA.

Valentini, C. (2010). Personalised networks of influence in public relations. *Journal of Communication Management, 14*(2), 153–166.

Verhoeven, P., & Aarts, N. (2010). How European public relations men and women perceive the impact of their professional activities. *PRism, 7*(4), 1–15.

Watson, T., & Sreedharan, C. (2010). The senior communicator of the future – competencies and training needs. In M. D. Dodd & K. Yamamura (Eds.), *Ethical Issues for Public Relations Practice in a Multicultural World, 13th International Public Relations Research Conference* (pp. 889–897). Gainesville, FL: Institute for Public Relations.

Zerfass, A., Moreno, A., Tench, R., Verčič, D., & Verhoeven, P. (2008). *European Communication Monitor 2008. Trends in Communication Management and Public Relations – Results and Implications.* Brussels, Leipzig: University of Leipzig/ EUPRERA.

Zerfass, A., Tench, R., Verčič, D., Verhoeven, P., & Moreno, A. (2014). *European Communication Monitor 2014. Excellence in Strategic Communication – Key Issues, Leadership, Gender and Mobile Media. Results of a Survey in 42 Countries.* Brussels: EACD/EUPRERA, Helios Media.

Zerfass, A., Verčič, D., Verhoeven, P., Moreno, A., & Tench, R. (2015). *European Communication Monitor 2015. Creating Communication Value Through Listening, Messaging and Measurement. Results of a Survey in 41 Countries.* Brussels: EACD/ EUPRERA, Helios Media.

Zerfass, A., Verhoeven, P., Moreno, A., Tench, R., & Verčič, D. (2016). *European Communication Monitor 2016. Exploring Trends in Big Data, Stakeholder Engagement and Strategic Communication. Results of a Survey in 43 Countries.* Brussels: EACD/EUPRERA, Quadriga Media Berlin.

Zerfass, A., & Viertmann, C. (2016). Multiple voices in corporations and the challenge for strategic communication. In K. Alm, M. Brown, & S. Royseng (Eds.), *Kommunkasjon og ytringsfrihet i organisasjoner* (pp. 44–63). Oslo: Cappelen Damm.

Commandment 9
Solid: Strong, Sensitive and Savvy

Personal solidity, with all its ups and downs, is one of the storylines in the famous Danish television series *Borgen*. The series revolves around the female Danish Prime Minister Birgitte Nyborg, her 'spin doctor' Kasper Juul and Katrine Fonsmark, the anchorwoman of the most important Danish news show. These three characters symbolise politics, public relations and journalism, the tension between those fields and what these interrelationships can do to people personally. The importance of personal solidity and what it entails becomes clearer and clearer in the course of the series' 30 episodes. In one episode, for example, Birgitte Nyborg fired her spokesman Kasper Juul and replaced him with the highly educated professor of rhetoric Tore Gudme, to handle the press. That did not go very well. Why not? Because Tore delivered 'tone-deaf, elitist responses' to the media.[1] He lacked a feeling for journalistic reasoning and media dynamics. He lacked the critical savviness and antennae for public opinion. Birgitte quickly rehired the experienced 'professional' Kasper Juul.

The Borgen example shows that working in strategic communication requires extensive knowledge of communication theory and media but also a solid sensitivity to other social, political and interpersonal dynamics with their related tensions and how to manage them.

Our final commandment for the book's series of nine is, therefore *solid*. By this we mean having explicit individual solidity driven by personal,

---

[1] See the Borgen website at https://www.dr.dk/tv/se/borgen and https://en.wikipedia.org/wiki/List_of_Borgen_episodes.

© The Author(s) 2017
R. Tench et al., *Communication Excellence*,
DOI 10.1007/978-3-319-48860-8_9

organisational and professional ethics and frameworks as well as exploring issues of pluralism and diversity in the workplace to facilitate and deliver the satisfaction our framework calls for. Before drawing conclusions about solidity let's first take a look at three aspects of it: the forgotten skill of listening, ethics and gender.

Commandments in Practice: Solid

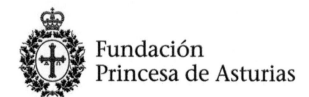
Fundación
Princesa de Asturias

Communication Practitioners Striving for Excellence Help to Reposition the Organisation

The Princess of Asturias Foundation is a non-profit private Spanish institution that has granted the Prince of Asturias Awards (now Princess of Asturias Awards) since 1981. Intended to reward scientific, technical, cultural, social and humanitarian work carried out at an international level by individuals or institutions, they are conferred in eight different categories: the Arts, Literature, Social Sciences, Communication and Humanities, Technical and Scientific Research, International Cooperation, Concord and Sports.

The annual presentation ceremony of the Awards is presided over by The King and Queen of Spain. More than 800 journalists from different countries come to Asturias every year to provide media coverage on the cultural events organised around the Awards Ceremony and the ceremony itself. Many of the leading figures of our time have graced the stage of the Campoamor Theatre in Oviedo, the capital of Asturias, to receive the Award: Nelson Mandela, Woody Allen, Mario Vargas Llosa, Martha Nussbaum, Stephen Hawking, Annie Leibovitz, Peter Higgs, Tzvetan Todorov, Susan Sontag, Michael Schumacher, Jürgen Habermas, Sebastian Coe, Howard Gardner and Michael Haneke, among others.

Mindful of the need not to stand apart from the world around us, the Board of Trustees of the Foundation started to work on designing the future of the institution a few years ago. The Trustees realised that the world had changed a great deal since the Foundation was created in 1980: new social changes, different (online) means of communicating our message and values and a new King was expected to assume the throne not many years later. All of these things led to a profound process of change.

The Board decided that the organisation needed to adapt to these new times without losing its essence and that new management dynamics were required. Accordingly, a new director took up the post seven years ago, implementing a more innovative management model, one that is more professionalised and more demanding than the one the institution had followed for the previous 30 years.

Within this context, in 2014 the Foundation underwent its first major transformation since it was created 36 years ago. The then Prince of Asturias was proclaimed King of Spain and his eldest daughter assumed the title of Princess of Asturias. Consequently, the Honorary Presidency of the Foundation is now held by a ten-year-old girl (the Princess of Asturias, Leonor de Borbón).

Rubén Vigil, the Director of Communication and Media Relations, explains the challenge and how it was approached:

We need to rethink how we do things. The main strategic objectives are to generate trust in our institution, engage the public, reinforce our organisation's impact on society, attract young people and increase the impact of the Foundation's activities in the international media. Nevertheless, we are aware that the main value we bring to society is intangible and that prestige must never be equated with impact.

I began working with the Foundation in 2002 and became a member of staff in 2004. I have been Head of the Communications Department since January 2005, supporting the director in the areas of representation and institutional communication, in addition to designing, implementing and assessing the institution's strategic communications. I am also responsible for ensuring the compliance of all in-house media to the corporate identity manual.

Throughout these years of heading the Foundation's Communications Department, I have seen the importance of professional development in order to maintain the high levels of expectation of a job of these characteristics. I regularly take part in different training schemes that allow me to evolve and improve as a professional. I hold a degree in Information Sciences from Salamanca Pontifical University, as well as a European Master's Degree in Conference and Events Organisation from the University of Deusto and an Expert in Protocol qualification from Miguel Hernández University, Spain. More recently, I have been awarded a certificate of completion of the 'Leadership Decision Making: Optimizing Organizational Performance' program by the John F. Kennedy School of Government at Harvard University.

The staff of the Princess of Asturias Foundation's Communications Department is made up of three men and one woman who work for the organisation on a full-time basis. Extra staff are brought in during September in all areas of work to cover the official as well as cultural events organised on the occasion of the Awards Ceremony, which is held in October. For this purpose, I count on a team of more than 20 people in the Communications and Credentials Department to help me with the work.

When building my team of co-workers, I seek to obtain the highest possible professional diversity in the backgrounds of the people I am going to hire. Staff members are skilled in communication and protocol, photography, public relations, journalism, video and social networks and are able to speak some of the following languages: Spanish, English, German, French and Italian. In recent years, we have also introduced hiring policies aimed at integration. We accordingly have someone working with us who belongs to a group in risk of social exclusion.

In addition to the necessary training, in a job such as this, the common factors defining the team are an interest in culture, a strong sense of responsibility at work and attention to detail. The job demands a constant commitment to excellence from everybody so as to minimise the public impact of unforeseen events.

Any gesture or message may give rise to different interpretations due to the links between our institution and the King of Spain as the Head of State. Therefore, self-control and prudence are two fundamental aspects when interacting with others. As a result, the level of pressure and stress experienced over a period of several weeks a year is very high and requires a great deal of self-discipline.

Any communications department knows that it must earn the trust of journalists in order to get support for the messages that matter most to the organisation. Always providing accurate information whilst achieving a balance between maintaining a certain distance and generating trust with the media is vital. Journalists and other media professionals are largely the ones who will act as the chain of transmission of the image we seek to project.

That is no longer enough, however. We are now facing a new context populated by an increasingly educated public that is more demanding about the kind of information it wants to know, less forgiving of any mistakes that may be committed, and whose habits of consuming information seek immediacy. Thus, one of the main tasks of the Communications Department is to identify the perceptions and expectations of key stakeholders. This allows us to adapt messages to the new communication paradigms.

We are aware that we must safeguard the public image of the institution. So we develop strategic communication plans that are very mindful, not only of the opinion that society has of us, but also of the self-evaluation that we ourselves carry out regarding our own work. It is a system of across-the-board active listening that is applied throughout the organisation. Each year, this system allows us to carry out an in-house analysis of all those elements that may be fine-tuned to achieve an even higher degree of excellence. Therefore, in addition to encouraging the participation of the whole team in the development of internal assessment reports, we ask those people who work with us in each edition of our Awards to do the job with a fresh approach, devoid of self-censorship, bringing new ideas that enable greater efficiency in the work we do.

Another part of this active listening system at the Foundation that allows us to establish strategic lines of action is conducting external surveys with the help of consultants. This allows us to focus attention on those areas susceptible to improvement and identify changes in society that may affect us. In this respect, one of the aspects that we have worked on most in recent years is that of transparency. For some time now, there has been a greater demand from society to learn more about what lies behind certain institutions, how they work, the way they are funded, and so on. For this reason, we are currently working on matters of transparency with the aim of being leaders in this field among Spanish foundations. We have likewise introduced new elements in our work, such as the Spanish Association of Foundations and the European Foundation Centre's principles of good practice in this field. At the same time, we are undertaking environmental awareness projects, improving accessibility for disabled people at our events, measuring the impact of our activities and strengthening our international links with our Laureates and other prestigious institutions from all around the world.

An added difficulty is that our message, associated with the highest values, is aimed at a spectrum of the public covering all backgrounds and ages. Also our actions may be interpreted in a way that transcends the institution itself and affects the Head of State. This constitutes a major challenge that we face with both professionalism and rigour.

Rubén Vigil
Rubén Vigil is Head of Communication and Media Relations at the Princess of Asturias Foundation (Fundación Princesa de Asturias) in Oviedo, Spain.

About the Princess of Asturias Foundation
The Princess of Asturias Foundation is a non-profit private institution whose essential aims are to contribute to extolling and promoting those scientific, cultural and humanistic values that form part of the universal heritage of humanity and consolidate the existing links between the Principality of Asturias and the title traditionally held by the heirs to the Crown of Spain. The Foundation's net assets are about 31 million euros; its income comes from donations by the different individuals and institutions that form part of its Board of Trustees and Patrons, revenue from its assets and public grants.

The Forgotten Skill of Listening

For communication professionals listening is a multi-level activity.[2] Multi-level listening has four levels: listening to yourself, listening to co-workers and colleagues, listening to customers and listening to the other stakeholders of the organisation and to society. Part of being solid is to be able to listen well on all these levels. This starts with knowing your own listening style. And, as a practitioner being able to create a good listening climate in your own communication team. Listening to customers requires empathy. Empathy is the skill to sense what others feel and mean, to find out what others really need and to react actively during and after the conversation.[3] Listening to stakeholders and society at large is the fourth level of listening and can prevent conflicts between the organisation and the involved stakeholders. To whom should we listen and when and what shall we do with the information obtained? These are all questions for any professional responsible for creating a culture of listening in and around the organisation. At all levels tests are available to give insights into listening skills and into ways for improving listening capabilities.[4]

According to the International Listening Association (ILA), listening is 'the process of receiving, constructing meaning from and responding to spoken and/or non-verbal messages'.[5] This is a pretty straightforward definition and

---

[2] Siere (2014).
[3] Drollinger et al. (2006).
[4] Siere (2014).
[5] See www.listen.org.

clearly an important part of communication. Still, it is sometimes referred to as 'the forgotten skill'[6] especially in a world saturated with mediatised messages. Audience fragmentation and proliferating media channels and speakers demand more 'work of listening'[7] on all levels. The label of forgotten skill even applies to communication management. Practitioners often argue to their superiors that listening is important and therefore communication is relevant, but listening strategies are often not in place.

According to our empirical data, a vast majority of organisations in Europe have an overall communication strategy and are focused on messaging strategies.[8] A bit more than half of them have also developed an organisational listening strategy. The most active listeners are joint stock and private companies and the least are governmental organisations. There are also significant differences between countries, organisations in countries in Southern and Western Europe more often have listening strategies in place than organisations in Eastern and Northern Europe.

For the most part listening is limited to media and issue monitoring in the broadest sense of the word. Dialogues and specific research on stakeholders are much less practised. Furthermore not many professionals have listening tasks in their official job description or have them ascribed as an explicit objective for the communication department. It is clear from the findings of the Monitor that joint stock companies lead the way in the practice of organisational listening. That is probably because their publicly traded stocks can be sensitive to the dynamics of opinion formation among shareholders, investors, the media and the public.

Organisational listening is perceived as a task for the communication department. About a fifth of them can be labelled as listening-minded and being well ahead of the rest. They are better in contributing to overall objectives of the organisation by identifying opportunities. Also they are better able to explain the benefits of listening and therefore the value of communication. This leading group made listening an explicit objective for the communication function and part of the communicators' job description. They conduct stakeholder research and dialogue on a regular basis and pay more attention to issues monitoring and management. This relatively small group of pioneers shows that systematic listening is an important part of communication and can enhance the value of

---

[6] Burley-Allen (1995).

[7] Macnamara (2013, 2016).

[8] Zerfass et al. (2015), pp. 58–69.

communication in the organisation. Good multi-level listening skills therefore definitely contribute to being a solid professional (see Box 38).

> **Box 38 What we have learned from excellent departments concerning listening**
>
> Excellent communication departments:
>
> - Illustrate the benefits of listening to stakeholders and identify opportunities.
> - Implement listening strategies more often (like defining contact points for collecting feedback, instruments to listen to stakeholders, to monitor discussions, to initiate dialogue and integrate the knowledge gained).
> - Are forerunners in listening to stakeholders.
> - Use a greater number of techniques as well as applying more advanced modes of listening.
> - More often have listening tasks as part of the personal job description of communicators.

The New Relevance of Ethics

In an era of banking scandals, personal and corporate tax avoidance and evasion, like anyone else, communication professionals sometimes face situations where particular activities might be legally acceptable, but challenging from a moral point of view.[9] In our 2012 survey six out of ten communication professionals in Europe reported that they had encountered such situations in their daily work over the past year and more than one third of the respondents experienced several ethical challenges.[10] The ECM data suggest that, year-on-year, ethical issues are becoming more relevant again. For the profession ethics have always been an issue, if not at the front than at the background of it. The profession and practitioners are used to being criticised about their ethics or ethics being ignored. Perceived as sinners, downright impostors who try to deceive the public and society for the benefit of organisations or saints that only communicate dialogically and symmetrical.[11] Perceived as cultural and ethical relativists that set their sails to every wind,[12] proclaim that perception is all there is,[13] or caught between

---

[9] Bowen (2010); Bentele (2015).

[10] Zerfass et al. (2012), pp. 18–35.

[11] Fawkes (2012).

[12] Pearson (1989).

[13] Brown (2012).

relativist and universal values,[14] the profession has sought several solutions for the dilemma's and criticism, for example, by looking for ethical communication *processes* instead of content.[15] In practice though ethics in organisations are often driven by compliance and transparency rules.

The European Communication Monitor data demonstrate high levels of awareness of ethical problems in the world of strategic communication.[16] Professionals working in governmental relations, lobbying, public affairs, as well as in online communication and social media encounter the most ethical challenges. Two-thirds of them face such problems at least once a year. Less ethical questions or challenges were perceived in the fields of internal and international communication. The results show that ethical questions are more prevalent in Eastern Europe, compared to Western, Northern and Southern Europe. Also professionals working in consultancies and non-profits face ethical challenges when working in strategic communication more than professionals working in governmental organisations, private companies and joint stock companies.

Despite the variety of challenges and the intense debate on codes of ethics in the profession over many years (e.g. the Code of Athens), the majority of European communication practitioners have never used such a code to solve moral problems. Only a minority of them has ever applied a code in their daily work. Male communication professionals and members of professional communication associations use ethical codes more often than female professionals or professionals who are not affiliated to associations. A country-by-country analysis revealed that the use of codes is surprisingly not greater in countries with an elaborated system of regulations and institutions like Germany.[17] A third of the professionals think that typical ethical codes provided by the communication profession are outdated. Nevertheless, an overwhelming majority thinks that the communication profession really needs such rules. This suggests a clear opportunity for professional associations to take a lead and provide up-to date ethical guidelines made to fit the digital age across Europe.

Dealing with ethical issues on individual level and on the level of the organisation and society certainly is one of the most important aspects of working in communications. It's also a challenge in a world where no clear

---

[14] Kim (2005).

[15] Pearson (1989).

[16] Zerfass et al. (2012), pp. 18–35.

[17] Avenarius and Bentele (2009).

ethical rules exist anymore, not in organisations, not in society and not for individual behaviour. Being solid also means being able to handle the grey and ever changing area of ethics well.

The Gendered Profession of Communicators

When it comes to communication management, women have taken over in numbers, and the industry is nowadays a predominantly female industry.[18] It is a so-called gendered profession. In the United States, 70 per cent of the professionals are female.[19] and similar estimates of the amount of women working in the field are made for the Netherlands, Germany and Sweden.[20] This feminisation of the profession raises all kinds of questions. What does it mean for the power of the profession in organisations? And for equality of men and women? For leadership in the field? And for the communication style of organisations?

The high numbers of women in the field do not, for instance, mean that women are equally occupying senior and powerful positions.[21] This connects communication management to the leadership issue being brought forward in the third wave of feminism about a rising role of women in education and employment, but insufficient participation of women in politics and leadership.[22] An additional problem with communications is that because it became a 'profession' where there is a majority of female employees, stereotypes of practitioners emerged such as the PR Bunny or a PR Girl.[23] These are also reflected in film and other popular culture products with PR women such as Samantha Jones in Sex and the City.[24] As soon as women started to enter the profession in higher numbers, debates on why this has happened occurred.[25] Some scholars argue that the reason why women managed to enter communications in such high numbers is because women are more inclined towards emotional work and they are more friendly and kind, all of which are skills necessary in the field[26]

---

[18] Wyatt (2013); Fitch and Third (2010); Aldoory and Toth (2002).

[19] Aldoory and Toth (2002).

[20] Van Ruler and Elving (2007); Bentele and Junghänel (2004); Flodin (2004).

[21] Grunig et al. (2001); Rush et al. (2004).

[22] Merchant (2012).

[23] Fröhlich and Peters (2007).

[24] Ames (2010); Johnston (2010).

[25] Yeomans (2010); Aldoory (2005).

[26] Hochschild (1983, 2003, 2008); Yeomans (2010).

with which traditional prejudices against women have actually been enforced, even by scholars. What did we find in the European Communication Monitor about gender and communication management over the years?

Still Traditional Views on Personal Traits of Men and Women

When it comes to personal characteristics ascribed to women, communication practitioners report traditional views on differences between men and women. Men are seen as seen as more aggressive, more able to promote themselves, self-confident, political savvy, more motivated for managerial positions, more analytical and with stronger managerial and operational skills. On the other hand, women are seen as more emotional and sensitive to people. Curiously men and woman value all these characteristics differently, except political savviness. Political savviness is seen equally strongly by men and women alike. For the rest of the characteristics the values differ. Figure 34 shows all the values and differences reported about personal traits for men and women. Generally speaking

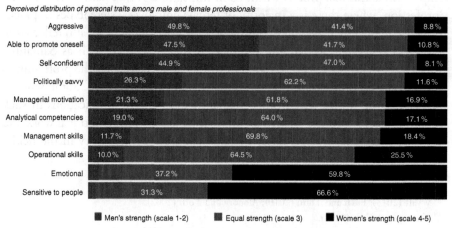

Perceived distribution of personal traits among male and female professionals

Aggressive	49.8%	41.4%	8.8%
Able to promote oneself	47.5%	41.7%	10.8%
Self-confident	44.9%	47.0%	8.1%
Politically savvy	26.3%	62.2%	11.6%
Managerial motivation	21.3%	61.8%	16.9%
Analytical competencies	19.0%	64.0%	17.1%
Management skills	11.7%	69.8%	18.4%
Operational skills	10.0%	64.5%	25.5%
Emotional	37.2%	59.8%	
Sensitive to people	31.3%	66.6%	

■ Men's strength (scale 1-2)   ■ Equal strength (scale 3)   ■ Women's strength (scale 4-5)

Fig. 34 Differences between male and female communicators[27]

---

[27] Zerfass et al. (2014), p. 130. *n* = 2,777 communication professionals across Europe. Q: How do you believe the following personal traits are distributed among male and female communication professionals? Scale 1–2 (men's strength) – 3 (equal strength) – 4–5 (women's strength).

women think more stereotypically about men and also about themselves. They think men are more aggressive, self-promotional and self-confident than women and women are more emotional and sensitive to people than men.

These views largely fit into stereotypes against women as compassionate and emotional while men are more predisposed for managerial and leadership position. On the other hand, there is a drop in characteristics ascribed to men when it comes to managerial motivation, analytical competences and managerial and operational skills. It seems that women are slowly finding their way through acknowledgement of their efforts and an increase in self-esteem. These skills are more seen as equally strong than the other characteristics. However, they are still seen as emotional and compassionate as opposed to men, which fit into traditional stereotypes against women held by both sexes.[28] Men and women interpret the issue of gendered personal traits and skills quite differently.

Perceived Consequences of a Gender Shift

What does feminisation mean for the industry? According to the practitioners interviewed for our survey a female majority can have both positive and negative consequences upon the profession. First of all women's engagement with the industry is, in general, not labelled through negative stereotyped images of women. It is labelled through increased professionalism. Moreover, it could be said that increased professionalism and characteristics associated with the alleged dialogic nature of women, as the prescriptive model of symmetrical communication, are positively attributed to the feminisation of the profession. Women think this is so more than men. The fostering of professionalism is also linked to an increase of salaries for communication professionals. On the negative side professionals are afraid that feminisation might perpetuate the soft image of the profession, increase the process of encroachment and that it will slow down the technological evolution of the profession. Men are more afraid of this technological slowdown than women are. Figure 35 provides an overview of the answers on the statements.

---

[28] Van Zoonen (2004); Eichenbaum and Orbach (1999); Templin (1999).

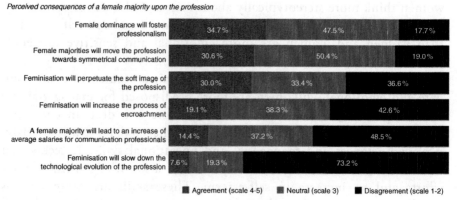

Fig. 35   How women might change the profession[29]

Lower Job Status and Payment for Women

The European Communication Monitor identified that male and female professionals agree on a lot of things about their jobs. For example they think their tasks are interesting and manifold, their work-life balance is all right and overall they are equally satisfied with the job (see Fig. 36 for the total list). The only difference is reported on job status. Male professionals report a higher job status than their female colleagues. This goes in line with feminist views that women still have lower positions even if they work in an industry where women form the majority of employees.[30] However, the difference between men and women is not large, which might mean that women report slow progress towards equality in work in general.

However, as emphasised by feminist activists, when it comes to assigning important roles, women seem to be treated unfavourably, and these roles are more often assigned to men. For example, mentoring roles are more assigned to men than women in the communications industry. These two results are in line with frequently discussed views on women's position in management literature that largely demonstrates the unfavourable position of women against their male colleagues.

---

[29] Zerfass et al. (2014), p. 120. n = 2,777 communication professionals across Europe. Q: Please state whether you agree or disagree with those statements. Scale 1 (strongly disagree) – 5 (totally agree).
[30] Merchant (2012).

	Female	Male	Overall
My tasks are interesting and manifold	77.2%	77.5%	77.3%
The job has a high status**	46.4%	53.0%	48.9%
My work-life balance is all right*	36.2%	36.4%	36.3%
The salary is adequate	37.0%	38.6%	37.6%
I have great career opportunities**	36.7%	35.2%	36.1%
My job is secure and stable*	46.1%	47.0%	46.4%
Superiors and (internal) clients value my work	65.9%	68.0%	66.7%
Overall, I am satisfied with my job	65.2%	68.6%	66.5%

Fig. 36 Job satisfaction of communication professionals[31]

One other visible consequence of this is unequal payment for the same jobs. Even though women are the majority in communications, a wage gap still exists. For example, the Chartered Institute of Public Relations (CIPR) in the United Kingdom reported a significant wage gap between men and women working in the field. This difference exists, even though it cannot be explained by part-time positions or any other factor that could normally affect the wage gap.[32] In addition, the European Communication Monitor has systematically also identified a wage gap between male and female strategic communication professionals.[33]

Women Experience More Barriers to Success

Climbing the ladder of success is not the same for male and female communication professionals. Men and women really have different experiences in organisations. Men are much more optimistic about – or blind to – the

---

[31] Zerfass et al. (2014), p. 40. n = 2,777 communication professionals across Europe. Q: How do you feel about your actual job situation? Scale 1 (strongly disagree) – 5 (totally agree). Percentages: Agreement based on scale points 4–5. * Significant differences (chi-square test, $p \leq 0.05$). ** Highly significant differences (chi-square test, $p \leq 0.01$).

[32] CIPR (2015).

[33] Zerfass et al. (2007); Zerfass et al. (2008); Zerfass et al. (2009); Zerfass et al. (2010); Zerfass et al. (2011); Zerfass et al. (2012); Zerfass et al. (2013); Zerfass et al. (2014); Zerfass et al. (2015); Zerfass et al. (2016).

experiences of women in organisations than are women. Women more than men think it is true that they have to accomplish more in order to achieve the same success as men. They also feel, more than men, that women have to work harder to secure quality long-term relationships with superiors or top executives in the organisation. Also women think there are more invisible barriers hindering their career path to the top. Also they experience less advancement opportunities despite the same qualifications and think they perform work that is less valued in relation to organisational success. Finally they think, more than men, that women are excluded from informal power networks and receive less support by mentors. All in all there is a high level of agreement that women find progression in their careers harder, and face invisible barriers. This might be even worse in practice, but it is impossible to estimate this based on the results of the Monitor since there are records showing that women deny the *glass ceiling* issue and blame themselves for not progressing in their careers.[34] In organisations with an excellent communication function gender equality is more prevalent, the results of the monitor show.[35]

Closely connected to this issue is that over the years we have consistently found that women think the advisory influence of the communication function is lower than men do. Also women think that the executive influence of communication, the likelihood of to be invited to senior-level meetings dealing with organisational strategic planning, is less than men do.[36]

Moving Beyond Male and Female Communication Stereotypes

When it comes to communication styles, scholars systematically report on differences between men and women.[37] Often the theory of Deborah Tannen, an America sociolinguist, who tape-recorded and analysed numerous conversations for a better understanding of miscommunication

---

[34] Wrigley (2002).

[35] Zerfass et al. (2014), p. 149.

[36] Verhoeven and Aarts (2010).

[37] Coates (1989); Tannen (1990); Merchant (2012); Zerfass et al. (2014).

between men and women, is used to explain the differences.[38] A key aspect of Tannen's theory is that men and women have different ways of speaking. Men and women express themselves differently and construct different frames in interaction for different reasons. Men more often use communication to express and maintain independence, whereas women try to maintain intimacy when communicating. Tannen also found that women use communication more to connect emotionally and express their feelings, and men talk to increase their status. Put differently, men are understood to speak the language that expresses independence, competitiveness and enforces status while women are seen to speak in a way that enables connection and intimacy.[39]

However, when it comes to the preferred methods of communication of male and female managers in communication management, the results of the Monitor have showed surprising findings, that contradict the 'difference' approach that is often taken for granted. If we take into consideration the proposition that sees women and men as different, men are seen as less compassionate and more task-oriented, while women are seen as more interested in building relationships with their employees through interpersonal communication.[40] It is quite surprising that we found that women are more inclined to use emails and social media as methods of networking and men prefer face-to-face and phone calls to network with their peers. Men are seen as task-oriented, while women are seen as relationship-oriented, and while task orientation might have something to do with face-to-face and phone preferences, it is quite inexplicable how emails and social media fit into compassionate and caring communication methods meant to build intimacy and personal relationships. These contrary results might actually signal that women are more inclined towards rationality and professionalism in their approach to networking, while men seem to be more inclined to build personal relationships with their peers even if they are more task oriented. Whatever the explanation is, it is time to think beyond stereotypes about men and women's communication styles. Figure 37 shows the differences in communication preferences for networking between men and women.

---

[38] Tannen (1990).

[39] Tannen (1990).

[40] Eagly and Johnson (1990); Gray (1992); Eagly (1987); Eagly and Karau (2002); Martell and DeSmet (2001).

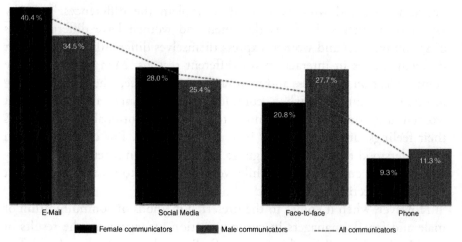

Female communicators   Male communicators   ----- All communicators

Fig. 37 Networking practices preferred by male and female communicators[41]

Communication Professionals' Views on Leadership

Building on the discussions from the earlier chapters, when we look at views of communication practitioners on what constitutes effective leadership for organisations, we see that the perceived most important characteristic for effective leadership is communicating in an open and transparent way. This is congruent with the widely accepted symmetrical and dialogic prescriptive models of public relations. Providing a clear overall, long-term vision and handling controversial issues or crises calmly and confidently are the numbers two and three in the list of important characteristics for effective leaders. These two are more reminiscent of the male stereotyped styles based on objective orientation. Women have more expectations with regard to all the analysed characteristics of effective leadership (see Fig. 38), but results don't show a preference of female practitioners for stereotyped feminine styles or with men for stereotyped male styles of leadership. That is in line with more recent studies in gender and leadership styles.[42]

---

[41] Zerfass et al. (2014), p. 65. n = 2,738 communication professionals across Europe. Q: Which form of professional networking do you practice most often? Pick one or state another form. In a typical week, I use most of my networking time (on the) ... Highly significant differences for all items (chi-square test performed without 'another form', p ≤ 0.01, Cramér's V = 0.093).

[42] Cuadrado et al. (2015).

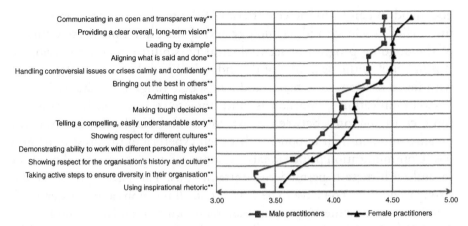

Fig. 38 Difference in expectations of effective leadership of male and female professionals[43]

In other words, effective leadership entails – among others – communicating in an open and transparent way, showing the importance of communication for organisations today.

What It Means to Be Solid

What does it mean for a communication professional to be solid in today's world? Individual solidity first of all means that you have to able to handle *paradoxes*. The paradox is seen as one of the most important features of our hypermodern world and our hypermodern organisations.[44] A hypermodern society is a society that is characterised by hyper consumption (an increasingly large part of life is characterised by consumption), hypermodernity (characterised by continuous change and flexibility) and hyper narcissism (the expectation that every individual behaves responsibly automatically). A hypermodern culture produces contradictions; for example, a firm belief in the market and consumption that

[43] Zerfass et al. (2014), p. 81. n^{min} = 2,695 communication professionals across Europe. Q: Listed below are specific behaviours often seen as being characteristic of effective leaders. When it comes to being an effective leader, how important is it to demonstrate each of the following characteristics or behaviours? Scale 1 (not at all important) – 5 (very important). Mean values. * Significant differences (independent-samples t-test, $p \leq 0.05$). ** Highly significant differences (independent-samples t-test, $p \leq 0.01$).

[44] Lipovetsky (2005); Roberts and Armitage (2006).

goes hand in hand with fierce criticism of the market and consumption. A firm belief in science and technology and at the same time fierce criticism of the ongoing progress of technological possibilities that are developed. A firm belief in the flexibility of the individual and the organisation paired with fierce resistance to change and a nostalgic longing for the past.

Communication professionals find themselves constantly amidst all those contradictions. Between management and employees, between the organisation and their opponents, between experts and the press to name a few. Communication professionals are supposed to give answers about how to deal with these hypermodern contradictions. You have to be solid and strong to do that. You have to be sensitive to all positions and to listen to all who have to say something about the organisation or an issue. You have to be sensitive to ethical considerations of the time and savvy about public opinion fluctuations to guide the organisation in the dynamic world of traditional and new media.

Being solid also means you as a communication professional need to be *reflective*, reflective on yourself, on the organisation and on the culture and society you and the organisation are a part of. You have to understand your own feelings, those of others and the dynamics of the system you are part of. Personal solidity is at the heart of reflective communication management.[45] You have to be able to see the organisation from the position of the outside world, from the public sphere perspective and coach all members of the organisation in how to deal with that. Locally, regionally and globally. This fundamental boundary position requires personal integrity, credibility for all parties involved and an ability to deal with diverse and different populations. Dealing with inequality and power differences between groups inside and outside the organisation and trying to effectively bridge them with communicative solutions is also part of solidity.

Perhaps the most important part of personal solidity for communication professionals is to be *prudent*. Prudence is a bourgeois virtue in our age of commerce, says Deirdre McCloskey, distinguished professor of economics, history, English and communication at the University of Illinois. She defines prudence as good judgement or practical wisdom. Prudence is connected with words like wisdom, common sense, savviness, rationality, self-interest, foresight, calculating, caution, policy and good sense.[46]

---

[45] Holmström (1997); Van Ruler and Verčič (2005); Holmström et al. (2009).
[46] McCloskey (2006), pp. 253–254.

Prudence does justice to the complexity of the internal and external environment communication professionals find themselves in. Being prudent helps to deal with complex issues and problems in practice and to gain relative independence from the top management of the organisation and also of the publics and stakeholders you are dealing with. Prudence leaves room for being asymmetrical *and* symmetrical at the same time, for bonding *and* bridging and for strategic *and* communicative action. Being prudent acknowledges the complexity of strategic communication and strategic framing – or the more popular term of spinning – that are ineluctable parts of communication management. Being prudent releases the professional from the burden of the accusation of being always on the edge of unethical behaviour.

Maybe the most important aspect of being solid is to understand that *conflicts of interest* are a fundamental part of living together as humans and therefore also of organisational life. Solving one conflict often gives rise to another one. Tensions inside and around the organisation are a constant and unsolvable. Coping with these conflicts and with trying to reach consensus at the same time is the key aspect of the communication function of organisations. The ideals of symmetry and consensus go hand in hand with the practice and the reality of conflict.[47] Being strong, sensitive and savvy about that makes a satisfied communication professional.

References

Aldoory, L. (2005). A (re)conceived feminist paradigm for public relations: A case for substantial improvement. *Journal of Communication, 55*(4), 668–684.

Aldoory, L., & Toth, E. (2002). Gender discrepancies in a gendered profession: A developing theory for public relations. *Journal of Public Relations Research, 14*(2), 103–126.

Ames, C. (2010). PR goes to the movies: The image of public relations improves from 1996 to 2008. *Public Relations Review, 36*(2), 164–170.

Avenarius, H., & Bentele, G. (Eds.) (2009). *Selbstkontrolle im Berufsfeld Public Relations.* Wiesbaden: VS Verlag für Sozialwissenschaften.

Bentele, G.(2015). Responsible advocacy? Reflections on the history, system, and codes of public relations ethics, with comments on education and research. In A. Catellani, A. Zerfass, & R. Tench (Eds.), *Communication Ethics in a Connected World.* (pp. 19–32). Brussels: P.I.E. Peter Lang.

---

[47] Holmström (1997, 2005); Holmström et al. (2009).

Bentele, G., & Junghänel, I. (2004). Germany. In B. Van Ruler & D. Verčič (Eds.), *Public Relations and Communication Management in Europe*. (pp. 153–168). Berlin: Mouton de Gruyter.

Bowen, S. A. (2010). An examination of applied ethics and stakeholder management on top corporate websites. *Public Relations Journal*, *4*(1), 1–19.

Brown, R. E. (2012). Epistemological modesty: Critical reflections on public relations thought. *Public Relations Inquiry*, *1*(1), 89–105.

Burley-Allen, M. (1995). *Listening. The Forgotten Skill*. New York: Wiley.

CIPR Chartered Institute of Public Relations (2015). *State of the Nation, 2015*. London: CIPR.

Coates, J. (1989). Gossip revisited: Language in all-female groups. In D. Cameron & J. Coates (Eds.), *Women in Their Speech Communities*. (pp. 94–122). New York: Longman.

Cuadrado, I., Garcìa-Ael, C., & Molero, F. (2015). Gender-typing of leadership: Evaluations of real and ideal managers. *Scandinavian Journal of Psychology*, *56*, 236–244.

Drollinger, T., Comer, L., & Warrington, P. (2006). Development and validation of the active empathic listener scale. *Psychology and Marketing*, *23*(2), 161–180.

Eagly, A. H. (1987). *Sex Differences in Social Behavior: A Social-role Interpretation*. Hillsdale, NJ: Lawrence Erlbaum Associates.

Eagly, A. H., & Karau, S. J. (2002). Role congruity theory of prejudice toward female leaders. *Psychological Review*, *109*(3), 573–598.

Eagly, A. H., & Johnson, B. T. (1990). Gender and leadership style: A meta-analysis. *Psychological Bulletin*, *108*(2), 233–256.

Eichenbaum, L., & Orbach, S. (1999). *What do Women Want? Exploding the Myth of Dependency*. New York: Berkley Books.

Fawkes, J. (2012). Saints and sinners: Competing identities in public relations ethics. *Public Relations Review*, *38*(5), 865–872.

Fitch, K., & Third, A. (2010). Working girls: Revisiting the gendering of public relations. *Prism*, *7*(4), 1–13.

Flodin, B. (2004). Sweden. In B. Van Ruler & D. Verčič (Eds.), *Public Relations and Communication Management in Europe* (pp. 413–424). Berlin: Mouton de Gruyter.

Fröhlich, R., & Peters, S. B. (2007). PR bunnies caught in the agency ghetto? Gender stereotypes, organizational factors, and women's careers in PR agencies. *Journal of Public Relations Research*, *19*(3), 229–254.

Gray, J. (1992). *Men are from Mars, Women are from Venus: A Practical Guide for Improving Communication and Getting What You Want in a Relationship*. New York: Harper Collins.

Grunig, L. A., Toth, E. L., & Hon, L. C. (2001). *Women in Public Relations: How Gender Influences Practice*. New York: The Guildford Press.

Hochschild, A. R. (1983). *The Managed Heart: Commercialization of Human Feeling*. Berkeley, CA: University of California Press.

Hochschild, A. R. (2003). *The Managed Heart: Commercialization of Human Feeling* (2nd edition).Berkeley, CA: University of California Press.

Hochschild, A. R. (2008). Emotion work, feeling rules, and social structure. In M. Greco & P. Stenner (Eds.), *Emotions: A Social Science Reader* (pp. 551–575). New York: Routledge.

Holmström, S. (1997). The inter-subjective and the social systemic public relations paradigms. *Journal of Communication Management, 2*(1), 24–39.

Holmström, S. (2005). Reframing public relations. The evolution of a reflective paradigm for organizational legitimation. *Public Relations Review, 31*(4), 497–504.

Holmström, S., Falkheimer, J., & Nielsen, A. G. (2009). Legitimacy and strategic communication in globalization: The cartoon crisis and other legitimacy conflicts. *International Journal of Strategic Communication, 4*(1), 1–18.

Johnston, J. (2010). Girls on screen: How film and television depict women in public relations. *Prism, 7*(4), 1–16.

Kim, H. (2005). Universalism versus relativism in public relations. *Journal of Mass Media Ethics, 20*(4), 333–344.

Lipovetsky, G. (2005). Time against time: Or the hypermodern society. In G. Lipovetsky & S. Charles (Eds.), *Hypermodern Times* (pp. 29–71). Malden, MA: Polity Press.

Macnamara, J. (2013). Beyond voice. Audience-making and the work and architecture of listening. *Continuum: Journal of Media and Cultural Studies, 27*(1), 160–175.

Macnamara, J. (2016). *Organizational Listening: The Missing Essential in Public Communication.* New York: Peter Lang.

Martell, R. F., & DeSmet, A. L. (2001). Gender stereotyping in the managerial ranks: A Bayesian approach to measuring beliefs about the leadership abilities of male and female managers. *Journal of Applied Psychology, 86*(6), 1223–1231.

McCloskey, D. N. (2006). *The Bourgeois Virtues. Ethics for an Age of Commerce.* Chicago, IL: University of Chicago Press.

Merchant, K. (2012). *How Men and Women Differ: Gender Differences in* Communication Styles, Influence Tactics, and *Leadership Styles* (CMS Senior Theses, Paper 513). Retrieved from: http://scholarship.claremont.edu/cgi/view content.cgi?article=1521&context=cmc_theses.

Pearson, R. (1989). Beyond ethical relativism in public relations: Co-orientation, rules, and the idea of communication symmetry. *Journal of Public Relations Research, 1*(1), 67–86.

Roberts, J., & Armitage, J. (2006). From organization to hypermodern organization: On the appearance and disappearance of Enron. *Journal of Organizational Change Management, 19*(5), 558–577.

Rush, R. R., Oukrop, C. E., & Creedon, P. J. (Eds.) (2004). *Seeking Equity for Women in Journalism and Mass Communication Education: A 30-year Update.* Mahwah, NJ: Laurence Erlbaum Associates.

Siere, R. (2014). *Ongehoord. Waarom luisteren uw organisatie beter maakt.* Amsterdam: Adfo Groep.

Tannen, D. (1990). *You Just Don't Understand: Women and Men in Conversation.* New York: Ballantine Books.

Templin, C. (1999). Hillary Rodham Clinton as threat to gender norms: Cartoon images of the First Lady. *Journal of Communication Inquiry, 23*(1), 20–36.

Van Ruler, B., & Elving, W. (2007). *Carrière in Communicatie.* Amsterdam: Boom.

Van Ruler, B., & Verčič, D. (2005). Reflective communication management: Future ways for public relations research. In P. J. Kalbfleisch (Ed.), *Communication Yearbook 29* (pp. 239–273). Mahwah, NJ: Lawrence Erlbaum Associates.

Van Zoonen, L. (2004). *Entertaining the Citizen: When Politics and Popular Culture Converge.* New York: Rowman and Littlefield.

Verhoeven, P., & Aarts, N. (2010). How European public relations men and women perceive the impact of their professional activities. *PRism, 7*(4), 1–15.

Wrigley, B. J. (2002). Glass ceiling? What glass ceiling? A qualitative study of how women view the glass ceiling in public relations and communications management. *Journal of Public Relations Research, 14*(1), 27–55.

Wyatt, R. (2013). The PR Census 2013. *PR Week* (UK online edition). Retrieved from: http://www.prweek.com/article/1225129/pr-census-2013.

Yeomans, L. (2010). Soft sell? Gendered experience of emotional labour in UK public relations firms. *Prism, 7*(4), 1–14.

Zerfass, A., Van Ruler, B., Rogojinaru, A., Verčič, D., & Hamrefors, S. (2007). *European Communication Monitor 2007. Trends in Communication Management and Public Relations – Results and Implications.* Leipzig: University of Leipzig/EUPRERA.

Zerfass, A., Moreno, A., Tench, R., Verčič, D., & Verhoeven, P. (2008). *European Communication Monitor 2008. Trends in Communication Management and Public Relations – Results and Implications.* Leipzig: University of Leipzig/ EUPRERA.

Zerfass, A., Moreno, A., Tench, R., Verčič, D., & Verhoeven, P. (2009). *European Communication Monitor 2009. Trends in Communication Management and Public Relations – Results of a Survey in 34 Countries.* Brussels: EUPRERA.

Zerfass, A., Tench, R., Verhoeven, P., Verčič, D., & Moreno, A. (2010). *European Communication Monitor 2010. Status Quo and Challenges for Public Relations in Europe. Results of an Empirical Survey in 46 Countries.* Brussels: EACD/ EUPRERA, Helios Media.

Zerfass, A., Verhoeven, P., Tench, R., Moreno, A., & Verčič, D. (2011). *European Communication Monitor 2011. Empirical Insights into Strategic Communication in Europe. Results of an Empirical Survey in 43 Countries.* Brussels: EACD/ EUPRERA.

Zerfass, A., Verčič, D., Verhoeven, P., Moreno, A., & Tench, R. (2012). *European Communication Monitor 2012: Challenges and Competencies for Strategic Communication: Results of an Empirical Survey in 42 Countries.* Brussels: EACD/EUPRERA.

Zerfass, A., Moreno, A., Tench, R., Verčič, D., & Verhoeven, P. (2013). *European Communication Monitor 2013. A Changing Landscape – Managing Crises, Digital Communication and CEO Positioning in Europe. Results of a Survey in 43 Countries.* Brussels: EACD/EUPRERA, Helios Media.

Zerfass, A., Tench, R., Verčič, D., Verhoeven, P., & Moreno, A. (2014). *European Communication Monitor 2014. Excellence in Strategic Communication – Key Issues, Leadership, Gender and Mobile Media. Results of a Survey in 42 Countries.* Brussels: EACD/EUPRERA, Helios Media.

Zerfass, A., Verčič, D., Verhoeven, P., Moreno, A., & Tench, R. (2015). *European Communication Monitor 2015. Creating Communication Value Through Listening, Messaging and Measurement. Results of a Survey in 41 Countries.* Brussels: EACD/EUPRERA, Helios Media.

Zerfass, A., Verhoeven, P., Moreno, A., Tench, R., & Verčič, D. (2016). *European Communication Monitor 2016. Exploring Trends* in Big Data, Stakeholder Engagement and Strategic Communication. *Results of a Survey in 43 Countries.* Brussels: EACD/EUPRERA, Quadriga Media Berlin.

Epilogue
The Future of Excellent Communication: From a Soft to a Hard Discipline

Strategic communication is today one of the key competitive advantages available to organisations. It has to be purposeful, it has to be planned and it has to be managed. And, above all, it has to be developed as carefully as any other key management function: it has to be regularly assessed and compared to the best in the world. It has to be evidence based, underpinned with scientific research. This is the essence of the concept of excellence: no matter how good you are, you always have to become better; others are developing, evolving and even jumping ahead, so you should too, preferably faster and better.

This is exactly what the *nine commandments of communication excellence* presented in this book say: strategic communication resides in connected organisations with influential communication departments in which ambitious professionals work. Organisations need to accept the whole world as a field in which they have to benchmark, so they must be purposefully globalised. Organisations have to grow their 'connectors' (axon terminals) around the globe to see, listen, smell and feel what is going on and be able to present themselves – so they must be purposefully mediatised. And they ought to reflect on what they are and what they sense about others and the world as a whole, they are required to act, interact, reflect and learn to reinvent themselves every single day – so they must be reflective.

© The Author(s) 2017
R. Tench et al., *Communication Excellence*,
DOI 10.1007/978-3-319-48860-8

193

Connected organisations can only emerge as a result of careful guidance supported by influential communication departments. These should be literally embedded in their organisations, influencing the top management and be interlinked with other functional departments, like controlling, human relations, marketing, operations, sales, etc. They need to be comfortable with numbers, as datafication is one of the major consequences the Internet has brought to organisational life. And they are obliged to be strategised in the sense that only by linking communication to organisational objectives makes communication relevant to an organisation as a whole. Listening, planning and messaging are meaningless unless they are integrated in strategic decision-making at the top.

But influential departments in connected organisations only exist because ambitious professionals bring them to life. They have to be well educated, extensively trained and possess explicit competencies in order to perform excellent communication. They ought to be able and willing to personally link with stakeholders inside and outside organisations, and they must understand interdependencies with their colleagues and the world out there, providing a climate fostering mutual collaboration and support.

And, last but not least, they need to be solid people and professionals, driven by personal, professional, organisational and societal ethics. They must be prepared to recognise and value pluralism and diversity, and in a world that is unimpressed with formal experts and looks for personalised assurance for trust they must be able to build respect and reliability at a human level, before they try to convert them to group or organisational levels. Solid organisations stand on solid professionals.

The nine commandments of excellent communication are shown in Fig. 39. They focus attention to what is important in making assessments about one's worth. But they don't automatically produce excellence. On the contrary: by following these guiding commandments, professionals have to deal with paradoxes that are associated with each of them. Nobody has said that life is simple; the beauty of the world around us resides in its uncertainty and in its paradoxes.

The Nine Paradoxes of Excellent Communication

Paradoxes are a key characteristic of the global hypermodern culture of today. The hypermodern society is a society featured by overdrive in every sense of the word. Life is characterised by consumption, continuous change, flexibility and

Fig. 39 Nine commandments of excellent communication

individualisation. It is a society of freedom, hedonism and autonomy. But there is still a gap between the ideal of a free hypermodern individual and the realisation of that ideal. This results in disappointment or and a so-called paradoxical happiness[1]: an individual can reach happiness but can be depressed and sad at the same time. Everybody is freer than ever but also more dependent on others. These kinds of paradoxes also exist for the economy and for organisations. An interesting example of a hypermodern paradox on this level is that more consumption and spending is necessary to be able to build a sustainable way of production. Hyperconsumption and sustainability are two sides of the same coin.[2] Paradoxes will also be central to communication. Each of the nine commandments therefore has its own paradox in itself. Communication professionals as well as top executives are advised to know them and keep them in

---

[1] Lipovetsky, 2005.
[2] Kruk and Vloemans, 2011.

mind when making judgements about strategic communication. Let us present them in the same order as we have organised the book:

1. The Paradox of Globalisation: Cosmopolitan and Cultured

Globalisation is the first commandment because we have to go out and compare to the best in the world, or the world is going to come to us and we may not be prepared and able to live up to it. In that way globalisation is egalitarian and cosmopolitan. At the present time, the global *lingua franca* of business, science, politics . . . is English and many people use it to communicate not only internationally, but also internally in their own organisations (e.g. in multinational companies and inter – and non-governmental organisations). It looks like globalisation is a force driving us all closer, making us all similar, even the same.

But globalisation in order to compare with the best is anything but just copying the best. Value(s) reside(s) in culture(s). Global comparisons make sense for benchmarking and learning about possibilities, but their exploitation has to become localised and enculturated. All existing organisms, including social organisations, are alive because they are good at what they are doing, at least to a certain degree. Just changing them without regard to what makes them good in the present is the quickest way to their demise. The majority of organisational restructurings and turnaround don't succeed. The reason is precisely that organisations are not machines that can be dismantled and reassembled at will. Cultures can be nurtured, not managed.

Globalisation as our first commandment must be understood in its full paradox. On one side, it is cosmopolitan in enabling comparisons with others. But at the same time it is cultured in its intention to do that precisely for the reason to preserve one's organisation's life and prosperity, identity and, therefore, culture. This is not easy because it forces everybody to move beyond inertia and comfort zones. It is also risky: it is not impossible that by being really inferior or just impressed with other's superiority one loses his or her soul. Globalisation is about both opportunities and threats, and outcomes are not given in advance. But there is no alternative: human history is a graveyard of groups that were trying to preserve their cultures in isolation. The only result of that was inferiority and, in the final consequence, decay. If evolution is about adaptation, it is about communication and interaction.

2. The Paradox of Mediatisation: Control and Openness

Whatever humanists say, from an evolutionary point of view, media were invented in an attempt to control the environment. People and organisations must observe their environments so that they are not surprised by enemies, and they send messages to attract or detract attention. The growing mediatisation we are recently witnessing is a result of lower costs for the production and distribution of media. While this gives mediatised organisations incredible amounts of power and control, it also produces an illusion.

To be able to see something at the same time means blindness to something else. To talk to somebody at the same time means ignoring somebody else. Media are formidable extensions of our nervous system, but they are no less misleading than our senses are. There is no way to produce a general media system that communicates about, with and to everybody. All authoritarian regimes dreamt about them, but were never able to produce one. If organisations were able to do so, they could succeed forever. But the opposite is the truth: the more an organisation tries to produce a total media system, the more fragile it becomes. The artful use of owned, earned, paid and social media creates a demand for balancing between those quite different fields. In the long run and more generally speaking, it creates a need to balance between control and trust.

Trust has to be earned and learned: organisations must be trusted by their key stakeholders or their transaction costs become excessive. And they must also learn to trust, because they cannot simply control everybody – trust and control are functional equivalents. And if they attempt to try to control everybody they will only diminish any trust they possess. This is anyway only a figure of speech: one can never 'have' trust, but the trustee always possesses trust. Mediatisation has to be situated in an environment in which organisations work on their images and reputations, in an environment in which own media coexist with other forms and owners of media. In that sense mediatisation of organisations should purposefully contribute to media pluralism and richness. Excellent communication can handle the paradox of control of media messages and let go of control when dealing with gate kept media, whether they are classical journalistic media, partisan state media, or bloggers, video bloggers or social media influencers.

3. The Paradox of Reflection: Contemplation and Expediency
The paradox of reflection simply means that analysis should not produce paralysis, and at the same time, efficiency should not affect efficacy. The very idea of reflection presupposes that one stops and thinks; and the very idea of action presupposes that one stops thinking and does something. These two processes, action and reflection, are different, but they must be exercised simultaneously.

Historically, scientific management was invented as something different from production. Headquarters with staff were moved away first in armies from the trenches and then in factories from machines. Some were to think and others were to fight or work. But this made sense only as long as staff in the headquarters were more educated than workers in production. In our contemporary knowledge society, the opposite is true in many organisations. When knowledge is dispersed across an organisation, the whole organisation must learn to switch between the modes of thinking and acting.

This transformation which makes organisations leaner and flatter has brought tremendous new opportunities to communication professionals. They are involved in listening, thinking and talking, but more and more are also responsible for developing structures and programmes to empower others to listen, think and talk. It is the need for organisations to become reflective which is inventing new roles for professional communicators and which is making communication ever more central to the core of contemporary organisations.

Structures and systems for listening need to be designed in such a way that they enable a wide internal distribution of data and information through a process of collective organisational learning. What makes sense to whom and who understands what cannot be programmed in advance. It is precisely this uncertainty of information and knowledge sharing that brings about innovation. Innovation, in turn, is necessary for the continuous improvement of existing goals, policies and routines. Reflection is always also about thinking the unthinkable, about being bold to go beyond the presently given and obvious.

4. The Paradox of Embeddedness: Integration and Differentiation
Professional communication can be only as strategic as it is involved in the strategic management of an organisation. It has to enrich the top management's perspective of the world and its understanding of key stakeholders.

If media are extensions of their nervous system, which enable organisations to experience much more than they can do directly, then communication structures form the spine within an organisation. As such, communication must extend to all parts of an organisation. It is severely deficient if it closes itself off and into a silo. Instead it must be an integrated part of all organisational functions, while keeping its own identity at the same time: strategic communication departments and professionals might work with finance on financial communication, with marketing on marketing communication, with operations on work-related communication, with human resources on internal communication and so on. In that way strategic communication is differentiated in subfields with specific rules that practitioners must master. It makes a big difference whether one is interacting with a local journalist or a global investor, an employee across the globe or a member of the board. Yet, an excellent communication department always represents the same organisation.

Communication departments must have a communication leader who is part of or at least is associated with the top management of the organisation. At the same time, the department must have its representatives in all parts of an organisation, linking many into one. Furthermore, integration is not only spatial in that it embraces all parts of an organisation, but is also going into depth. More and more work in organisations is about communication and the communicative part of many organisational roles and positions is on the increase. Leaders expect ever more people to know and master how to communicate. Communication incompetence, on the other hand, is becoming one of the deadly sins for excellent organisations. This gives communication departments additional responsibility to nurture and develop the communicative abilities of co-workers and associates within their organisation.

Communication has always been embedded in the whole of an organisation – what is new is the importance it is gaining both at the core of the organisations and in all its constituent parts.

5. The Paradox of Datafication: High-Tech and High-Touch

Datafication of strategic communication and of organisational and social life as a whole has surprised many professional communicators. It is even greater for those who entered the communication profession because they 'like people', but are not necessarily so enthusiastic about the numbers. The Internet has allowed rich and reliable descriptions of humans and their multifarious interactions in numbers. With the advent of artificial intelligence we can anticipate that even more of this automated interpretation of our behaviour will happen. Already today search engines and social media platforms are largely automated. Many think that communication on the Internet resembles real-life communication. But it does not. Much of the content seen on media portals is also visible on social media. But in the latter case it is not only selected by producers and senders, but to a large part by software algorithms that use data from many sources to determine what a recipient will see on the screen. The content presented to a user in a specific situation on a particular device is not known in advance, but is generated in the course of the interaction.

But although the Internet is changing everything and communication is becoming increasingly automated, no computer can make order out of (social) chaos. Humans do things that no machine in a foreseeable future can do: make sense out of data and information, understand the present and envision the future. Datafication of communication may be digging a hole between the organisational high-tech environment and high-touch interactions that people need. It is a new paradox organisations are facing. They still have to learn how to deal with this paradox. It opens up new opportunities for communication departments who will have to reinvent themselves as custodians of a new renaissance, combining knowledge and experience in both sciences (for data and machines) and humanities (for people). Strategic communication as a discipline of the social sciences is entering the central stage. The performance of organisations and the world as a whole will in large parts depend on the competence to communicate appropriately in quite different settings.

6. The Paradox of Strategised: Focus and Politics

Strategy is basically about focus. One has to understand, where he or she is, where he or she would like to get to and what is the best way of travelling there. But the world is not flat. Organisations have multiple stakeholders and their borders are becoming porous.

Communication departments help top executives to articulate and symbolise what their organisations are and what they stand for. They are ultimately responsible for authentic and integral, clear and focused, consistent and transparent, yet culturally and politically sensitive communication in a world of increasing cultural, economic, financial, investor, linguistic, media and political complexity. Changing communication habits, the proliferation of media channels, degradation of journalistic standards and audience preferences for infotainment over facts are posing communication problems to leaders of all kinds of organisations. This is a challenge faced by politicians for more than a decade. Their responses have often led to questionable results, resulting in a loss of trust for the whole political system. At the same time there is an increased need for the personal presence of all leaders – alone and in teams. This becomes ever more complicated when organisations grow and start operating in different time zones.

There is a clear need to focus on the core purpose and mission of an organisation on the one side. On the other hand, sensitivity to other cultures and languages is key – but this may bring about the danger of de-centring key values of the organisation. For that reason we expect communication departments to move from structures predominantly linked to stakeholders and programmes to more integrated approaches.

There is no way out of the paradox of focus and politics: sensitivity to stakeholder expectations is becoming a norm for all large organisations, and while they engage not only in dialogue, but literally in polylogue, they must keep their eye on the ball: they have a purpose to fulfil and a mission to accomplish.

7. The Paradox of Sagaciousness: Professionalism and Humanness

There is a well-known saying in fiction, film and business: 'This is not personal, it's only business'. Professional communication is demanding that practitioners engage in a lifelong learning process. Top positions in strategic communication are becoming reserved for the best graduates with years of demonstrable practice. In some countries, for example, in Germany, we can see that many CCOs hold doctorates in a social science, and that they associate their practical work with research and teaching at universities – which is quite a common practice in more established professions like law or medicine. Integration of communication into the very core and decision-making structures of organisations comes with greater responsibilities and more demand for high-level knowledge.

But while this academic training and education enables specialisation, institutionalisation and professionalisation of communication, this doesn't have to come at the expense of humanity. Surgeons have to train until they can operate and perform their professional duties whilst overcoming the normal discomfort many of us would feel at the sight of so much blood, trauma and bodily intervention. But that does not make them less humane. On the contrary: they can practice their profession precisely because they can look at traumatic images and situations that other people cannot. The professional communicator must learn to do the same.

There is never a business that is not personal: all business is personal, and professional communicators must internalise that. There will be times in the life of organisations that force them to lay off people: it is a business decision, but it is very personal to those involved. Communicators have to deal with those situations in a professional way. Whatever they do in organisations affects other people: it is business and it is personal at the same time.

8. The Paradox of Linkedness: Centralisation and Dispersion

Professional communicators are highly linked with their colleagues and everybody around them: they are linked to 360 degrees. Structurally, and in the language of network analysis, they perform the function of stars – nodes through which many other units are connected. They are like crossroads on which communication travels. They are the ones who are knitting communication networks within and between organisations and stakeholders. But it is not possible to be equally connected to everybody else. People are closer to some people and more distant with others. Likewise, organisations have stronger and weaker links to other organisations, people and systems. Wisely linked professionals understand the importance of their weak just as much as their strong links. They invest in nurturing both. Being close to people who matter at a given moment is essential for success; but having broad networks of connections with other people who may at some point in the future be critical may be a well-kept secret for success.

Ambitious communicators are purposefully working on linkages they have within and across organisational boundaries. They are boundary spanners with double loyalties to the organisation and to a certain extent also to the stakeholders that they represent – the decision makers within the organisation. It is precisely this paradox that gives communicators a special value. They can see and say more than the vast majority of organisational members can. In that respect they also resemble from history the fools that kings and queens kept in their courts: since the very beginnings of our civilisations, rulers knew that because of their authority many people around them say what they think the 'leader' would like to hear – but not what they really need to know. It was the 'funny' fools who were allowed to say whatever they wanted, even the truth, because it was part of their role. Excellent communication professionals are neither fools nor people known for their jokes. They are serious managers, but they often have a privileged position to say more than others can. Being connected with the key decision-makers on one side and also to a dispersed network of stakeholders on the other side is a great source of power.

9. The Paradox of Solidity: Ethics and Efficiency

Professional communicators should be ethical, but they also make things happen. Many people believe that being ethical or true to one's core values is the opposite of being opportunistic or taking advantage of a situation. But the opposite is true: ethical dilemmas and paradoxes are only relevant when they are connected to opportunities. If there is no situation of choice there is no place for ethics, just for obedience to necessity.

This means that communication professionals have to understand their specific role in situations of managerial choices. Top management in corporations, governmental organisations and non-profits is there to deliver: they have fiduciary responsibilities to their owners, shareholders, voters, members, etc., to make as much or the most out of whatever is valued. They are there to exploit opportunities and many times they have to go all the way to the borders of what is conceivable, or even beyond that. The best leaders are capable of delivering more than anybody could have imagined beforehand. But while they are fighting for success in the middle of the battle, they can be carried away. Communication professionals are there to help and protect them from their own mistakes. Not to paralyse, but to offer a sounding board, warnings, advice or even therapy. But communicators have to understand that the buck stops at the top. There are decisions to be made or forgone, and organisations are not an environment for innocent souls. Organisational life is about making decisions.

It takes a solid personality to survive the stress that comes with the job of juggling with paradoxes, of evaluating values and offerings that are out of hand's reach, to control effort and maintain stamina for the long-term perspective in the face of short-term offerings. It requires wisdom that is founded on good education and bred on extensive experience. Hypermodern times are both ethically hypersensitive and opportunistically hyperefficient. It is possible to complain about it, but this also opens new routes to improvement for professionals, organisations and societies at large.

Where Do We Go from Here?

Strategic communication and public relations was created as an applied discipline rooted in communication studies, business administration and the social sciences. In the contemporary hypermodern world, its growth and further development is dependent on a productive interaction between practice and research, academics and professionals. Practice without research is blind. The practice has to become much more evidence based instead of being based on personal experiences and anecdotal evidence. In other words strategic communication has to go from a soft to a hard discipline. A discipline that underpins its practice with results and insights from empirical-analytical research. Productive tensions between theory and practice benefit both. The ideas presented in this book and the decade of fruitful cooperation around the European Communication Monitor, Asia-Pacific Communication Monitor and Latin-American Communication Monitor show that this is possible and rewarding for all sides. It is this collaboration that is helping to transfer and transform a practice into a profession.

References

Kruk, M., & Vloemans, P. (2011). Twee Gucci tassen pas de problem, maar meer dan dat?. *De Groene Amsterdammer, 16*(02), 32–35.

Lipovetsky, G. (2005). Time against time: Or the hypermodern society. In: G. Lipovetsky & S. Charles (Eds.), *Hypermodern times* (pp. 29–71). Malden, MA: Polity Press.

Where Do We Go from Here?

References

Appendix

About the European Communication Monitor and Its Methodology

The European Communication Monitor (ECM) explores current practices and future developments of strategic communication and public relations in companies, non-profits and other organisations including communication agencies. It has been conducted annually since 2007 and has been complemented by biannual surveys in other regions (Latin America, Asia-Pacific) since 2014. The communication monitor series is known as the most comprehensive research in the field worldwide, altogether covering more than 80 countries. It is the only continuous global research in the field which adheres to full standards of empirical research and provides transparency about its sampling procedures and respondents.

A joint study by academia and practice, the ECM is organised by the European Public Relations Education and Research Association (EUPRERA) and the European Association of Communication Directors (EACD), supported by different partners and sponsors over the years. The study has been created and is led by Ansgar Zerfass from the University of Leipzig in Germany and BI Norwegian Business School, Oslo, Norway. It is co-authored since 2008 by Ángeles Moreno (University Rey Juan Carlos, Madrid, Spain), Ralph Tench (Leeds Beckett University, United Kingdom), Dejan Verčič (University of Ljubljana, Slovenia) and Piet Verhoeven (University of Amsterdam, the Netherlands). A wider board of professors and national research collaborators ensure that the survey reflects the diversity of the field across Europe (see below

© The Author(s) 2017
R. Tench et al., *Communication Excellence*,
DOI 10.1007/978-3-319-48860-8

for an overview of national research contacts). Results have been reported in more than 160 peer-reviewed journal articles, book chapters, contributions in professional magazines, keynotes, presentations and webinars in multiple languages on various continents. Full reports for each annual study along with articles, web videos and other content explaining key results are available at www.communicationmonitor.eu.

Sample

Over the last ten years more than 21,000 European communication professionals from over 40 countries participated in the survey of the monitor, ranging from 1,087 in 2007 to 2,710 in 2016. Every year tens of thousands (40,000 in 2016) throughout Europe are invited with personal emails based on a database provided by the EACD. Additional invitations are sent via national research collaborators and professional associations. The online questionnaires (in English) are based on research questions and hypotheses derived from previous research and literature; they are pre-tested with communication professionals from various countries.

A strict selection of respondents is a distinct feature of the ECM and sets it apart from many studies which are based on snowball sampling or which include students, academics and people outside of the focused profession or region. The sample is not a representative sample of the communication profession in Europe. Such a sample is not possible because the population of European communication professionals is unknown. Looking at the demographics of the respondents we certainly can state that the respondents of the monitor are decision makers in the profession and important opinion leaders in the field. In Table 1, the demographics of the respondents are presented from 2007 to 2016.

Statistical Analyses

For describing and analysing the data described in this book the Statistical Package for the Social Sciences (SPSS) was used. Cluster analysis and factor analysis (Explorative Factor Analysis) was used for classifying subjects. Results have been tested for statistical significance with, depending on the variable, chi^2, Pearson correlation, ANOVA/Scheffe post hoc, Kendall rank independent-samples T and Kendall rank correlation tests. Statistical indicators (Cramer's V, F, r, tau) are reported in the footnotes of the chapters. Results are marked as significant ($p \leq 0.05$) * or highly significant ($p \leq 0.01$) ** where applicable.

Table 1 Demographic background of respondents: European Communication Monitor 2007–2016

Year	2007	2008	2009	2010	2011	2012	2013	2014	2015	2016
Number of respondents	1,087	1,524	1,863	1,955	2,209	2,185	2,710	2,777	2,253	2,710
Gender (%)										
Female	–	54.8	50.7	55.8	55.6	57.6	58	61.7	59	58.1
Male	–	45.2	49.3	44.2	44.4	42.4	42	38.3	41	41.9
Number of countries	22	37	34	46	43	42	43	42	41	43
Education (%)										
Doctorate	–	–	7.4	7.3	6.7	7.3	6.4	6.7	7.9	6.3
Master	–	–	60.2	59.3	58.8	57.6	59.9	60.8	60.8	62.6
Bachelor	–	–	25.1	26.9	27.8	27.6	26.5	26.6	26.1	25.6
Age (mean)	41.3	39.4	41.7	40.6	41.2	41.5	40.9	40.9	41.4	41.6
Experience (%)										
More than 10 years	48.9	45.3	58.3	52.1	56.7	57.7	58.3	57.7	62.2	59.9
6–10 years	27	24.2	26.9	28.6	27.4	26.3	25.5	24.4	23.4	22.9
Up to 5 years	24.1	30.5	14.8	19.2	15.9	16	16.1	17.9	14.3	17.3
Type of organisation (%)										
Joint stock company	–	27.9	29.7	28.5	28	29.3	26.2	24.7	25	19.5
Private company	–	17.8	18.4	21.5	18.2	19.9	18.9	18.9	17.6	17.9
Government-owned, Public sector, political	–	12.1	12.7	16.9	14.1	16.4	16.3	18.4	17.4	13.1
Non-profit, association	–	9.5	11.5	11.6	10.9	12.8	13.4	13.2	11.1	11.9
Consultancy	–	32.6	27.8	21.6	28.8	21.6	25.2	24.7	28.9	37.5
Position (%)										
Head of comms/Agency CEO	–	–	53.8	47.9	48.8	42.7	43.2	40	44	37.2
Unit leader	–	–	29.8	32.3	28.8	29	28.4	27.6	27.2	32.1
Team member/consultant	–	–	12.7	16.5	17.6	20.7	22.5	26.1	22.7	24.9
Other	–	–	3.7	4.4	5.7	7.5	5.9	6.3	6.1	5.8

– = not measured in that year

The Comparative Excellence Framework

In the Comparative Excellence Framework for communication management (see introduction chapter), theoretical considerations are combined with self-assessments of communication professionals and statistical analyses to identify the characteristics which make a difference. Excellence is based on the internal standing of the communication department within the organisation (influence) and external results of the communication department's activities as well as its basic qualifications (performance). Each of these two components is calculated on the basis of four dimensions. Influence is a combination of perceived advisory and executive influence and performance is a combination of perceived success and competence. Only organisations clearly outperforming in all dimensions are considered as excellent. Clearly outperforming means scoring 6 or 7 on a seven-point scale.

National Research Collaborators

A large number of academics from renowned universities have supported the European Communication Monitor surveys over the years. The current team as of 2017 includes Prof. Dr. Andrea Catellani, Université Catholique de Louvain, Belgium; Prof. Dr. Milko Petrov, Sofia University St. Kliment Ohridski, Bulgaria; Dr. Denisa Hejlová, Charles University Prague, Czech Republic; Prof. Finn Frandsen, Aarhus University, Denmark; Prof. Dr. Vilma Luoma-aho, University of Jyväskylä, Finland; Prof. Dr. Valérie Carayol, Université Bordeaux Montaigne, France; Ass. Prof. Dr. Eleni Apospori; Athens University of Economics and Business, Greece; Dr. John Gallagher, Dublin Institute of Technology, Ireland; Prof. Dr. Emanuele Invernizzi, IULM University Milan, Italy; Prof. Dr. Øyvind Ihlen, University of Oslo, Norway; Assoc. Prof. Dr. Waldemar Rydzak, Poznan University of Economics, Poland; Evandro Oliveira, University of Minho, Braga, Portugal; Assoc. Prof. Dr. Alexandra Craciu, University of Bucharest, Romania; Prof. Dr. Liudmila Minaeva, Lomonosov Moscow State University, Russia; Prof. Dr. Jesper Falkheimer, Lund University, Campus Helsingborg, Sweden; Prof. Dr. Ayla Okay, Istanbul University, Turkey. Previous national collaborators include Ryszard Lawniczak, Posznan University of Economics, Poland, and Francesco Lurati, University of Lugano, Switzerland. Special support has also been given throughout the years by EUPRERA directors of administration Anne-Marie Cotton, Belgium, and Virginia Villa, Italy.

Research Team

Since 2008 the research team for the European Communication Monitor has included Dr. Ansgar Zerfass (lead researcher), Professor and Chair in Strategic Communication, University of Leipzig, Germany, and Professor in Communication and Leadership, BI Norwegian Business School, Norway; Dr. Piet Verhoeven, Associate Professor of Corporate Communication, University of Amsterdam, the Netherlands; Dr. Ángeles Moreno, Professor Titular of Public Relations and Communication Management, University Rey Juan Carlos, Madrid, Spain; Dr. Ralph Tench, Professor of Communication, Leeds Beckett University, United Kingdom; Dr. Dejan Verčič, Professor of Public Relations, University of Ljubljana, Slovenia.

The research team for the first edition (ECM 2007) included Prof. Dr. Ansgar Zerfass, University of Leipzig, Germany; Prof. Dr. Betteke van Ruler, University of Amsterdam, the Netherlands; the late Prof. Dr. Adela Rogojinaru, University of Bucharest, Romania; Prof. Dr. Dejan Verčič, University of Ljubljana, Slovenia; and Prof. Dr. Sven Hamrefors, Stockholm School of Economics, Sweden.

Statistical Analysis and Assistant Researchers

Valuable support in terms of project management and data analyses has been provided by several research assistants and associates at the University of Leipzig throughout the years. These include (in alphabetical order): Nadin Ernst, M.A.; Ronny Fechner, M.A.; Sandra Häberlein, M.A.; Anne Ihle, M.A.; Stephanie Krahl, B.A.; Dr. Peter Schmiedgen; Katharina Simon, M.A.; Sophia Charlotte Volk, M.A.; and Markus Wiesenberg, M.A.

Partners and Participants

The ECM has been made possible through support granted by valuable partners and sponsors since 2007: PRIME Research, Ketchum, Grayling, Infopaq, Cision and Hugin Group.

The authors thank all those partners involved in supporting this unique, longitudinal research project, as well as everybody who participated in the surveys over the years.

Index

© The Author(s) 2017
R. Tench et al., *Communication Excellence*,
DOI 10.1007/978-3-319-48860-8

Printed in the United States of America

MIX
Papier aus verantwortungsvollen Quellen
Paper from responsible sources
FSC® C105338

Printed by Books on Demand, Germany